Confessions of an Air Ambulance Doctor

My Life in Blood, Guts and Latex Gloves

DR TONY BLEETMAN

EBURY
PRESS

1 3 5 7 9 10 8 6 4 2

This edition published 2013
First published in 2012 by Ebury Press, an imprint of Ebury Publishing
A Random House Group company
Originally published by Ebury Press in 2012 as *You Can't Park There!*

Copyright © Tony Bleetman 2012

The Random House Group Limited Reg. No. 954009

Addresses for companies within the Random House Group can be found at
www.randomhouse.co.uk

A CIP catalogue record for this book is available from the British Library

The Random House Group Limited supports the Forest Stewardship
Council® (FSC®), the leading international forest-certification organisation.
Our books carrying the FSC label are printed on FSC®-certified paper. FSC is
the only forest-certification scheme supported by the leading environmental
organisations, including Greenpeace. Our paper procurement policy can
be found at www.randomhouse.co.uk/environment

Designed and set by seagulls.net

Printed and bound by CPI Group (UK) Ltd, Croydon, CR0 4YY

ISBN 9780091947279

To buy books by your favourite authors and register for offers visit
www.randomhouse.co.uk

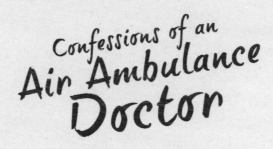

Confessions of an
Air Ambulance
Doctor

This book is dedicated to the memory
of Peter Ryan Boatman QPM

CONTENTS

PROLOGUE

The Right Wrong Stuff?

During open-chest resuscitations, I've held a non-beating, recently stilled human heart in my hands. And, should you ever get to hold one, you will find the human heart to be rubbery and shockingly light considering all the work it has to do: approximately eleven ounces in a man, nine ounces in a woman, one ounce in a wheel clamper.

Occasionally I'd get those stopped hearts started again; most times I didn't. Sometimes these operations were carried out on pavements, sometimes in a prison yard, sometimes in a living room. A living room that in turn could become a morgue or delivery suite, depending on whether the patient died or was reborn.

I knew from a very early age that I had to be a doctor. I had always respected the family's GP. Dr Hyman was kindly but firm and very no-nonsense. It was obvious to me even as a young child that this man had great intelligence and compassion. He loved his job and he made me feel better. Each consultation ended with an anecdote, which was about how exciting it was to have studied medicine and become a doctor. His obvious enthusiasm for medicine had a big impact on me. I wanted to be just like him: strong, clever and happy. Even though I was encouraged to go into the family's optician business, I knew that I had to become a doctor, no matter what. Dr Hyman died a few years ago. I wish I could thank him for giving me the inspiration to embark on an exciting, fulfilling and adventurous career – with the added bonus of helping people along the way.

My desire to become a doctor was matched only by my desire to become a pilot. My parents told me that as a two-year-old, one of my first utterances was 'up car' as I looked up and pointed at an aircraft. Seems logical to me even now. I saw a vehicle (car) that was up in the sky. Must be called an 'up car' then.

During summer holidays with my grandparents in Oxford-shire, I occasionally saw Concorde flying overhead during her flight trials. I was mesmerised by her beauty and power. My interest in aviation grew and became a little obsessive. I collected pictures and books on aircraft and read everything that I could about the subject. My first flight was in a Vickers Viscount from Heathrow to Jersey on a family holiday. As we boarded, the pilots welcomed us on to the aircraft. The flight deck door was open. I stopped to look at the dials and switches. The captain looked down at me and smiled. He looked so important and suave in his BEA uniform and cap.

The flight was much better than I could have imagined. I still remember looking out the window transfixed by the passing landscape and the clouds. In fact, the flight was far more exciting than the holiday itself. By the age of four I knew that I had to be a doctor and I had to be a pilot.

Here are two facts for you: trauma injuries, whether at home, at work, on the road or through crime, are the largest killer in Britain of people under the age of 40. And all of the 20 or so air ambulance units in this country are run by charitable donations. This means that whenever you hear that distinctive sound of helicopter blades slicing up the sky above you – often on the way to one of those trauma injuries mentioned above – and you see one of our red or bright yellow metal birds flying by, the jet fuel it's running on hasn't been bought by the NHS or the government but from donations given by strangers. And it's not cheap: an hour's flying time costs about £1,000, so the news that the Helicopter Emergency Medical Service – or HEMS, as we like to call it – is able to exist solely on the generosity of the public is both brilliant and shocking.

And, to be honest with you, when I tell people what I do, their reaction is that my work is both brilliant and shocking too. I have friends who are not involved in the worlds of either medicine or aviation who just don't know how I can do it. Whether it's cutting through the breastbone of a patient so you can plug a stab wound in their heart or barrel-rolling a light aircraft at 5,000 feet, the general reaction is one of disbelief. I'm often asked how I could put my life on the line like that, and how I feel about having the lives of other people in my hands.

To answer that question means I have to make a confession: the truth is I'm an adrenaline junkie. Sometimes that means piloting my little blue and white Beagle Pup up there where the air is thin. When I flip the plane over so I'm upside down, and the green of the earth is suddenly above me and the blue of the sky is under my wings, it feels fantastic. It's freedom.

And then there are the times when I'm fighting to save someone's life, rather than risking my own. When everything goes right and you're able to help someone in a critical condition – when you've genuinely made a difference – it's that adrenaline rush all over again. Different kind of barrel roll; same feeling.

In his famous book about NASA and jet aircraft test pilots, *The Right Stuff*, Tom Wolfe coined that term to describe that certain something the pilots needed to have in their psychological make-up to be able to do what they did. And this same theme crops up whenever I have to give a talk about my work as an emergency physician: I'm often asked what characteristics make a good emergency doctor. I tell people about that strange kind of detachment you need, the distance that all doctors, surgeons and medical professionals must have in order to function calmly while someone's life is in the balance.

Maybe there has to be something equally 'wrong' about both doctors and flyers for them to function normally in often very abnormal circumstances; but I would say this in their defence – it is, I think, at least the *right* wrong stuff (if that makes sense).

The right wrong stuff is vital when you get an emergency call-out on New Year's Eve and you respond by scrambling into a bright yellow Agusta 109 helicopter, which then screams you across the sky at near-200mph to drop you into a head-on accident crash scene. You find the young driver is so close to death that you have to operate on her immediately while she is still trapped in the wreck; and all the time you're surrounded by the smell of spilt petrol, the sound of fire engine generators and power tools used to cut open the vehicle and you see flashing blue lights illuminating pooled blood. There's no time for emotion in this sort of scenario, no time for anything but the job at hand. And if I need to be detached from the situation, so be it. It's what makes me good at what I do.

And being a good HEMS doctor means that you have to be prepared for the adventure, thrills and the adrenaline rush that comes with the job. It also involves a lot of laughter and comradeship with some very interesting people. And how much do they pay me for doing this? Nothing, not even petrol money. The truth is, if I had to, I would pay *them* to let me do it – but please don't tell them I said that.

CHAPTER 1

The Man on Two Trolleys

The horizon levelled out after a reasonable barrel roll about 5,000 feet over the English countryside. As the light G-loading dissipated, I throttled back and began my descent. I found the big lake just where I hoped it would be and having worked out where I was, I pointed the Beagle Pup towards the airfield. After the pre-landing checks, I called the tower and got the expected response: 'G-AWWE, report downwind, left hand, 23'. I banked to the left and lined up with the runway, making sure all the numbers on the dials were as they should be, correcting slightly for airspeed, height and angle of approach.

After an acceptable landing, I taxied the Pup towards the flying club hangar, slowly weaving gently from side to side so that I could see over the aircraft's nose as we trundled along. I opened the door slightly and shut down the engine. It had been a particularly good flight: some gentle aerobatics on a perfect summer's afternoon, sun shining and only a light wind. It felt good; all the stresses of work and my increasing pre-occupation with encroaching middle-age had been replaced for 45 minutes by the concentration and mental discipline required to safely fly and aerobat a beautifully preserved and cherished vintage British light aerobatic aircraft.

A few minutes later, the aircraft was inside the hangar. I checked the control locks, made sure that the master switch was off and pulled the cover over the canopy.

I looked at my oil-stained hands and wiped them on my grubby flying suit. I considered washing up and changing, but with a start, realised that I was due to meet with Derek, the air-operations manager for the soon-to-be launched air ambulance unit a couple of hundred yards further down the airfield. After glancing at my watch, I decided that I should walk towards the fire station where the new unit was going to be located.

It wasn't difficult to find Derek. I entered the fire station, climbed up an impossibly narrow metal spiral staircase and walked towards the noise. The noise all emanated from a tall man with a Seventies-style porn-star moustache, walking at speed across the floor while issuing instructions to two cowering ambulance staff. He had a mobile phone pressed to his right ear and was managing to conduct an energetic conversation into it while continuing to delegate. 'The aircraft is offline but we've got the car,' he barked into the phone.

The floor was wooden and had clearly only been installed that afternoon. There were carpentry tools carefully piled in one corner and the smell of sawdust permeated the air. Over to the left of the room, someone in ambulance uniform was trying to assemble a computer. Derek caught sight of this and briefly broke off his phone conversation to shout over:

'That's the monitor cable, you muppet! It won't fit in the back of the printer!'

Someone else was assembling flat-pack shelves, and on a filthy green couch sat the tubby pilot who had introduced himself to me a couple of weeks earlier at the hospital and had got me involved in this fledgling service. Right now I couldn't decide whether or not he'd done me a favour. Also, I couldn't remember his name. He was leafing through a lads' mag, seemingly oblivious to the noise and activity going on around him. As he caught my eye, he gave me a smile and then a shrug, glancing towards Derek so that I would understand it was just Derek's way.

From the window I could see a sleek and powerful-looking yellow helicopter being tended to outside the building. I knew it wasn't the standard red EC135 air ambulance that I was used to seeing at my hospital, but I couldn't yet identify it.

There was a series of Ordnance Survey maps mounted on a board on one wall. Someone had drawn the controlled airspace areas in marker pen. A metal eyelet was screwed into the map board at the point representing the airfield. Around this was a transparent compass rose. Through the eyelet there was a string attached to a small metallic representation of a helicopter glued onto a small circular magnet. The string ran upwards to the upper-left corner of the board, where it passed through another eyelet. A weight was attached to the end of the string. There was a series of numbers running alongside the left side of the map board.

Even I could work this one out. If you put the toy helicopter somewhere on the map, it would pull the string and bring the weight up the scale of numbers. It must be a way of estimating distance or flying time to a location from base. The string's angle on the compass rose would give you the outbound track from the airfield.

I could sense the energy but also some tension in the room. I approached Derek and before I could get a word out he halted his phone conversation and said, 'You must be Bleetman?' I was about to open my mouth when he broke off eye contact and turned his attention back to his mobile: 'We'll take the job!' he said into the phone. He hung up.

'Right,' he said, without looking at me, 'we've got a job, let's go.'

He went over to the map and moved the toy helicopter far over to the south-east. The little weight indicated 20 on the numerical scale on the left side of the map board. I guessed that this probably meant 20 minutes of helicopter flying time in a straight line. There were no motorways linking the base to the point where Derek had stuck the toy helicopter on the map board; it was all A and B roads. I wondered how we could possibly respond to an emergency in a reasonable time frame over that distance.

'Er... Derek,' I ventured, 'I'm wearing a flying suit.' I was also concerned about whether or not I was insured, but he was ready to go.

'Get the *A–Z* from the grey cabinet and get into the yellow

Seat parked outside,' was his response. 'We've got no doctor here today, the Agusta's offline, so we'll take the car. Quick!'

At least I now knew what the aircraft was: an Agusta 109. I knew by name that it was the fastest, most powerful commercial helicopter available – cruising speed just shy of 200mph. I also now knew that, unexpectedly, my first run out on a job was would not be in the helicopter but a car.

I quickly found the map book and went out to the Seat. It was a Cupra R, the fast rally-spec version. The body was emblazoned with the name of a local car dealership. Clearly, it had been donated. I jumped into the passenger seat and started to work out our route.

The inside of the car was a mess. There were CD boxes, maps, latex gloves and empty cans of energy drinks strewn over the floor and seats. It looked like 12 teenage boys had been living in it for a week – apart from the fact that in the back there were some medical bags and a heart monitor. The car had blue lights and a siren selector panel, a mount for a mobile phone and a standard ambulance radio. As I strapped in, I felt a little ridiculous sitting in a car in my grubby flying suit. I was bewildered by everything happening so quickly, but sensed that I was about to start a whole new adventure.

The driver's door opened, Derek jumped in and placed his mobile phone on the mount and started the engine. The Seat's wheels spun and we accelerated away fast. The CD player came on automatically as soon as the car had been fired up, and dance club anthems blasted out at high volume. In the few seconds it took us to reach the airfield gate, Derek cracked open an energy drink, necked the contents of the can, belched then crushed and tossed the can towards the back seat. His mobile lit up brightly again and he started responding to a text with one hand on the wheel and an eye on the phone.

'It's the Bitch,' he informed me as he texted a brief response.

We screeched to a halt at the airfield gate, leaving two tyre stripes of black rubber. The gate opened painfully slowly by an electric motor activated by a swipe card in Derek's right hand through the open car window. As we accelerated away and over the music he shouted, 'Look up Church Road on the map!' Then he hit the lights and sirens.

I was usually quite comfortable on blue-light runs, having had many years of either driving myself or being taken to accident scenes in emergency vehicles. This, however, was different, *very* different. With the lights, sirens, booming music and mobile phone text pings going off, it felt as if we were belting along in a high-speed pinball machine. And the rally-spec Seat accelerated fast enough to pin you back in your seat – suddenly I'd found myself in a real-life *Grand Theft Auto* computer game.

Derek approached the cars in front of us at frightening speed, anticipating that the flashing lights and siren would get them out of the way before we hit them at over 140mph. The cars in front rapidly increased in size as we approached them, but then vanished to a small dot in the rear-view mirror as we blasted past. They always swerved out of the way, or we swerved round them if they weren't quick enough for Derek's liking. To this end, he employed several carefully chosen phrases to tactfully instruct the cars ahead, including 'Wake up, fuckwit!', 'Move over, Granddad!' and 'Out of my way, muppet!'

'Get me directions, you muppet!' Derek shouted, and I realised that this time the muppet was me. 'We'll be there in a few minutes and it would be useful if I had a sodding clue where the job is!'

I looked at the map. The job was on an A-road, not too far away. 'It's just before we hit the market area,' I said.

After an impossibly short journey time for the distance covered, we arrived at the accident scene. The little Seat shuddered to a halt in a cloud of tyre smoke. We jumped out into the smell of cooked rubber and brake dust and, having grabbed the medical kit from the back, quickly made our way towards the scene.

I was nervous; I knew that I was about to be assessed. Derek was watching my every move as he walked just behind me down the dark country lane, bordered by trees. A wrecked motorbike was in the middle of the road – smashed glass, oil, petrol, bent metal – and there was a large fresh chunk missing from the nearest tree. There was also some flesh, blood and scraps of torn clothing on the tarmac. A motorcyclist's boot lay by the verge. An ambulance was parked just ahead.

I opened the back door to find two ambulance crew working on a pale and lifeless young man. There was a severed, bloodied stump where his left leg should have been. One of the crew was ventilating him with a bag-valve-mask; the other was trying to insert an intravenous line (IV), presumably to start fluid replacement. Something caught my eye over towards the left side of the ambulance cabin. It took me a second or two to identify what it was – it was the young man's severed leg, lying on a bench seat. I knew Derek was still watching me.

It was very clear to me that this unfortunate man was dead. I moved further into the vehicle and checked his pulse – nothing. His pupils were dilated and fixed; he wasn't breathing.

In this kind of situation, it's not helpful to just wade in and stop all attempts at resuscitation. The crew had been working on him for a while. To stop them makes you look arrogant and uncaring. They were giving their all for this man and I had to carefully and tactfully make them realise that they should stop. Most ambulance crews don't witness major trauma very often; much of their work involves taking an old lady to hospital after a fall or because of feeling unwell, or something similar. It sounds odd, but a severely injured motorcyclist is the job they've been waiting for. You can't trample all over that and ever expect to be taken seriously again, especially when they have no idea who you are or why you're wearing a grubby flying suit. The best way is to diplomatically engage with the case and then wind things down at the right pace, taking them with you. It's also a safeguard against getting it wrong. Snap decisions often land you into trouble, so careful involvement, even with an apparently hopeless case, is always worthwhile.

I felt very self-conscious in my dirty flying suit. Nothing about me could have possibly conveyed the image of a senior hospital consultant. I tried to gently establish my credentials as a responsible, serious doctor. First, I tried to get some information about the patient and his case. It was difficult to start up a dialogue because, apart from my unconvincing appearance, the two ambulance crew were fired up and totally immersed in their efforts at resuscitation. Being very wary of me and uncertain of who I was, one of them eventually said, 'Okay, Doc, can you help me get venous access? We can then start fluids and run to hospital.'

I did as he asked and got a line into the external jugular vein. We started fluids and continued the chest compressions, which had been underway since before Derek and I had arrived.

I've always thought that cardiac arrest is God's way of telling you that you're dead. There are few exceptions, especially in blunt trauma cases like this one. And this is true, despite the popular depiction of patients surviving on *Holby City* and *Casualty* after a couple of chest compressions and an electric shock or two. There are some patients who do survive cardiac arrest, and with those patients you go all the way, knowing they've got a fair chance of recovery. But not in a blunt trauma case where a limb has been violently torn off and the patient has bled out through the stump. Given the mechanism of the accident, it was also likely that there would be other non-survivable injuries in addition to the missing leg.

The fluids were running through the IV line, the chest compressions continued, we added adrenaline. I took a minute or two to look closely at this poor young man: short cropped hair, not yet able (it would appear) to grow a full beard, a tattoo design thinly outlined on his upper arm, waiting to be inked in with colour at some later stage. That wouldn't happen now; the tattoo would be buried as an outline. There was absolutely no point taking this man to hospital.

When the second crewmember said, 'Doc, can you help in the back while I drive us to hospital?' I knew it was time to start the process of letting the young man rest.

'I don't think we need to go to hospital,' I told him gently. 'This man is unlikely to survive. In fact, I think we should review this and consider taking some difficult decisions.'

'But I've already alerted them and they're waiting for us,' he replied. He was keen to go.

I knew the nearest hospital: it was a sleepy rural district general and the best we could hope for on our arrival would be a junior doctor with a 'how to practise Emergency Medicine' handbook in his pocket, certainly not a full trauma team. And even if they had the capability to assemble an operating theatre comprised of the world's best trauma surgeons, this man was dead and had been for some time. No one apart from a priest and an undertaker could help him now. I had to get the ambulance crew to acknowledge this, and ensure the motorcyclist's dignity.

It was also about my credibility. Derek had been standing behind me throughout and had said nothing. I was really being tested now. Would I avoid the temptation to embark on a series of pointless 'heroic' procedures? Was I assertive enough? How would I interact with land ambulance crews in this sort of situation? Would I yield to their unrealistic demands to run to hospital with a fresh corpse?

It was time to do what needed to be done; we had to stop. Firm but sympathetic, I carefully explained the rationale for ceasing our efforts and declaring this poor boy dead. It was difficult, but eventually we got there. Resuscitation efforts ended. I pronounced him dead and completed the paperwork that Derek had thrust into my hand.

The police, who by that time had arrived at the scene, also struggled to accept that I was a doctor. I had no ID but they scribbled down my details and eventually let us go.

I got into the Seat with Derek. He put a can of some kind of high-caffeine fizzy pop into my hand and dialled a number on the mobile. It was on speakerphone. It was the Bitch.

'Got a late job, sweetheart, sorry. Went out with Bleetman – new doc, motorcyclist versus tree, dead at scene. Poor fucker.' I thought that about summed it up.

The voice of the Bitch was pleasant, female, reassuring. They chatted for a while about Ambulance Service politics and the conversation ended. She sounded as if she cared. I immediately liked her. 'Bitch' was clearly a very affectionate nickname. Derek explained that she would be one of the paramedics working on the new air ambulance unit, although he would actually be her boss. I thought that would make for some fairly interesting dynamics in any couple.

As we drove back, Derek seemed to be deep in thought. While he crumpled and tossed another empty can into the back, he said, 'Doc, can you fly Saturday? Be at the base for eight o'clock, you're flying with me and Porky.'

I wasn't sure if I was free – I was still processing the events of the last hour. I said to Derek that I would check and get back to him. His next comment shook me a little.

'Which part of "Get your fat lazy arse to the base at eight o'fucking clock on Saturday" didn't you understand, Bleetman?' He turned to look at me, smiled and raised his eyebrows.

I had passed the test. I was a Helimed doctor.

CHAPTER 2

Are You Bleetman?

Two weeks earlier a man with a beaming face and boyish smile had approached me at work. He was wearing a pilot's uniform shirt and airline trousers and was a little overweight. 'Are you Mr Bleetman?'

'Yes,' I shook his hand.

'I'm Nigel Brown, chief pilot of Helimed 999. We're a new charity-funded air ambulance. I'm surveying hospital landing sites. We open for business in a couple of weeks and I've come to look at your hospital's helideck as you're on our patch.'

I had been a consultant in Emergency Medicine for about 12 years since returning to the UK after completing my medical-school training in Israel. I'd then trained in Surgery in Glasgow and then Emergency Medicine. After several posts, including that of a deputy police surgeon and a senior registrar in A & E Medicine, I was now an established consultant at a hospital. It was a full-time, full-on job – equal parts occupation, preoccupation and obsession – with lots of nights and week-ends. Pretty standard then for medical work.

Despite the workload, I'd been fortunate enough to have been given the chance to combine my love of medicine with my love of flying, because one of my roles at the time was to manage the helicopter work that the North Central Ambulance occasionally brought into our hospital. I had worked with our hospital estates department to plan and get the hospital's elevated rooftop helideck ready to respond to the need of air ambulances to deliver patients to hospital. Previously, they had had to land in a playing field near the hospital and get a land ambulance to transfer the patient from the aircraft to the Emergency Department. This added about ten minutes to the whole process of delivering a sick patient to hospital and made a mockery of using a fast aircraft in the first place. I got lucky: the hospital had commissioned a new building to house a fracture clinic. I was able to influence the designers into ensuring that the building would be strengthened to enable helicopters to land on its roof. This required additional planning for ramps and fire-fighting equipment. I became quite knowledgeable on the intricacies of Civil Aviation Authority regulations on helicopter landing sites. It is far more involved than simply having a flat roof with a large 'H' painted on it in white; the Civil Aviation Authority require helidecks that are more than three metres in height to have a fire crew in attendance for every aircraft movement. So I had coerced hospital porters, carpenters, electricians, healthcare assistants and even hospital security guards into getting trained as firefighters and they learned how to respond for incoming and outgoing helicopter flights. I had then negotiated with their managers and conducted their firefighter medical examinations, blagged some used firefighter uniforms and also managed to get free training from a contact at the airport, who I had got to know through some emergency planning work.

The whole set up here had been a labour of love and a lot of hard work, and I was very proud of it.

As I showed Nigel around the helideck, he seemed genuinely impressed, which was a relief. He asked me, as I knew he would, to show him the operational response to an incoming aircraft. I dialled the 2222 emergency number on the hospital switchboard and advised, 'Incoming helicopter, code green, ETA seven minutes!' The message was acknowledged by the switchboard operator who initiated the well-rehearsed call-out procedure.

We stood on the helideck. Within a minute, we could see three figures running from the hospital workshops towards the building. Three minutes later they were on the helideck, wearing firefighter uniforms and manning their firefighting stations at the perimeter of the helideck. All of them were breathing hard. One had the ground-to-air radio in his hand and was ready to talk to any incoming aircraft. Only minutes later, the clinical retrieval team arrived with their trolley and were waiting at the side of the helideck in their allocated position, ready to receive our 'casualty'.

It had all gone smoothly. Nigel was clearly impressed. I introduced him to the fire crew and the clinical team. Theory and practice can be two very different things, as you soon learn as a doctor, so to see all this come off exactly as planned was very rewarding. But when you're setting up any new venture, as well as the procedures running smoothly, the people also have to gel. Nigel had a great personality and within a very short time even our hardened A & E nurses had warmed to him (no mean feat); one even flirted outrageously.

After the crew dispersed, Nigel and I chatted. He told me that Helimed 999, the new air ambulance unit, would be based at the local regional airport. He then confessed something that made me even more excited about the venture, and something that would make it, and us, unique: they planned to operate a medical Helicopter Emergency Medical Service model of air ambulance and *not* the traditional paramedic-led air ambulance model. This was big news.

The North Central Ambulance helicopters that I was used to seeing at the hospital operated the very traditional paramedic-led service. Some of their paramedics were a little gung-ho and on any occasion when we debated the role of doctors out in the field, they were adamant that there was no role for doctors outside the hospital. These paramedics were sure that they could hack anything. To them, doctors would just get in the way, cause delay and boss them around, because all doctors were prima donnas with attitude. They were determined not to be anyone's bag carrier.

I could see their point, in a way, but I also knew that doctors had a role to play and that it might be time for things to move on from where they had started. And I thought that I could be the right man for the job.

*

Flying for Helimed 999 wasn't my first foray into pre-hospital care, as it is now known. And it also wasn't my first experience of screaming around the skies in a helicopter.

After growing up in London, in 1979, at the age of 17, I packed up my flares and *Saturday Night Fever* album and went to live in Israel. I had always felt different as one of a handful of Jews in a Church of England school. The class bully, having told the only black kid to 'Fuck off back to wog land!' advised me to 'Fuck off back to yid land!'. Even though I had been brought up in London, I thought the idiot had made an accidental point in that I wouldn't be in a small ethnic minority if I fucked off to yid land, so I gave it a go.

For six years I trained at medical school in Tel Aviv. I went on to have a long association with the Israeli Defense Forces as a soldier, combat medical technician, a failed trainee Air Force pilot and finally, as a military doctor in an elite unit. I had my first taste of combining medicine with helicopters when I witnessed medical helicopter work on the battlefields of Southern Lebanon in the 1982 invasion. It all looked so glamorous.

While training in the Israeli Air Force, we were assessed by our peers every month to ascertain how we functioned within the group on the flying course and to identify those with annoying behaviour and habits. Essentially, we completed a questionnaire on each other in our group. It was important to score well as this was an important part of assessment during the flying training. On those days, I would always ask my wife Jacqui – whom I had married when I was a medical student training in Tel Aviv – to bake some cakes and cookies before the monthly assessments so that everyone in the group would give me a high score. That became a habit and worked well. It was one area of the course assessment in which I scored highly.

As a junior doctor in Israel, I worked shifts on a doctor-crewed ambulance. Our role was to get to heart attack victims and administer clot-busting drugs as soon as possible. They needed a doctor on board to do that. We also attended other types of emergency and I was therefore exposed to the whole range of emergency work. During my time working on the ambulance unit, I developed a healthy respect for the para-medics who educated me in pre-hospital survival and how best to do something useful for seriously ill or injured patients before we got them to hospital. They kept me straight, and kept me safe. I learned a whole new way of communicating with patients who only minutes earlier had experienced some-thing traumatic. We worked inside overturned lorries, in bathrooms, on the street, in the cinema or on the beach. Anywhere and everywhere, we delivered advanced medical care. It was one of the best groundings and crash courses (sometimes literally) in pre-hospital care that I could have received.

I also learned how to blag free food and medical kit, which would later come in very useful back in the UK when estab-lishing the Helimed units and, crucially, I learned how to improvise in highly challenging situations.

The paramedics taught me how to interact with the other emergency services, which sometimes had different and competing priorities at the scene. This was an eye-opener in itself as I had assumed that everyone would pull together in an extreme situation, but I soon realised that this was not always the case. I learned how to control busy scenes, traffic, hostile crowds, onlookers and grieving relatives. Most importantly, I learned the value of how and when to rely on each other and we developed mutual trust in our respective skills and abilities.

I had been dropped from flying training in the Israeli Air Force because I was impulsive and cocky. Still, some of that impulsiveness and cockiness can work well in Emergency Medicine and also in pre-hospital care. You have to make rapid assessments without knowing the whole story. In the field, you need to make snap decisions, take calculated risks and perform surgical procedures and operations that in hospital would require scrubs, gloves, two assistants, bright lights, powerful anaesthetic drugs and trays of sparkling surgical instruments laid out in a logical order. But in pre-hospital care out in the field, you have none of that: you're out on a high wire – but instead of holding a balancing pole in your hands, you have someone else's life. And there is no colleague to ask for help if it all unwinds: it's you and your paramedic. If it turns out well you're heroes; if it goes wrong you are vulnerable to criticism and ridicule.

In 1994, having returned to the UK in 1991 after 12 years of living in Israel, I began work in Cambridge as a Registrar in

Emergency Medicine. I encountered the occasional serious trauma victim accompanied to hospital by local doctors, who tended to be dressed in a suit and tie beneath a large fluorescent jacket with 'BASICS DOCTOR' printed on the back. My boss, Howard Sherriff, whom I admired a great deal, also occasionally came into our hospital with ambulance crews delivering seriously injured patients. He too had the jacket.

According to Howard, in the sixties, Ken Easton, a local GP, had started to respond to serious road accidents on a notoriously dangerous stretch of the A1 in Yorkshire. His efforts giving care and treatment at the crash scene saved lives, and the Ambulance Service were grateful. Word spread around the country. Local volunteer doctor–responder schemes were established in most counties. These were largely run by local GPs, although a few hospital consultants also joined in. Members of these schemes carried pagers and had some medical equipment in their cars. The Ambulance Service called them out for difficult accident scenes where patients were trapped in vehicles until the Fire Service could cut them out. In many areas, the police had allowed these doctors to fit their cars with blue lights and sirens.

In 1977 the doctors and their volunteer schemes formed an organisation called the British Association of Immediate Care Schemes, or BASICS. BASICS continues to this day, offering education and representing doctors in dealings with the government and professional bodies. I am proud to serve as their honorary secretary.

The idea of the pre-hospital emergency doctor called out to exciting crashes and disasters was right up my street: I was always easily bored and needed stimulation from new things and different challenges, so swapping the hospital ward for blue-light driving to accident scenes was perfect. And it felt good to be involved in something still comparatively new and evolving. I fitted my old Volvo with a magnetic blue-light bar, which had an integral, old-style 'nee naw' claxon siren. I carried a pager and responded to the occasional crash on the A14 and M11.

To my surprise and disappointment, nine times out of ten I had little to offer at accident scenes. Most of the time, we gave a little morphine or advice to the paramedics; advanced skills were not required for the majority of the jobs we were sent to. And, at that time, when I did get to the one-in-ten serious job, I didn't have the advanced skills required to really make a big difference: I was too junior a doctor and not yet trained or competent enough to offer hospital-level interventions.

Up until the 1980s, an ambulance's function hadn't changed since the post-war founding in 1946 of the modern service: the ambulance was simply a means of transport for the patient. Ambulance crews could offer a kind word, a blanket, some bandages and splints and promises of a cup of tea, followed by a bumpy, noisy nee-naw of a ride to the nearest hospital.

Then, in the mid-eighties, paramedical care was slowly introduced into the service. These paramedics were no longer 'ambulance drivers' or 'stretcher bearers' but rather professionals trained to perform a series of advanced procedures and administer a limited number of drugs. The ride was just as bumpy and noisy but you no longer had to lie there bleeding and dying; you could be attended to. Hopefully you'd get to hospital in a survivable enough condition to secure that cup of tea.

This explosion in paramedic skills narrowed the gap between what they couldn't offer and what a doctor could. The number of additional skills that the GP could bring to any scene was small and was rapidly becoming smaller. However, this handful of skills would most certainly be life-saving for those patients who needed them.

Most GPs who responded as BASICS doctors did not and do not have these advanced skills. When they attend a scene they can offer a slightly wider array of drugs. Usually they cannot perform surgical procedures or administer a general anaesthetic. They do, however, still have a role. Their presence allows paramedics to operate outside rigid ambulance protocols. A doctor can take responsibility for operating beyond the constraints of carefully controlled paramedic practice. In other words, they can facilitate certain procedures being done then and there to try to save lives.

The few remaining original BASICS GPs look a little old-fashioned now. They are useful as another pair of hands and in being able to offer clinical judgement, experience and wisdom. The reality is that the practical skill sets of the GP and the modern paramedic are closer than ever. In fact, many paramedics routinely outperform GPs in the delivery of advanced skills. Even so, there are situations where only a specialised emergency doctor will do. This resulted in the development of medically-led HEMS units.

The first air ambulance unit in the UK was established in Cornwall in 1987 (today its helicopters carry the legend '1ST IN THE UK') and after initial funding by the local health authority was withdrawn after a few months, it quickly became a charity organisation. It was, and remains, a paramedic-led service – essentially, an airborne ambulance that can quickly get to difficult and dangerous locations and then package and transport patients to hospital.

To put it simply, trauma is when someone has been injured in a way that means that they cannot continue normal life without intervention. This could mean broken bones, internal bleeding, a severe case of shock, anything that means they need help. Often, such injuries happen in places that are hard to access or would just take too long if we were to go to them by ambulance. While paramedics can do an awful lot, some people saw that even more might be done. Two years after the Cornwall Air Ambulance took flight – and following a Royal College of Surgeons' report criticising pre-hospital trauma care – Dr Alastair Wilson and consultant surgeon Richard Earlam had the vision to form the London Air Ambulance unit (LAA).

The LAA was different. Working out of the Royal London Hospital, they responded to trauma cases within the M25. And they didn't attend medical or paediatric emergencies, just trauma. What was to be so pioneering about this HEMS service was that the LAA unit decided to use not just paramedics but to also put a trauma doctor on board. This changed everything. Their rationale was that advanced skills can make a difference to trauma victims provided you get the right doctor to the scene in time. The idea was that no longer would the trauma patient have to be transported to hospital to see an emergency doctor who could save his life but instead the doctor would be taken directly to the scene to immediately tend to the patient. There are a number of advanced interventions that make a difference in trauma survival for severely injured patients. At the time, only doctors could deliver these skills.

The London HEMS service stood alone for many years while the rest of the country developed more and more traditional paramedic-only units. Doctors were expensive, usually out of their comfort zone working on the streets, and many paramedics didn't want a doctor stealing their thunder.

But the founders of Helimed 999, like Wilson and Earlam in London, had bigger, more ambitious ideas. Helimed 999 was actually going to be the first unit outside of the London Air Ambulance to put doctors up in the air on an air ambulance. Not just for trauma cases but for all types of emergency work where they could make a difference. It was revolutionary stuff. In addition to trauma, the unit would respond to paediatric, cardiac, medical and even psychiatric emergencies. The potential to make a difference would be huge.

Hearing that Helimed 999 was to be this kind of doctor-led service was really exciting. I loved flying, I loved Emergency Medicine and combining the two was irresistible. But to also learn that we would be the country's first all-emergency HEMS unit was a dream come true. It felt like all my doctoring and aviating birthdays had come at once.

I wanted to be in on this so I probed a little and Nigel told me that they were looking to recruit suitable doctors, and he gave me the name of their medical lead. He was Dr Martin Wilson, a consultant anaesthetist. I vaguely knew him and remembered him as being quiet and controlled. He had a good reputation and was, reassuringly, an ex-London HEMS doctor so he saw the value of putting doctors with advanced skills on the aircraft

I called Dr Martin Wilson almost immediately after Nigel had left. He remembered me and we chatted. I told him that I was interested in joining the new unit. He said that there was no money and that it would all be voluntary. A lot would depend on how I got on with the crew and Derek, the unit's air operations manager. Dr Wilson told me that I would need to commit to a minimum number of shifts to justify the cost of issuing me with a flight suit and helmet; he wanted a tight and cohesive doctor-led service. He talked about clinical governance and strict standard operating procedures (SOPs). I respected that; this was just as it should be.

Dr Wilson seemed to be thinking it through as we talked because it took him a while to suggest that I went along to meet Derek. He promised to call him and tell him to expect me.

I went home and discussed it with Jacqui, although to be honest, the 'discussion' mostly consisted of me enthusing about this potential new Helimed service. I didn't exactly offer it up for debate and she knew me well enough to see that I'd found a new love in my life. She was quite used to it whenever I seemed to have discovered a new way to work more hours, and she was always incredibly supportive. Jacqui was one of that rare breed of women – doctors' wives – who, through strength and capability, enable their husbands to have functioning home lives even when their working hours and practices can be quite dysfunctional. Behind every good doctor there's a woman who is, amazingly, not getting royally hacked off with him – or, as likely as not, an understanding husband not getting hacked off with his doctor wife.

My children, David (then 14, the eldest), Laura, Rachel and Mim were all equally understanding of Dad's time away from home when at work – for a few years I'd already been responding in my own car with flashing lights as an Ambulance Service volunteer. So, me going into HEMS would be cool for them and just another aspect of what I did. They were all equally unimpressed too by what I did, as kids tend to be with Dad, though David got the bug for medicine at an early age and did start to show a genuine interest in my work. Being naturally studious, stable and inquisitive, he was, I thought, pretty good future doctor material, an assessment endorsed by the way his face lit up when Jacqui and I bought him a micro-scope – his best *ever* birthday present, he said. And, as he grew older, we two boys even 'talked shop' over dinner, which Laura grew to hate.

So, with the new Helimed service in mind, over the next few days I had a lot to think about. I did some research, explored the workings of other air ambulance units around the country and started to read about contemporary models of aeromedical transfer work.

I began to get a warm glow about all of this.

CHAPTER 3

First Two Jobs, First Two Complaints

Derek and Porky rattled through the challenge and response pre-flight checklist:

'Both Engines'	*'Flight'*
'Pumps and fuel cocks'	*'Forward'*
'Captions'	*'Clear'*
'Instruments and Radios'	*'Set'*
'Front'	*'Secure'*
'Back'	*'Secure'*
'Area'	*'Clear'*

This countdown, as well as being operationally important and crucial for flight safety, also sets you up psychologically for what you're about to do: leave the relative safety of the earth and get pulled up into the wild blue yonder in a little painted tin can with a big, massively powerful fan on top of it, spinning at about 400 revolutions per minute.

It had been nearly 20 years since my encounters with military 'CASEVAC' air ambulances in the Israeli Army during the Lebanon War, but it now seemed like only yesterday. The pre-flight excitement of being imminently airborne came flooding back as I looked out the window and saw the grass nearby obediently lay back flat and trembling in the downdraft, and the horizon seeming to shudder in the waves of immense engine power. I was in a beautiful Agusta 109, the fastest civilian helicopter available – top speed nearly 200mph and with a fully digital programmed engine system, heaving us into the air in under a minute. With its streamlined profile and aggressive snout, the thing was like a Ferrari with blades. It was even the right colour: bright yellow.

The Agusta's engines whined and then roared into life, chucking the rotors around until we lifted into the air and hovered for a second or two at about six feet. Its nose tipped forward, as if in salute to the earth we were about to leave, and then we gathered speed – and fast. The helicopter surged upwards as it developed translational lift; Porky, who I now realised was the overweight pilot I'd met previously, selected gear up and we screamed off towards the south-east, leaving the wail of the engines behind us like an aural contrail. From the back I had a prime view of what was happening in the cockpit. So mesmerising, it was was easy to forget why we were airborne. The adrenaline of the scramble and the job details were almost forgotten but my enjoyment didn't last long.

'Get me the Land Ranger map and mark the grid, you muppet!' Derek shouted from the front cabin. 'Helpful for me to know where the fucking job is!' He was in full flow. It was a slightly scary but also magnificent sight. He made you feel that you were going to war. If the high-speed joyride in the Seat had made me realise anything, it was that I had to quickly over-come the excitement of the launch and start honouring my mission duties as a HEMS crewmember.

Looking up at the laminated map-guide that had been attached to the top panel in the rear of the cabin, I worked out which map I needed. I took out the map from the very organ-ised rack above the patient cot, opened it up and plotted the grid reference for the job. It was on a relatively nearby A-road. I circled it with my pen and passed it forward to Derek.

He snatched it from my hand and immediately started a narrative to Porky: 'Wires two miles ahead, slightly to the left of track. Then *more* wires, four miles ahead, also slightly to the left of track. The job is to the west of a triangular-shaped wooded area just before we hit the village.'

Porky responded, 'First wires identified, second set identi-fied, well clear! I can see blue lights and traffic queues both directions. Pre-landing checks, please.'

'Landing area'	*'Selected'*
'Gear down'	*'Three greens'*
'Captions'	*'Clear'*
'Front'	*'Secure'*
'Back'	*'Secure'*

Porky pulled us round hard to the left and started his approach. 'Doors open!' he ordered. Derek opened his door. I slid open the door on the starboard side of the aircraft and immediately the cabin was filled with the noisy whirr of the blades. After rotating my seat, I sat with my legs dangling out in the slipstream, feet buffeted by the disturbed air. Visions of colour-saturated Vietnam War footage popped into my head, with GIs sitting in the open doors of Huey helicopters with their feet hanging out, hands resting on the warship's heavy machine guns.

For an introduction to HEMS work, this was pretty cool! The ground blurred past beneath me.

I knew there were direct connections between what we were doing now, skimming over England at a rate of knots, and what had gone on 30 years previously in Vietnam – and the connections were more profound than just the similar level of adrenaline pulsing through our veins and those of the GIs. In Vietnam, by 1969, the American Army was using specially trained medics on battlefield helicopter ambulances, and using them with such success that US researchers found that wounded American soldiers had better survival rates than civilian motorists involved in a car crash on a Californian freeway. And that incredible realisation led directly to the world's first experiments in using civilian paramedics. As is often historically the case, battlefield developments during a time of war would drive innovations in medicine and care delivery. (Famously, Super Glue was first used on the battlefields of Vietnam to retard blood loss and also to enable soldiers' open wounds to be quickly closed, rather than using traditional suturing.)

The purpose of opening the helicopter's doors during the landing approach served to enhance safety, enabling us to be able to see any unexpected obstacles and debris, and also to check for clearance between the rotor blades and trees or other obstacles. Wires were always a big fear: hard to see, easy to hit, bloody impossible to escape. Only a few years before the entire crew of the Kent Air Ambulance unit had been killed when their aircraft hit power lines, crashed and exploded.

'Clear left, down at that!' Derek advised. 'Clear right!' I offered back as I hung out the open door. Porky acknowledged, and lowered us. And then with a slight bump we were down. I thought about how it could not have been more than five minutes since the Bat Phone had rung back at base with the call-out. This was fast.

'Clear out,' Porky advised. 'Caution the slope,' he added. The rotors were still winding down and the engines' whine dying as I tossed the rucksack and cardiac monitor onto the grass outside and hopped out. Once outside the aircraft, I pulled the rucksack onto my back, lifted the monitor and made eye contact with Porky, who gave me a thumbs-up sign, indicating I was clear to leave the aircraft under the running rotors.

Derek led us down the embankment. We removed our helmets and placed them on the grass before continuing down to the job.

Two cars had collided, pretty much head-on. Two young women were sitting at the side of the road and were being attended by a land ambulance crew. The women looked fine and didn't appear to need our services.

A young man on a spinal board was being manoeuvred out of a car from which the roof had been cut off by the Fire Service. He was alert and didn't appear to have any obvious immediate problems. I made the decision to let them get on with it and we would have a look at him once he was out.

At that point, a middle-aged man in a suit and tie with a fluorescent jacket brushed me aside by pushing his right elbow into my back and made his way into the mêlée of the rescue. On the back of his fluorescent jacket was a label that read 'BASICS DOCTOR'. 'Basics' certainly described his attitude. I thought he might be a local volunteer GP and so I followed him through to see what this was all about. As I approached, he turned and said, 'We don't need any helicopter heroes here, thank you! I'll take it from here.' Well, that's a big fat zero out of ten on the bedside manners too, I thought.

To quell the annoyance I felt I tried counting to ten but then I thought, aw fuck it, and bailed out at 'six'. I asked him who he was. He answered sharply that he was a consultant from the local hospital and had been called out by the ambulance service. After informing him that I was a consultant in Emergency Medicine working on the air ambulance, I suggested that we could examine this patient once he had been pulled out of the wrecked car. He blanked me and went into a dramatic and loud monologue for the benefit of everyone within range, explaining that any idiot with an ounce of clinical experience could see that this patient was fine and didn't need a helicopter. Then he shooed us away. I hadn't been professionally 'shooed' since I was a junior doctor. This time I only made it to 'three'…

The conflict between us escalated for a while until Derek pulled me back and said, 'Just leave it, he's a cock.' (Cock, by the way, is a clinical term for another medical professional you don't like.)

We got airborne. There was silence for the first few minutes, and then Derek started cackling like Sid James in *Carry On Doctor*.

'Well, that went well, Bleetman!' he said.

Porky joined in, 'Yeah, Doc, I think that went *ever* so well, don't you?' Derek was still laughing, 'I mean, after that, what could possibly go wrong?'

As we climbed up the spiral staircase back at base, the phone rang. I knew that it was going to be a complaint. Derek answered, and after listening for a while he grew very animated and launched into some more clinical definitions: 'Martin, your orthopaedic colleague was a *cock*! I don't give a toss who he is, he's bloody ignorant. So no, we *won't* phone him… there's no complaint to answer… bye.'

Derek's feet went up on the desk and he cracked open an energy drink. We switched on the TV. Later I learned that all air ambulance stations, by law, have to have a TV permanently tuned into re-runs of *Top Gear* on digital channels. I settled into the filthy green couch to watch a tall man in a creased leather jacket slide his arse around a track in a sports car. The phone rang again.

Derek answered. He handed it to me and mouthed, 'It's for you.' Porky choked on a sandwich he was in the middle of demolishing as he tried to suppress a laugh. I knew what was coming.

The BASICS doctor started by introducing himself and went on to explain that had he known that I was a consultant he wouldn't have behaved like he had. It was almost an apology. I pointed out that whether I was a consultant or not wasn't really the issue, it was the primacy of the patient that was most important. After a little chat, we exchanged a few pleasantries and promised each other that we would be nicer next time we met on a job.

Derek's intervention had clearly made this potential problem go away. He had taken on the medical director and defended my position. Sometimes that's all it takes to stop someone in their tracks, but not everyone has the balls to do it. Luckily, we had a team leader who did.

Derek was now smiling, 'Not bad, Bleetman – first job, first complaint!' Surprisingly, he seemed perfectly happy with that. He downed the rest of his fizzy drink and belched violently.

Only a few minutes later, the Bat Phone rang again. Simultaneously a claxon loudly went off outside the building. Porky immediately dropped his copy of *FHM* and his second sandwich and zipped up his flying suit as he ran towards the spiral staircase. Derek took the call. He looked unimpressed: 'Minor rear-end shunt? Where?' He moved the toy helicopter, pulling its string across the map board to the extreme top-right corner.

The little weight moved up the distance/time scale by the side of the board and indicated 25 minutes of flying time.

Outside, the Agusta 109's Pratt & Whitney engines were already squealing into violent life and the increasing velocity of the rotors getting up to speed was generating an immense noise. Porky was outside and ready and eager to fly.

In the crew room, Derek was still on the phone interrogating the dispatcher. 'So, he's conscious, talking, and the car is undamaged? So why do you want Helimed?'

He listened and seemed unimpressed. 'Okay, but if you get anything more exciting while we're away, please call us. *Not* happy!' he barked.

I looked at the string and read off the outbound track and distance, then hurried out to the aircraft. After plugging in my helmet communication cable, I told Porky, 'Outbound 030 degrees for 25 minutes, clear of controlled airspace.' He turned to me and smiled. I was beginning to get the hang of it.

Derek got in and connected his helmet lead. 'It's a crock of shit, Porky – a minor rear-end shunt and whiplash – but he's apparently just had surgery on his cervical spine so they won't move him and want a doctor there. And all we've got to offer them is *Bleetman*.'

Porky laughed.

With the flight checks complete, we lifted and headed north-east. We had loads of time to sort out maps, the grid reference, airspace restrictions and radio communications with Ambulance Control.

We found the job and even from the air we could tell that it was a trivial accident. This is where the Vietnam analogy loses some of its lustre; whereas those guys might have looked down out of a Huey gunship and seen a smoking bomb crater decorated with severed legs and puddles that were black with blood and flashing white with reflected light, we just looked down on a Ford Mondeo that had been bumped slightly from the rear. It was less *Apocalypse Now* and more *Coronation Street*.

Though it did make me think about another similarity between doctors and soldiers: the tension between what we are and what we do. Both professions don't want to see people hurt and yet we *do* want to see action; that's the dichotomy. All that practice and all that theorising means you just can't wait to put the training to good use, even though you know something pretty bad – war or disaster – has to happen to allow you to function.

After landing the Agusta, we approached the car and spoke to the driver, who was sitting bolt upright and tightly gripping the steering wheel. I struggled to see any damage even to the paint on the rear bumper of his car. The other vehicle involved in the collision had long gone. I tried to work out what the fuss was about. Apparently, our patient had recently undergone disk surgery in his neck at a major hospital in the extreme south of our patch. Immediately after the impact of this minor road collision, he had felt a jolt in his neck and experienced an electric shock feeling down his back. I spent some time examining his neurology and worked out that there had been no damage to his spinal cord. But he was scared.

We gave him a little morphine for his pain but also to alleviate his obvious anxiety. We then got him out carefully and packaged him on a rigid spinal board with a neck collar and blocks for flight.

Porky advised us that we had enough fuel to get to the hospital. Derek was not happy. 'This job will keep us offline for two hours,' he protested.

'No choice, Derek,' I countered. 'They'll have all his records and scans there. We should take him.' Derek reluctantly called the receiving hospital to alert them of our planned arrival and to give them details of our patient.

I put a headset on the patient so that he could talk to us inside the Agusta. I spent most of the flight enjoying the view because I didn't have much else to do apart from reassuring him and asking him if he was okay from time to time.

We landed at the hospital and unloaded our patient. As we pushed him on the trolley through the door of the Emergency Department, we encountered a short black-haired nurse wearing a corrugated frown. The archetypal hard-faced A & E sister, she gruffly asked us where we had brought our patient from. Derek told her that we had flown him about 60 miles from the north. She thought about it and then asked sharply, 'So what made you bring him here then?' She was rude and irritating; she didn't want us there and we didn't want to be there either.

CHAPTER 4

Meet the Gang –
the Gang's All Here

Perhaps we did get off to an uncertain start at Helimed 999, although considering the pioneering nature of what we were doing that was understandable. But several things started to come together to galvanise the unit and produce a very forward-thinking and novel way of delivering air ambulance work. We made sure we had the right doctrine, the right crew, the infrastructure and the important working relationships with the Ambulance Control centres and ground crews.

Martin, our medical director, introduced some good standard operating procedures to ensure we practised our craft to the highest standards. This process took a few months but once we got there, we knew without doubt that no one could touch us; we really were the best in so many ways. We also liked each other as friends, which is important. It was an extra bond that allowed us to become a tight and cohesive unit.

Within days of first gaining access to the empty upper storey of the fire station at the airport, it had been well and truly transformed. The semi-decorated mess that I'd walked into for my first meeting with Derek had now been kicked into shape.

Now what I should have done at that point was to explain that he had recently undergone surgery at this hospital and it seemed prudent to bring him back as the accident had caused him to feel pain at the operation site in his neck. Unfortunately what I said was something entirely different.

'Your first problem is that there's a sign outside your door which says "Emergency Department". Your second problem is that some twat has put a helipad outside, so you're going to attract air ambulances.'

She didn't look at all pleased at this answer. She pointed us towards a cubicle and we unloaded our patient. He was still fine and we handed him over to one of the doctors in the department.

We flew back to base and were still chuckling about the 'so you're going to attract air ambulances' punchline when ambulance control radioed through asking us to call the medical director on the phone after landing back at base. We all looked at each other like schoolboys recently caught misbehaving.

Back at base we got a surprisingly pleasant phone call, but still, the message was made clear: I had to be a little more careful or this adventure might come to an abrupt end. Derek cocked an eyebrow at me.

'Even better, Bleetman. First two jobs, first *two* complaints. Good hit rate.'

There was now a very comfortable and functional area that housed the crew, administration offices, a training room, a large area for the charity fundraising staff and even a gym. Downstairs, at the back of the fire station, equipment and drugs stores appeared.

A carpet was fitted; two more filthy green sofas and some furniture arrived, along with a television with free connection to satellite TV. A games console materialised. Someone had plumbed in a fully fitted kitchen and there were a number of computers, all with internet access. A lot of thought had gone into planning the crew room. It was decided that the pilot should share the crew room with the doctor and paramedic. Each member of the crew had a workstation mounted on a work surface that ran beneath a long window, which looked out over the magnificent yellow Agusta 109 helicopter.

Not everything had changed, some of the original fixtures and fittings were still there – Porky, for example, was still lying on the sofa reading *Loaded*. And the telly was still tuned to reruns of *Top Gear*.

I was shocked when Derek told me that the entire base had been created on just 800 quid; Derek was a master in the art of gentle persuasion. Still, 800 quid to turn an empty shell of the upper storey of the fire station into a fully functioning and comfortable base was pretty good going. This was Olympic, gold-standard blagging here.

The world-class 'gentle persuasion' even extended to the three fast cars parked outside. Derek had blagged the rally-spec

Seat Cupra, and the unit also had two Rover 75s. The filthy green sofas came from a fire station but most other fittings, furniture and electronic gadgetry had simply been asked for. It worked like this: you went into a large retail outlet wearing your orange air ambulance flying suit and asked to see the manager. You looked sincere and told them that you were setting up an Air Ambulance Service nearby and you needed some help with a minor item. As the conversation unfolded, you told the manager that the NHS doesn't pay for air ambulances and the operation is entirely funded by charity and donations. You went on to say that every penny raised by the charity pays for precious fuel for the aircraft and there is no budget for whatever item you are trying to blag.

Often, the small item we were trying to blag escalated into a gift of anything we wanted in the store. We didn't even pay for stationery. And the kitchen was always full of cases of soft drinks and packs of snacks, all donated by the kindness of strangers to go towards the good cause.

So we had a superb base and a great helicopter. We now had to get the operation more established, so the recruitment of new medics continued. A handful of hospital consultants and senior medical trainees joined the service. We all helped to run a selection process designed to select the best possible paramedics to join the unit.

The selection process for paramedics was conducted over two days. The first day required the candidates to pass a physical fitness test after a day of professional exams. They were also assessed on their performance in simulated medical, paediatric and trauma emergencies that were remarkably realistic. They took written tests in maths and basic navigation to evaluate their ability to undergo training in aviation matters, which would be required if they were selected to join the unit.

On the second day of selection, the paramedics were tested on their leadership and team skills. These tests were conducted in the style of officer selection in the Armed Forces. They had to negotiate a 'minefield', cross a 'river' with barrels, rope and a plank of wood and similar exercises. We decided not to test whether or not they could stand Derek's high-speed driving in case we scared them all off. At the end of the second day they had an interview. The process worked: we got the best people possible.

Once they were recruited, the paramedics also underwent training in aviation skills so that they could function as qualified HEMS crewmembers. They were taught about the aircraft and its systems and sat exams equivalent to those required by private pilots. They also became proficient in air law, navigation, aircraft marshalling, refuelling, emergency drills, meteorology and, after a few flights, creative swearing. In essence, they became non-handling co-pilots. A big part of their training was Crew Resource Management (CRM), which encouraged effective communications and team-working in a busy cockpit. In the blag-of-all-blags, Porky even managed to get a Robinson-22 light helicopter for them to attempt to fly so they could feel the effects of controls and begin to appreciate what a helicopter pilot has to do.

Our freshly trained HEMS paramedics were then taught to work with doctors in delivering those advanced medical skills that would save lives. This was initially done in-house, but I saw an opportunity there. I got in touch with a lady called Linda, who had set up university-level advanced training for paramedics at a university in the Home Counties. As you do, I met her in a car park on the eve of a bank holiday and we hit it off immediately. Within three months we had three modules at Master's degree level established at our local medical school and I got the Ambulance Service to pay for it. The finished product of this training was a paramedic who operated well in the aircraft and could function alongside a doctor as an expert in delivering intensive care skills to the sickest patients. This is what made us good and effective.

Some of our paramedics had been recruited from the traditional paramedic-only style North Central Ambulance and were sceptical about all this doctor-led intensive care on-scene stuff. People are usually resistant to change, especially if they feel threatened by it. However, once trained, they became almost evangelistic in their enthusiasm. They now knew that we had only minutes to save the lives of the sickest patients. We showed the traditional paramedics how we took the intensive care unit directly to these patients – in the shape of a big Agusta-shaped mobile hospital – not the other way around.

Our job was to deliver critically ill and injured patients who were often under a general anaesthetic to hospital, their bleeding controlled and advanced life-saving surgical interventions completed in the field. Quite often, the hospital doctors were amazed as there was little for them to do once we delivered our patient to them. Eventually things got so slick that we began to take patients directly to the CT scanner in the receiving hospital before they hit the Emergency Department. We had done all the Emergency Department's work in the field.

Barry was one of our paramedic graduates. His heavy Irish accent was so unintelligible on the intercom and on radio calls that he always had to repeat his radio messages. We still never really understood him. Whenever he asked anything that sounded like a question, the standard response was 'Er... yeah, Barry, it's about half past two.' He was a superb paramedic, though, extremely focused and efficient under pressure. And he was very affable and good at smoothing ruffled feathers at hectic accident scenes, which turned out to be an invaluable quality.

Sean stood at just over five feet and, possibly because of his height, was very ambitious. He was a one-man emergency service, having been a paramedic before moving over to the Fire Service to become a training officer. His paramedic skills were kept current by flying shifts on Helimed 999. He also had another quality always welcomed by us – he was another champion blagger.

Also on board, both figuratively and literally, was paramedic Yvonne, who happened to be going out with Derek. She was also known affectionately by one and all by her nickname 'the Bitch'. Not because anyone thought that she was one, I hasten to add, but because it was an in-joke between her and Derek that we just grew to share, a bit like Arthur Daley referring to his wife as ''Er Indoors'. In fact, Yvonne was one of our most capable and invaluable crewmembers – fiercely intelligent, focused, methodical, not at all girly but very attractive, always a bonus when working with a bunch of ugly men. She clearly loved Derek but, as might be expected from someone dating a strong personality, she needed to be more than capable of standing her own ground. And sometimes their flaming rows spilled over into the base, shrapnel flying everywhere. On these occasions me and the rest of the crew would usually find a good hiding spot and wait for peace to break out... or at least for a ceasefire so we could run to the toilet.

Doctors were a different matter altogether. They were all volunteers, whereas the paramedics were salaried ambulance staff, so it had to be someone who wanted to give their time. There was no selection process for doctors as such. Our doctors didn't need to pass a fitness test or be tested on their clinical ability beyond the medical director's subjective assessment: natural selection led to the removal of doctors who did not get on or integrate with the pilots and paramedics. Any hint of being a prima donna was simply not tolerated. Such doctors never found a vacancy on the duty roster. To get on to the unit, a doctor had to have a reputation for being a good clinician and, most importantly, must be able to independently deliver the advanced procedures that the service sought to deliver and save lives. Martin, our medical director, must be convinced that you possessed the clinical credentials and credibility to deliver these advanced interventions in the field. Derek had to like you as well.

Gradually we got our selection of doctors down to the ones that worked best. There were some colourful characters among them, including John, who loved the ladies. And balancing up John's hetero dramas, we had Tom, a rotund and very camp doctor. A gifted clinician, the paramedics loved working with him, which balanced out quite nicely with the lesbian doctor we'd just taken on board. Being the sophisticated men-of-the world that we were, we all took it in our stride – apart from Porky, who thought it cut down on his chances of pulling. On one particular shift, the HEMS paramedic on board was also about as camp as our Tom, so after a job, when Porky, Tom and a gay paramedic wheeled the patient into hospital, Porky noticed that two young nurses were observing them. Porky duly inflated his chest in what he thought was a very manly fashion and bellowed, 'I'm straight, honest!'

Of course, we didn't let him forget that in a hurry.

We also had Steven, who was training as a colorectal surgeon. He had a bit of a wild-child past but nowadays was more introverted and deep. He was a very good doctor and although at times he could get a little anxious, his natural talent was more than enough to get him to become very slick. This was the minefield through which you walked when working on what we might call the civilian battlefield. You had to have the confidence and know-how to quickly decide what to do, and then do it.

And then there was Klaus – a tall, lanky German, who was highly skilled but also very, very quiet. We sometimes called him 'Mouse' because he was so stealth-like you wouldn't even hear him come up behind you. He only spoke when it was an absolute necessity. It wasn't a case of 'Ssh! Don't mention ze var!' – it was a case of don't mention anything at all!

We got another pilot too: young Maurice, or Goose as we liked to call him (after the *Top Gun* character). Maurice was a temp pilot, or a 'floater', but ended up coming out on a lot of jobs with us. Fresh out of the RAF, he was beyond keen and loved the drama of it all. His favourite part of the job was the flying – anything that got the adrenaline pumping. If he wasn't a pilot, and he had the right build, I think he'd have been in the SAS. He even used to come to work wearing a T-shirt with the 'Who Dares Wins' logo on it and the latest Chris Ryan book, which provided us with hours of entertainment.

In general, we decided that most of our docs would fly once a week but would fill the duty roster as their time allowed – which, if they were anything like me, would probably lead to even more widowed doctors' wives. We thought that two shifts a month should be the absolute minimum; in fact, most of them would end up doing at least four.

We needed all the doctors and all the hours they could spare to be able to build up a rota of unpaid volunteers. And as our reputation in critical care grew, other air ambulance units who didn't carry a doctor began to call us out to assist them in complex jobs. So, we ended up covering a huge part of the country.

Finally, by the end of the first paramedic university course we had a small group of highly trained and motivated individuals, most of whom were relatively normal – a sort of cross between the A-Team, the Dirty Dozen and the doctors on *M.A.S.H*. I was actually surprised and quite pleased at how little they were fucked up. Result!

As we relied solely on charity donations, we had to attend countless public relations events. A friendly local DJ called Jonny Riff (I'm guessing not the name his mother gave him) usually accompanied us to these things. At the next engagement, Jonny got a bit more than he bargained for when he thrust a microphone in front of each member of the crew as we stood in front of a crowd of thousands at a summer fair. The JCB formation diggers had just finished their display. We had the Agusta in the background for dramatic effect, and all the better to raise money.

Jonny moved along the line, asking us all what we did. When he got to Steven, the colorectal surgeon, he said, 'So, Doctor, you give your time for free to the Air Ambulance – that's great. What's your day job?'

Steven, thinking that a lot of the crowd wouldn't know on what part of the body a colorectal surgeon operated, replied,

'Well, Jonny, I'm an arse doctor.' The crowd went quiet for a few seconds, and then burst out laughing.

Steven was also a champion blagger. We wanted to give the doctors and paramedics practical training in opening chests. Opening a chest is known as a thoracotomy and when done quickly on victims of penetrating chest wounds, gives a reasonable chance of saving the victim of a knife or a gunshot. Often it's the *only* thing that will save them. But you've got to be quick: you need to cut and open the chest fast, open the sac that surrounds the heart and then stop the bleeding with a finger or clamp and some stitches. This skill was a 'must have' for our teams but it was very difficult to train people in thoracotomy in hospital, as emergency management of a desperately ill victim of a stabbing does not provide a controlled training situation for aspiring emergency chest surgeons. In other words, if you're on a bed bleeding out, you don't want some fucker practising on you!

So, one day, Steven told everyone to attend the medical school at an arranged time. The crew were amazed when they arrived to see a roomful of cadavers laid out on slabs that Steven had arranged for them so that they could undergo practical training in opening chests in a controlled way. These had been blagged from the anatomy department of the medical school. He even arranged a second session for the crew on duty that day. Everyone got to split and crack open a real human chest and plug holes in the damaged hearts. Even the pilots attended – Porky with sandwich in hand and *Nuts* magazine in his pocket.

Who says we didn't know how to show our crews a bloody good time?

In the second summer of my involvement with the unit, I met Simon Knott-Mason, a new doctor who went on to become a very close friend. Simon was on loan from the Royal Air Force. He was tall and had the look of a lovable rogue. The crews loved him, which was always important. He had bounced around some other careers before falling into medicine. Always referred to as SKM, he was the life and soul of any gathering. His Air Force connections came in useful and got us invited to spend the weekend with an RAF search and rescue unit at RAF Valley. I flew us all up to the Air Force station in a borrowed aircraft from the flying club. We got free accommodation in the officers' mess and spent two days being shown round the unit waiting for a job for them to go to. They offered us seats in the back of the Sea King to accompany them to any jobs and provide some medical care.

While we were killing time at the base, Porky started chatting to their pilots. 'How long does it take you to launch your Sea King?' he asked.

I thought, uh-oh, I know where this is leading. The RAF Flight Lieutenant proudly informed us that they could be airborne within 15 minutes of a call. At the time, we aimed to be airborne in Helimed 999 within *two* minutes of the first ring of the Bat Phone. Porky, ever the diplomat, immediately started laughing and then loudly informed them of this fact. Don't get me wrong: we were all proud of how quickly we could 'scramble', but only Porky would so shamelessly crow about it to a group of RAF pilots.

However, the Sea King crews earned our deep respect in many other ways. They showed us videos of their missions. The Sea Kings flew in the most awful weather imaginable and we were humbled by their ability to hover this large helicopter close to a cliff edge or over a moving target in a choppy sea. I couldn't decide whether we were unlucky or lucky that no jobs came in for the Sea King crew while we were with them.

Our own beloved Agusta 109 helicopter had a spare seat in the back and we used it to train new paramedics and doctors, and also when we brought along observers. Observer seats were supposed to be used for ambulance officers, potential new paramedics and doctors in training. More often, though, the fourth seat was occupied by an attractive female medical student that John had chatted up at work.

During this time, our man Porky had established himself as a very credible chief pilot and Maurice was putting in the hours when he could, but another full-time pilot was still needed. We found Chris, an ex-army infantry officer who had learned to fly helicopters in the Army Air Corps. A very gifted pilot, he was also a spiritualist which, among us sceptical atheist cynics, went down like a fart in a spacesuit.

Chris's spiritualism did lead him to come out with some bizarre things at times. Unnervingly he was often right. At one of the first jobs I attended with him, we were at the side of a seriously ill patient when Chris turned to me and said, 'His aura has changed colour. When it's yellow, his spirit is leaving.' The patient did die, but then it was on the cards anyway. Then the next time it would be, 'Tony, this chap's aura is red, he's fighting – you must keep going.'

His other weakness was for playing the stock market. He was always so optimistic, forever hoping for that big windfall. Between jobs at the base, we'd all be sat there chilling out with a coffee, watching *Top Gear* on telly or playing video games, but Chris would sit for hours on the internet and watch the little FTSE graphs move up and down. For him, mostly down. Even while we were at jobs, he would use his mobile phone to do the same. I could be working on a patient and in the background hear, '*Bugger!* Chinese mining is not doing well, just lost £12k. Never mind, can probably recover with the French truffle industry. Worth a punt!'

We were sitting around the crew room one day watching Richard Hammond on *Top Gear* trying not to crash himself into another coma when Sean looked up from his paper. 'Chris, I was reading the other day about these magic beans. Apparently you can buy three for the price of a cow. You plant them and they grow into a huge beanstalk. At the top of the beanstalk is a goose that lays golden eggs. You climb the beanstalk, grab the goose and get back down. You'll be made for life. One problem, though: there's a giant at the top of the beanstalk who might chase you if you take his goose. Probably best to keep an axe at the bottom of the beanstalk so that you can chop it down if the giant pursues you.'

As this fantastically ridiculous advice hung in the air, we all turned to look at Chris and, amazingly, he was actually looking into the middle-distance, seemingly mulling it over.

After a few months, we got another new pilot. Crewe was a civilian who had started his working life as a photocopier repair technician. Now, that might not seem like the most obvious route into aviation, but he had self-financed his flying training and we respected him an awful lot for that: it showed a real love of flying. Crewe brought enthusiasm and commitment to the unit, as well as common sense and new ideas. He was our new chief pilot in waiting and everybody knew it. Porky wouldn't stay for ever; his attention span was too short. And Chris might follow the aura of a girl into a bank and give her his stock market winnings.

Crewe was a good pilot; you could sense his mastery of the aircraft when he flew us to jobs. He transformed the atmosphere at the base. One of his first tasks was to tidy the place up and, of course, blag us some new furniture (blagging was almost a rite of passage for new incoming crewmembers).

With Crewe on board, things became tighter and more organised. He quickly familiarised himself with the equipment so that he could help the medical crew at the scene. When we attended the sickest patients, Crewe would have the next item of equipment ready for us, being able to predict what we would need next. He was very keen and would often sing 'I love my job, I love my job' to different tunes.

One early Sunday morning, we sat around the base peering out at the dense fog. Maurice was on stand-by as pilot and advised us that the weather was not likely to improve for several hours, if at all. If we got a call we'd have to respond in one of the unit cars. We sat down to watch *Top Gear*.

The Bat Phone rang. I took the call and it sounded very serious. A car had come off a nearby A-road and was over-turned in a ditch, person reported trapped. The job was not too far from base so we could get there quickly in one of the unit's cars. Crewe, who was shadowing Maurice at this point, looked like a mournful puppy as we got up to leave: as the redundant pilot, he didn't want to be left behind.

'Come on then, Crewe,' I offered. 'An extra pair of hands might be useful.' We ran out to the rapid response vehicle and piled into the Rover 75 but it wouldn't start. Great. The battery was flat. The second rapid Rover 75 was mysteriously missing and the Seat Cupra would be at home with Derek. So there was only one thing left to do: get Wicked.

I was driving a 14-year-old Ford Sierra because all of my money was used for paying for school fees and my recently acquired Beagle Pup aeroplane, having moved on from my beloved Chipmunk when the repair bills got too high. The Sierra had dark tinted windows – the boys on the unit often referred to it as the 'Sierra Wicked' in a hoodie voice because they said it looked like a gangsta car. Which it did, but I loved it. I'd had it fitted with blue lights and sirens as I used it on occasion to respond to jobs. But I was always getting stopped by the police, even when driving sensibly. They found it quite difficult to accept that a senior hospital consultant was responding to jobs in an old banger with blacked-out windows and a full array of blue lights. The police were also getting twitchy about blue-light use and were becoming increasingly vigilant in ensuring that there was no abuse of this privilege. On top of all that, they feared that terrorists or criminals could use blue lights while getting up to no good. On one single day I was stopped four times on the motorway while driving the old Wicked, and every time I was made to wait until the traffic officers were able to verify my status as an authorised blue-light responder. They even came to my house once and searched the car.

Over time, the local police began to recognise the car and their suspicions turned to mild ridicule. When I pulled up at jobs in the Wicked, they could barely hide their amusement. Still, none of the patients that needed their hearts jump-starting seemed to care. It doesn't matter what transport the doctor turns up in so long as the patient doesn't leave in a hearse. I'm sure they'd agree.

So, on this particular day, we had a problem. We couldn't fly because of the fog, the one rapid response vehicle on base had a flat battery and the second rapid response vehicle was missing. 'We'll have to go in the Sierra Wicked then,' I said. We threw the kit in the back of the old car and screeched off to the job.

Without realising it, I had left the stereo on high volume and when I turned on the engine, we were deafened by Phil

Collins's 'In the Air Tonight' blasting out on the radio. I reached over to turn it down.

'Leave it,' commanded Crewe, who was sitting in the back with a beaming grin. It was the first time that he had been on a blue-light ride and he clearly wanted a soundtrack to go with it. Remembering my first mad car ride in the Seat, I thought, 'Welcome to the unit.'

The weather presented problems for rapid response driving as well as flying: the flash and glare from the blue lights and the beam of the headlights reflected back off the wall of fog as we sped along, sirens blaring.

Still, we got to the job quickly, before even the Fire Service. Straight away we could see that it was a bad scene, really bad. There was an overturned car that was half immersed in a waterlogged ditch, one of its rear tail lights glowing dimly underwater – and that, I knew, was where we were going to have to work. Not in a bright white hospital room, not in a sterile operating theatre, but in a cold, dark, dirty ditch. I bent down and inside the car I scoped a single unconscious occupant with severe injuries. As the car was upside down, a lot of muddy water had creepes inside and was lapping over the interior headlining of the roof. Luckily, the guy was hanging supported from his seatbelt, which was the only thing that had prevented him from dropping headfirst into the filthy water and drowning.

Barry and I crawled into the ditch, kicked in the car window and then crawled into the wreck. The driver was struggling to breathe and I knew we didn't have a great deal of time. I could also smell petrol and see it swirling in rainbow ribbons in the water. We cut the guy free, lowered him down and dragged him out to the roadside. Then we delivered a general anaesthetic and got him settled on a ventilator. The ventilator was alarming, indicating excess pressure. His chest was barely moving. This was likely to be caused by pneumothoraces – collapsed lungs. Air from a ruptured lung will leak into the space around the lungs and progressively collapse them. You can fix this by cutting holes in the chest and draining the air out, allowing the lungs to re-inflate and work again. I cracked the seal on a freshly minted scalpel and sliced open both sides of his chest, inserted a finger and drained the trapped air. It was looking good for the patient. The ventilator stopped alarming and our boy's chest started to move with each cycle of the ventilator. The numbers on the monitor began to improve. Our patient started to recover further after being given some fluids and splintage; he now had a fighting chance.

We were working very well together. Maurice was preparing and handing us equipment, predicting what we would need next. It was an example of the highest-level possible medical response to a desperately ill patient and we felt good about it. Despite all the jokes and occasional cocking about, it was what we were all there for.

A land ambulance had joined us by this time and clearly this would have to be our mode of transport to hospital. I called the local hospital to alert them of our arrival. It was a strange call; they said they hadn't seen their overnight senior doctor for a while. Their senior on call happened to be Klaus, one of our own Helimed doctors.

We loaded our patient into the ambulance. I wasn't going to leave the Ford Sierra Wicked at the scene, so I tossed the keys to Maurice. I thought how I should probably have tossed the keys to one of the attending police officers, as they usually obliged in bringing abandoned response cars to hospital to reunite them with their owner, but I didn't.

'The blue-light master switch is next to the gear lever,' I instructed Maurice. 'Activate the sirens through the horn. One hoot to activate and cycle through the three tones, two hoots to turn the sirens off. Follow us to the hospital.' His face lit up like a kid with a new toy: he was going to drive on blues and bells. A little voice in my head suggested that perhaps this was not such a good idea but I had other things to worry about. Maurice might have been a great helicopter pilot, but he had never been trained to drive a blue-light response car.

We set off in the ambulance. I was very focused on our patient and wasn't paying any attention to the sirens and noise as we very quickly drove to hospital. I'd got over the adrenaline rush of a fast ambulance ride many hundreds of jobs ago and had learned to roll with the bumps and lurches of a blue-light journey. I still had a lot of work to do on our patient in terms of monitoring and adjusting the ventilator, drugs and fluids to maintain optimum numbers on the cardiac monitor. I was able to filter out the noise and I didn't bother to see if Maurice was following behind as I had instructed.

We got to the hospital and handed over our man to one of the consultants. Clearly he had just been called in very late – I knew that bedraggled look well. He was wearing the first thing that he had found in his bedroom, which happened to be his wife's red tracksuit, and he also had a 'bed-head' of ruffled hair and an unshaven chin. Not that the patient would care.

Klaus, our own Helimed doctor and the one who should have been on duty as senior doctor here at the hospital tonight, was still nowhere to be seen.

But the job had gone very well. And our patient was doing fine. The hospital team were clearly impressed and grateful; less work for them to do, and better chance of a good result. We left the resuscitation room to look for Maurice. He was standing next to the Sierra Wicked in the bright white glare of the ambulance bay. As we approached, he beamed. I'd never seen him so happy.

'That was great!' he said. 'I think I set off a few speed cameras and then I got a bit lost. Never mind, eh?'

Then a police car slowly pulled up behind us. The two police officers didn't get out but the driver was talking into his radio. Maurice was oblivious to their presence. I got a little knot of tension in my belly. There might be a problem here. And it might be more than the usual speed camera kill.

We often set off speed cameras when driving to jobs but we just reported them to Ambulance Control as we saw the flashes and they made the problem disappear by confirming to the police that we were authorised blue-light drivers on a bona-fide Ambulance Service job. Even if we didn't report the camera flashes, the Ambulance Service made the problem go away provided we were on their computer system allocated to a job. I was beginning to think that we might have a problem here with more than the cameras that Maurice had set off.

We piled back into the Ford Sierra and I drove us sedately back to base. There was a buzz from this job, which had gone extremely well, and it was too good to be killed by the appearance of the traffic cops. We had saved a life this early morning, and had also made a very positive impression at the hospital that could only enhance our reputation as a cutting-edge pre-hospital medical team.

We climbed up and around our impossibly narrow spiral staircase to the crew room. I wanted to brag a little about our exploits so I decided to call Derek. He was always interested in the high-profile jobs and liked to be informed immediately Barry switched on the telly so we could watch *Top Gear* (I think Jeremy Clarkson was pushing cyclists off their bikes or something like that).

I was expecting a simple *Boys' Own* chat with Derek about the job and I wasn't at all prepared for what I got when he answered the phone.

'Derek, we've just done a car job and—'

'Shut the *fuck* up and listen, you *fucking* moron!' he interrupted.

He went on to explain that our doc, Klaus, had used the rapid response vehicle to nip home because some work was being done to his own car. Klaus had been called on his mobile and had then hopped into the borrowed Rover 75 ambulance car to get back quickly to receive us. Unfortunately, he had collided with a Transit van on the way. Hence, the hospital had called in the on-call consultant.

Shit.

There were several issues here. First, the insurance arrangements were unclear as our honorary contracts with the Ambulance Service had never come through, and second, our doctor was therefore technically not on Ambulance Service books and the insurance status was, at best, uncertain as he was driving an Ambulance Service vehicle. I was shocked – it's always the quiet ones you have to watch!

Derek continued his tirade down the phone. When he was really angry, he tended to start a sentence with 'And another thing…'. I was having to hold the receiver further from my ear as he grew louder.

'*And another thing!*' he bellowed. I braced myself. 'What in the name of flying *fuck* were you thinking of sending Maurice off in the Sierra on blue lights?! Did you think no one would notice a fucking pilot driving at high speed on lights and sirens? I've had a world of pain from the police on this one, you *fuck*ing *moron!* AND ANOTHER THING… '

I became aware of a knot of tension deep in the pit of my stomach that tightened until it was dripping with gastric juice.

The word 'Oops' came to mind, but in fifty-foot tall flashing red neon letters – **OOPS!**

These dramas all led to a flurry of phone calls for the rest of the morning. Derek gave me regular updates and coached me on what I should say to placate each agency involved, if approached by them. As it turned out, we never heard anything. Somehow Derek made it all go away.

Privately, however, Derek 'debriefed' us quite... how shall I put this...? Robustly. If we'd only thought ahead and, for the duration of the debrief, had him sponsored for the use of the words 'fuck' and 'moron', we might have bought a brand-new helicopter. The debriefing was also another candidate for *The Guinness World Records*. I think the phrase '*And another thing!*' was used more frequently than at any other time in recorded human history.

CHAPTER 5

What Could Possibly Go Wrong?

Flying can be inherently risky, and because you're rushing to scenes when life is already in danger, you have to be even more careful. We took our pre-flight preparation and medicine checks and helicopter service duties deadly seriously. Air Ambulance shifts started at least an hour before we were ready to fly. We assembled at the base at seven in the morning and started with a cup of coffee and a chat. It was very important for us to gel as a team for the entire shift. Ten minutes with a hot drink and a friendly chat kick-started that process.

The day's pilot would check the crewmembers' weights and enter the figures into a spreadsheet used to calculate how much fuel we could carry.

After the hot drink, we would get into one of the rapid response vehicles and call Air Traffic Control on a handheld radio to get permission to drive along the taxiways to the hangar where the Agusta spent the night. The hangar doors were very heavy and it took two of us to push each one open so that we could access the aircraft. A little red tractor lived inside the hangar alongside the Agusta and, previously, Porky used the front end of our baby tractor to shunt the doors open. This practice had been banned after I had a go and promptly drove into the hangar door, smashing a headlamp.

Once inside the hangar the pilot would check the aircraft, opening panels and peering inside with a little torch. I would often follow the pilots around during the morning checks so that I could see what they were doing and learn about the aircraft.

Once the checks were completed we would attach a towbar to the hub of the nose gear and attach the other end of the towbar to the tractor. The pilot would always drive the tractor when it was towing the aircraft but we were allowed to play with the tractor when we ferried it between the hangar and the dispersal area.

Once on the tractor, the pilot would call Air Traffic Control to get permission for us to tow the aircraft from the hangar along the taxiway to the dispersal area outside the fire station. We would often sit in the open door of the aircraft when it was being towed, ostensibly to make sure that the rotor blades did not come into contact with many obstacles. Once at the dispersal area, the aircraft was towed to its position on the helipad and we would disconnect the towbar from the nose gear and the pilot would usually let one of us remove the tractor and put it in the small shed that kept it dry during the day. If the big Agusta was our mothership, the little tractor was our pup.

Then the serious business of preparing the aircraft for the day began in earnest. The pilots would often start the engines and check all systems. The shift's paramedic and doctor ran through meticulous check sheets for the medical equipment. Every pouch within the response bags was sealed once the content had been checked and accounted for. All drugs were checked for quantity and expiry date. We checked oxygen cylinders and our equipment; we ran checks on the ventilator and cardiac monitors. Every compartment, drawer and storage area was checked very carefully for equipment. There could be no excuse whatsoever for missing equipment or equipment failure on a job. Such oversights could cost someone their life.

Within the fire station we had an equipment and a drug store and a small room where we stored oxygen cylinders. Having checked the equipment on the aircraft and also on the rapid response vehicles, we would spend at least another half an hour going through the stores to make sure that stock levels were adequate and that all the paperwork was in order, particularly for the controlled drugs. Getting this wrong would put us at risk of criminal prosecution. Having done this, we would return to the aircraft to re-join the pilot and check the intercoms and headsets and make sure that the GPS and radios were all set up. This first hour of the day was taken very seriously indeed.

With our checks complete, we would head back into the crew room and run through a briefing. In the early days of the units these briefings were fairly informal and unstructured. We all knew that we had to cover the weather forecast, NOTAMS ('Notification to Airmen' reports), availability of backup from other units and other base admin duties.

With all those serious checks and double-checks out the way, for the rest of the day we could get on with the less taxing business of saving lives and sweeping up after.

In the beginning, on one occasion I asked Porky whether he would conduct a morning briefing and he scoffed and said, 'You mean like the Luftwaffe?' He was referring to our North Central Ambulance colleagues, who referred to us as 'the Cowboys'. But when Porky saw that I was serious, he cleared his throat and his face took on a stern captain-in-charge look. He peered out of the window, then turned towards the crew and said 'Gentlemen, it might rain today. End of briefing.' Sure enough, it did rain a little later, and as the rain began to fall, his face lit up as we flew back from a job. He said, 'See? How good was my briefing!'

However, as we matured as a service the briefings became far more formal and they were very useful. The pilots would start with the weather, NOTAMS and any technical issues relating to the aircraft. This would include any reported faults, numbers of hours until the next inspection and any serviceability items. The next part of the briefing would be conducted by the paramedic, who would talk through equipment, drugs and base admin duties planned for the day. Then the final part of the briefing was conducted by the doctor, who would address medical issues and identify other doctors on the patch who could be called upon for backup for any big jobs.

It was only after all this had been done that we telephoned the three Ambulance Controls in the region and advised them that we were online and ready to respond. That's well as also telling them who was on the duty crew that day in case we all crashed and died. It was always a sobering moment – to have to list the crew names.

Within a few months of Helimed 999's launch, we were running like a well-oiled machine. This was partly through sheer necessity – we had to be well drilled – but also practice: we were being called out so regularly. We were averaging about six jobs a shift. More than half the work was for road accidents and assaults, a significant chunk for equestrian accidents and a healthy smattering of medical, cardiological and paediatric emergencies.

'What could possibly go wrong?' is a phrase we used often on Helimed 999. We tended to use it when we knew we were flying into something nasty and this was our way of acknowledging that we were about to face an almighty challenge. 'So we've got 15 minutes of daylight, 20 minutes of fuel, the weather's turned to shit, we used all the kit on the last job and we're flying to a chest pain on the M6, position uncertain. What could possibly go wrong?'

A few years into your doctoring career you learn never to be surprised at what might be wheeled into the Emergency Department or carried twitching out of an ambulance. Sometimes it's not even the unusual accidents that shock you but the very ordinary ones so clichéd that you can't believe they ever actually happen outside of a bad sit-com.

Banana skins? Tick. Yes, people do slip on them. Garden rakes? Tick. People do step on them. Railings? Yes, people do get their heads stuck through them. Milk bottles? Yep, people (and here we mean men) do get them wedged firmly up their backsides. Vacuum cleaner attachments? Oh yes, people (and here again we mean men) do mysteriously somehow get their genitals stuck inside them – the difference here between suck and blow never before so painfully confused.

Sometimes I saw the life of the British public as one long real-life *Road Runner* cartoon with people running off cliffs (pause... hang... legs spin... fall), having anvils land on their heads, accidentally lighting boxes of dynamite, hammering their hands to tables, slicing themselves with circular saws, dicing themselves with wires, slamming windows and doors on bits of their throbbing bodies, having their faces flattened with frying pans, driving cars into brick walls and sticking bits of themselves into electrical sockets until they sizzled like bacon and their skeletons visibly glowed.

But the thing was, it was our job when we attended these scenes to make sure that that wasn't it for them. At one time it would have been the case that not a lot could be done – an open-and-shut case as well as a coffin; a land ambulance would have taken too long to get there and get back (and provided too little on-board care) to save many of the lives of accident victims. Our Helimed unit, however, could get there much quicker and we had the real chance to deliver potentially life-saving procedures on-scene or in the air.

*

We got a report in of a man impaled on a roof. As one, we all thought, hmmm, that sounds promising. Wonder what happened there: unlucky skydiver? Short-sighted burglar? A pissed and very late Santa Claus? An over-enthusiastic dad on a child's trampoline? It could have been any of those, and we were prepared for them all. Well, prepared to be amused by each one. Personally, I was hoping that it would be a combination of them all: a short-sighted and drunk skydiving burglar dressed as Santa, who had missed his target, landed on a child's garden trampoline and bounced all the way up onto the roof and become skewered on a TV aerial. I hadn't yet had a job matching that description so it would be nice to fill in the gap.

We ran past the Agusta and jumped in one of our cars as the job was in an urban area very close to the base. As we hared through the streets on lights and alarm bells, we ran through more possibilities, each one shouting over the woop-woop of the siren:

ME: A DIY moron that's drilled himself to the roof!

DEREK: A careless pervert trying to look in someone's bedroom! Or some idiot amateur stuntman trying to get on YouTube!

ME: A barbecue gone bizarrely wrong!

DEREK: A satellite dish fitter that's sat on his own aerial!

That last one got a big laugh, and also a collective wince and sharp intake of breath – none of us fancied having to extract a transmitter aerial from some hairy-arsed TV engineer.

We got to the scene to find it was a block of flats with a flat roof. Piling into the lift, we pressed for the top floor. This was always an odd moment, the bit whenever we had to travel in a lift, because after all the noise and the speed and drama of getting to the job, we then just ended up standing together in the lift as quietly as if we were in church, hoping no one would fart. There's something about lifts, and public urinals, that strikes men dumb. Maybe that's why lifts often smell of urine: one's easily mistaken for the other.

We got up onto the roof to find that between us we'd almost guessed it. We found two TV aerial fitters, one with a large drill bit through his foot and screaming at the heavens. Apparently, these two TV fitters were installing a large aerial to the block of flats and one was up on the flat roof, stamping hard so his mate in the flat underneath could work out exactly where to drill through. Guess what? The guy stamping had forgotten to take his foot away so the long drill bit had whizzed through the ceiling, drilled through the roof and chewed straight through the foot of the bloke standing on the roof. He was now very stuck... and very unhappy.

How do you sedate a man who is impaled standing up with a drill passing right through his boot? Answer: very carefully. I tried to get local anaesthetic in around his ankle for a regional block – but it failed. He screamed when we tried to free him.

The bloodied top of the drill point was a good two inches above the boot. We had to be careful with sedation because if he fell over he could badly twist an ankle and also rip out the drill bit sideways. It definitely made you wince just thinking about that. So with very judicious use of morphine and lots and lots of reassurance, we all gathered round and very carefully pulled him vertically up; the drill bit came away with him. We both winced when we saw our man's right foot well and truly skewered by the drill bit; we took him that way to hospital for its removal under an anaesthetic.

Afterwards Derek said that he thought it would have been easier to leave the guy standing there and just get him to hold the aerial. I had to point out the obvious fact that it wouldn't work because he wouldn't have been able to hold it at the same angle all the time so people in the flats would not lose their TV signal. Plus the screaming would have kept everyone awake at night. Derek had to agree. And we all agreed that the drill-bit-through-the-foot job made us wince whenever we thought about it.

So even though you could just about guarantee that a fair proportion of the British public could manage to make it out of their homes safely without burning, bleeding or electrocuting themselves to death, they would just get to work and do it there instead. Which always made things worse. Industrial accidents posed serious challenges for us in terms of access and rescue. And they often involved large-scale industrial machines that could do far more brutal things to the human body than simple domestic appliances. A home vacuum cleaner won't do you much damage unless you're silly enough to stick one of its attachments up your arse. But heavy industrial waste cleaning machines would suck your skeleton through the top of your head.

Getting called to an industrial accident meant that we often had to deal with limbs trapped in machines, workers trapped at height, patients on elevated platforms, victims high up in cranes and people in the midst of toxic or poisonous materials. These situations demanded some careful and quick thinking to keep ourselves safe and to offer medical care in precarious circumstances. A trapped and mangled hand, for example, could be anaesthetised with a carefully placed wrist–nerve block; and light sedation might help with freeing a victim of impalement – but not too much as they could fall over and make a precarious situation worse (as in our drill-bit-through-the-foot aerial fitter). What could possibly go wrong?

One early morning call turned out to be particularly hazardous. We were sent to a job at a metal foundry. Our patient had fallen between two vats of molten metal. He had trapped his right leg between the vats and it was slowly being roasted. He'd fallen and become trapped about six feet away from the end of the vats and therefore he wasn't accessible. He was in absolute agony.

The metal had a melting point of about 1,200°F, so you might say it was quite hot in the foundry and around the vats. It was, in fact, an earthly hell. A living furnace.

Our man was cooking, literally, so we knew we had to get him out pronto while at the same time making sure we didn't also end up as shish kebab. We rested a ladder on the edge of the vats; I was the lucky one who'd get to crawl along it. I knew had to work fast, not just for our patient but because as the ladders were metal, they conducted heat efficiently and would soon heat up themselves. I didn't want to be trapped on a red-hot limb over a vat of smoking, burning metal.

So, I carefully crawled along to our man, reached down and injected some local anaesthetic into the top of his thigh to anaes-thetise the leg – what we call a femoral nerve block. I tried a block myself – that is, to block out the smell of his leg flesh cooking.

As I was doing this, an on-site engineer was working away to insert a jack between the vats to try and ratchet them apart. We only needed about an inch or two to be able to tug the leg free. Finally the vats creaked apart just far enough for me to tug the poor man's leg free. I crawled back gingerly along the ladder, praying I wouldn't fall into the molten metal.

Not that we needed to prove that these things didn't get to us, but we went out that night anyway and had well-done steaks each. Sometimes you had to try and control what sensa-tions you were left with at the end of a potentially traumatic day. And it meant that the end of that particular day ended up smelling a hell of a lot better than the start of it.

The Agusta 109's turbines screamed into life outside the fire station. Porky was raring to go within a minute of the Bat

Phone's first ring. I took the call. A very English accident scene: cardiac arrest on an allotment. I was betting the guy was even wearing a cardigan. So, what you might call a 'double cardy'.

I plotted the location with the toy helicopter on the large map board on the wall. The string gave us an outbound track of 140; the weight on the string told me the job was four minutes' flying time away. Derek snapped down the visor of his flying helmet as he ran towards the aircraft, leaving only his porn-star moustache visible beneath it. I frantically ran behind him – my legs half the length of his, his strides twice as long.

I hopped into the back and plugged in my communications lead. 'Outbound 140, four minutes, clear of the zone!' I was getting good at this now. Derek drew a line on the ¼ mill scale aviation map and confirmed we would be clear of controlled airspace.

As we had run out onto the airfield and towards the aircraft, I'd been reminded again how I knew from the first time when I heard and saw a helicopter starting up and taking off that I would never tire of the sight and sound: it was mesmerising. The whine and then the little whoosh as the fuel mixture ignited in the turbine engines; the rotation of the blades from slow movement on engine start-up to their incredibly high-intensity drone in flight mode; the vibration of the cabin under the great power; the brief feeling of weightlessness as the wheels first lift off earth – everything below in the immense downdraft flattened or trembling – and then through the window the sight of the earth disappearing as the craft tilts, banks and screams across the sky towards the horizon.

As we lifted and surged up into the sky, Porky retracted the gear and I pulled out the 50 thou' Land Ranger map and marked the spot, double-checking the grid reference against the numbers on my kneeboard that Ambulance Control had given us. I tapped Derek on the shoulder and got visual confirmation from him that he had identified the map position that I had marked on the map. I then pulled out the Philip's *A–Z* and found the location again. The *A–Z* was useful in finding potential landing sites and identifying individual roads as it uses the same grid reference system as the 50 thou' maps so we get to see our target on both a large and a small scale. Within two minutes of getting into the aircraft, we had all the navigation sorted. We tore along the countryside at a height of about 1,000 feet. Treetops, fields and the occasional farmhouse zipped by beneath us.

'Two minutes!' Porky advised.

'We're looking for allotments to the west of the village,' Derek replied. 'No wires.'

We had a minute or so to go and there was total silence in the cockpit as the frantic map work had been completed. A moment of contemplation. At this point in a flight, I try to think ahead, to visualise the needs of the scene: what kit will I need? Where is the nearest hospital if the patient is very sick? Which hospital should we go to if we don't need a major trauma centre? It's also the time to discuss fuel and weight limitations with the pilot if I'm considering flying to a major hospital that may be some distance away from the job.

As I contemplated these issues, Porky decided to break the tense silence: 'Gentlemen, big nipples or little nipples? Discuss.' We all laughed.

The allotments were easy to find. 'We'll go for the patch of grass just to the left of the large greenhouse,' Porky advised. 'All happy?' he asked. That seemed reasonable to us as it was close to our patient, so we agreed. We quickly squared away the pre-landing checks.

'Doors open,' ordered Porky. I spun in my rotating seat and leant out the open side door. Derek did the same from his position, covering the port side of the aircraft. As the wind hit my face, I could smell the countryside. The scene was easy to pick out of the landscape. It usually is when there's a crowd of people standing around a man lying on the ground and looking alternately down at them and up at us. So that was our boy. The site was very tricky, though, for a helicopter landing: lots of sheds, greenhouses, piles of bamboo sticks, garden tools and, everywhere, bags of fertiliser. If we landed in that stuff the shit really would hit the fan... and be distributed far and wide.

Porky started the approach and, as we got lower, things started to happen. Bamboo canes and flowerpots flew every-where; even the bags of fertiliser started to lift and got thrown around. Two people in the small crowd surrounding our patient decided they'd had enough and fled. I saw the roof of a small shed tremble, lift and fly off. Then we noticed these small white objects flying all around the aircraft at high speed; the powerful vortex created by the rotor blades was pulling them in a circular motion towards the aircraft, and then flinging them far away. For a second, we all exchanged glances, puzzled, wondering what the hell they were. Then…

'Chickens! *Fucking* chickens!' Derek shouted. He was right. Past the open door of the Agusta was a whirling cyclone of chickens.

'Up! Up! *Up!* ABORT!' ordered Derek. Porky duly pulled on some power and abandoned the approach. We wheeled away in a spiralling cloud of white feathers and chicken shit, lifting back towards the sky. So we landed a short distance away, unavoidably trashing some more of the allotment in the process.

Derek stayed with the aircraft until it had shut down as we had landed on an unsecured site with the very real danger of people walking towards it and killing themselves by walking into the tail rotor. I'd noticed that people had a habit of excitedly running towards the aircraft in order to get us to get out and to quickly take us to the job. I didn't blame them – they're usually desperate for help for their loved ones. But we have to keep them – and us – safe. When landing in parks or housing estates, we tended to leave a crewmember with the aircraft until the rotors stopped. The last thing we wanted was someone walking towards us holding the top of their head in their hands and with scarlet fountains dancing brightly out of their skull. It tends to be bad for morale when someone is decapitated. And the dry-cleaning bill for our flight suits is enormous.

I ran with the kit to the job. My patient was an old chap in cardiac arrest. His face was blue and lifeless. His engorged tongue protruded between his teeth. His eyes, which already had worryingly little signs of life, stared up at the sky.

I was crowded by helpful onlookers, all fairly elderly. I needed some space but also some information. As I assessed the old man, I threw out a few questions: 'How long has he been down? Did you see it? Has anyone provided CPR?' I got back some blank stares and some mumbling. 'He's got a heart condition,' offered one elderly gentleman, casually supporting his weight on a spade.

A little old lady approached with a mug of tea and a tartan thermos flask. I wasn't really sure who the tea was for, me or the patient, but neither of us was in a position to accept.

I confirmed that he was in cardiac arrest. Having ensured that the rotor blades had wound down, Derek arrived within a minute and quickly intubated our patient, placing a flexible tube in the man's trachea to keep open his airway and allow us to ventilate him. I attached a cardiac monitor and inserted a cannula into a large vein on the man's forearm so we could administer drugs. We started CPR. The monitor showed ventricular fibrillation – VF is an abnormal heart rhythm, or arrhythmia, consisting of rapid and uncoordinated electrical activity in the heart. It ain't good, but at least it's a sign of some electrical activity – so we did have a chance. It was actually the type of cardiac arrest from which there is the best chance of survival. Electric shocks given across the chest serve to stop all random electrical activity and allow the heart's own pacemaker to work again and deliver a coordinated electrical stimulus to the heart providing a normal contraction and heartbeat.

We shocked him – no change. Shocked him again – no change. We continued CPR and gave him some cardiac drugs.

The lady with the tea leaned over and said, 'He complained of chest and arm pain while he was digging out his carrots and then he fell to the ground and his eyes sort of rolled back. He was gasping for a while and then he stopped just before you got here.'

Derek and I worked in silence. There was no need to talk; we were both working along the standard protocol for this sort of cardiac arrest. I thought it through and said to Derek, 'Thrombolyse? Nothing to lose, probably an MI.'

He thought for a second and answered, 'Sure.'

This meant I was going to administer thrombolytic – clot busting – drugs to try and unblock the artery which I figured had led to a myocardial infarction – MI – and then in turn, a cardiac arrest. I gave him the clot-busting drugs.

Derek and I got into our CPR rhythm. After about 10 minutes of CPR and electric shocks, our patient got back a pulse. It was time to take stock of the situation. We stabilised our man with a series of drugs. He began to bite on the tracheal tube. This was a very encouraging sign; at least some of his brain had survived and was working. We gave him a drug to stop him fighting against the tube. This was always one of the sweetest moments: feeling that simple, short *blip* that meant life was back and death was, at least for now, on the back foot. We always felt like punching the air in triumph. But even our muted inner victory celebrations had to be short-lived: we now had to keep our man alive.

It was time to plan our evacuation to hospital. Porky usually accompanied us to our patients. He had learned how to support us with medical tasks: he knew how to operate our equipment and get drugs out of the bag. He was also clever at cutting through wires, flattening fences, bridging trenches, kicking open gates, booting barking dogs up the arse, commandeering a nearby van, or whatever else it took to get us through any obstacles between us and the aircraft.

But Porky had been conspicuous by his absence on this job. I stood up to look for him. He was standing about 10 yards away, face to face with a tall man in Wellington boots. Both their faces were red, and both were shouting and waving their arms wildly. They were clearly about to hit each other. I left Derek with our patient and ran across to see what the problem was.

'You can't park there! What have you done?' The man in the wellies was practically screaming. 'I've reared those chickens since they hatched! They're all rare breed! You've *killed* them all! *LOOK!*' We couldn't help but follow his pointing finger, and indeed, strewn about the allotments, there were smashed eggs, ripped-out feathers and bits of bloodied pink meat. The guy's chicken coop was one of the many sheds without a roof and was also lying on its side. His few surviving chickens were clucking around in a mixture of cracked egg yolk and straw.

'Well, I'm sorry,' Porky shouted back, 'but I flew this crew in to save a life. We try to save lives – that's why we're here, you know. We're not on a picnic!'

'You've killed over 20 rare breed chickens! Who's going to replace them?'

A flurry of effing and jeffing followed from both camps. This was not good – time to break it up and get our man to hospital. I waded in, introduced myself (labouring the 'doctor' in my title for effect) and rattled through a quick apology.

'I'm truly sorry about your chickens (I wasn't). I really am (I really wasn't). But we had to get in quick to try and save a man's life (we really did). And I'm glad we did because we got here just in time to save him. Please call this number and ask for Jessie. She works at the charity's office and will guide you through the compensation process.' I thrust a card into his hand. He seemed to calm down a little.

I grabbed Porky by the back of his flying suit and dragged him away. 'Load and go, my friend,' I whispered. He could tell I meant business.

We got our old boy onto a stretcher and safely back to the Agusta. During takeoff, this time we managed to limit any more damage to just the killing of a cabbage crop and the possible manslaughter of several potatoes.

We flew off to hospital and delivered our patient to Intensive Care. We kept track of his progress and were very pleased to hear that he survived to dig another day. Good result! And, in another happy ending, even the rare-breed bird owner received compensation.

But we never did get into *The Guinness World Records* for tossing the world's biggest chicken omelette.

CHAPTER 6

Jumping From an Aircraft Without a Parachute

In Air Ambulance circles there is much debate about the merits of having wheels or skids underneath a helicopter. Our Agusta 109 had retractable wheels. Two other Air Ambulance craft, the Eurocopter 135 and the old Bolkow 105, had skids. Agusta pilots will tell you that wheels are preferable as they act as a tripod on soft ground (provided you apply the brakes). Eurocopter pilots tell you that skids allow you to land on just about any surface, and that the skids provide stability for the aircraft when it's on the ground. There are merits for both arguments.

Objectively, there were problems with us having wheels on the aircraft. When we landed on soft fields, we had to lean out and look at the wheels to see if they sank below the surface. If the wheels began to disappear from view into the ground and up to the level of the axles, then we couldn't let the aircraft settle and we couldn't land. This meant repositioning and taking us away from the scene. And this would mean that it would take us longer to get back to the patient.

We were always looking to shave time off everything we did, from getting 'scrambled' back at base to landing as near as possible to the patient. And then getting them safe, stabilised and back to hospital care. Taking a minute off each procedure could mean a big difference to the patient's life.

So Porky introduced the idea of jumping out of the aircraft. Without a parachute.

This meant jumping out while the helicopter was hovering just above ground. We trained on the airfield when returning from jobs. Porky would bring the aircraft to a hover at about six feet from the ground. He gave the order to 'Throw the doctor out in the hover'. We threw the kit out of the aircraft, unplugged the helmet lead and sat at the open door, leaping off to the ground. Forgetting to disconnect the helmet cable would lead to a snapped comms cable – or a snapped neck. He taught us to stay low on the ground until the aircraft had moved off. The paramedic stayed with the aircraft until it had landed as this was a legal requirement when going into unsurveyed landing sites. We started to use this technique a lot operationally if the aircraft could not land near to the scene because of soft ground, sloping ground, tall crops or other obstructions.

The Bat Phone rang. We'd got a call-out to a report of an overturned vehicle that had come off the M6 motorway. We quickly got airborne and searched the relevant area and after a few minutes saw a blue Fiesta on its roof in a field just off the motorway. The field had tall crops and so Porky could not put us down. We hovered for a while and it looked as if there were no occupants in the car. It seemed they had left the scene. This happens a lot with joy riders. Porky wanted us to be sure that there was no one injured inside the car and he decided that I should jump out to check while he hovered the aircraft nearby. I'd take my radio with me so I could advise him of the situation after surveying the scene. As it seemed likely that there were no occupants in the car, I decided not to throw the equipment out but rather just check out the car for myself. I opened the side door, slid across and sat over the side of the aircraft feeling the wind buffet me while we hovered about six feet above the crop. I disconnected the communications cable from my helmet and then slid out the Agusta and jumped, feeling the weird freedom of suddenly dropping through space. I remember thinking as I fell, 'This is taking quite a long time to reach the ground.'

My next feeling was of a huge, hard impact as I hit the ground and bounced. A few stars exploded into my vision. Then I was aware I was flat on my back and was badly dazed. It was surprisingly dark. I could hear our aircraft hovering close by but I couldn't see it; I couldn't even see as much of the sky as I should be able to. Mentally, I went through my body parts and established that there was no pain and that my arms and legs still worked. I rolled onto my side and then slowly got to my feet, feeling quite dizzy. When I straightened up, I realised that the crop (apart from the little bit I'd flattened) was towering in walls around me. It must have been about eight feet high. I realised why, when I was on my back,

I couldn't see much of the sky. And standing, I'm only five foot three inches tall.

I also realised I'd fallen more than 12 feet from the aircraft. I had been expecting a fall of perhaps five feet so no wonder it had seemed to take such a long time to hit the ground. God knows how it must have looked to Porky and the crew when I suddenly disappeared from view into the crops!

Once I remembered why I was in the field, I worked out that if the helicopter was in front of me, then the car must be behind. I made my way blindly through the crop, pushing it out of the way until it came to an end at the edge of the field and I stumbled across the car. The roof was crumpled from the vehicle flipping over. I peered inside. It had been abandoned. There was no blood or body parts inside it; no one lying around. Great. I bloody hated joy riders.

I called Porky on the radio and advised him that the car was empty. His crackly voice came back over the airwaves: 'What happened to you?'

'Next time we do that, can I have a parachute?' I responded. 'Now get me out of here!'

His voice got serious and professional, 'Okay, Tony, I'll hover-taxi across as close as I can get to your position and you'll need to climb in.'

'That's all copied,' I replied.

The Agusta 109 slowly hovered sideways towards me with the side door open, as I had left it. I could see Barry, our paramedic, peering out. Porky tried but could not get the Agusta to me at the flattened edge of the field due to some overhanging trees. So I re-entered the field, and after wading through the tall crop for a few yards, I could make out the wheel of the aircraft just above me. The door opening was at least a foot above that. I was still a little winded from the long drop. 'Lower Porky, but hold your position,' I pleaded. The wheel dropped another six inches directly into the crop. I was now struggling to keep standing due to being battered by the strong downdraft from the rotors. As I jumped up towards the hovering helicopter, my fingers struck the underside of the cabin. I fell back down to the ground. Crap. I stepped back a few inches and jumped higher. My fingers managed to grip onto the floor of the aircraft. But I couldn't hold on and slipped off again, back to the ground. I was getting worried now; also getting tired. I figured I had enough energy for one more go.

I jumped again and this time got both hands onto the floor and held on tight. The helicopter lifted a few inches and pulled me up, my head emerged from the top of the tall crop. The whole of the sky suddenly reappeared to me. Then a strong hand grabbed my right wrist and I was heaved up into the aircraft as it lifted off. I lay on my back looking up at Barry, beaming down at me. He said something in his impenetrable Irish accent.

'Yeah, Barry,' I said, lapsing into our standard response, 'it's about half past two… '

Later, we debriefed on the job and made some amendments to the procedure of jumping out in the hover – like make sure the doctor's not going sky diving without a parachute. Still, it remained a useful way to get a doctor into a scene quickly when the aircraft could not land.

But it was definitely a good idea to try and get the doctor to the accident scene alive.

Sunday afternoons in summer were often busy for us with equestrians and motorcyclists. I was out flying one day with Jenny, one of our newly qualified paramedics. We were sent to a motocross track to reports of a 14-year-old rider, unconscious and with severe injuries.

Chris, our spiritual pilot, was flying us to the job. When we got there we noticed that on one of the slopes on the motocross track there was a crowd of people. Their demeanour spelled trouble. We had learned to read scenes from the air. This one indicated two things: a very sick patient and a potentially hostile crowd.

'I can't get us in near the job,' Chris said, surveying the scene. 'We've got loose barrier tapes flapping about – don't want that in the tail rotor. Tents over there have blocked that area, kids on the other side – no good. Can't land on water, houses on the other side. Looks like we'll need to drop the doctor from the hover. Tony, you happy to jump?' he asked.

I confirmed that I was okay (if not happy) to jump; this was a serious job and I knew I had to get there fast. And as far as I could see there was no eight-foot crops about.

With all his expertise, Chris deftly hover-taxied the aircraft towards the scene. We made hand signals to the crowd of about two dozen leather-clad bikers to move away. But they didn't move. Clearly they were making a point. United around one of their brethren who was in trouble, they were not going to leave his side.

I knew we'd have to be quickly dropped here at the scene, allowing Chris to fly off and find a safer landing zone. For me, this was to be another jump-and-roll from a low hover. Our aircraft, like most HEMS, didn't have a winch for rope drops and pickups – that was RAF fly-boy stuff. Our patients and crew had to be loaded and unloaded on the ground.

'Right, Tony, I'm going to drop you here. Jenny and I will land just before the village, about 500 yards away. It will take us about 10 minutes to join you. Clear jump!'

So I threw out all the kit to the ground, unplugged my helmet cable, and jumped. I curled up on the ground until the downforce and the engine roar lessened as the aircraft moved away. I picked up the medical kit and made my way to the crowd standing around their injured comrade. They looked rough, distrusting, and were watching me very carefully. I looked back at this large human wall of black leather, blue tattoos and hard stares. Keenly aware of the sound of the Agusta 109 fading into the distance. I was now on my own.

I removed my helmet and put it on the ground, then I tried to make my way through the crowd. It wasn't easy as most of them towered over me and were clearly in no mood for a warm welcome. They had formed a defensive ring around the injured boy. He might have been their friend, but he was now my patient. Then they started making encouraging sounds and beckoning gestures to me. They reckoned I must be all right so reluctantly let me through, but they were still watching me intently.

I approached the injured rider. It was a heart-sinking moment. I knew we had a serious problem because above the general noise I could hear the wet, snoring sound of a partially obstructed airway. This suggested a big head injury, brain damage and a patient likely to die without rapid and advanced intervention. He was lying on his back on the ground, being shaken by a few of his mates, all encouraging him with, 'Come on, Billy, stop messing about! Wake up!' It was time for some careful assertion. Obstructive friends can sometimes be as damaging to a patient an obstructed airway.

'Okay, listen up, everyone. I am an Air Ambulance doctor; my name is Tony. Billy is very ill. I need your help and you need to help *me*. Please listen to my instructions carefully.'

Most of the bikers stopped and waited expectantly, two of them kept on shaking Billy, continuing to try and encourage him to wake. I could now see blood spattered on the inside of his helmet visor. Great, so we clearly had a big facial injury as well.

'You two, please step backwards and let me help him; you need to listen to me and do exactly as I say so we can all help Billy.' Very careful and deliberate use of language here – inserting 'all' to give us a sense of shared purpose and try to lessen some of their antipathy. The two bikers desisted in shaking him but were clearly not happy. Where the hell was Jenny, anyway?

I mobilised two of the crowd to assist with removing the helmet safely without disturbing his potentially damaged spine. I encouraged two others to open the kit and lay out the pouches in the order in which I would need them.

Once the helmet was off, strings of blood coming with it, it became clear that the situation was very bad. A brief survey identified that Billy had a serious head and facial injury and two broken femurs. Thinking ahead, I knew he needed, at the very least, urgent airway control and oxygenation, anaesthesia and intubation, cautious fluid replacement, advanced monitoring and leg splintage.

The intubation threatened to be challenging in this patient due to his facial injuries – it can be difficult getting an air tube into an undamaged face, let alone one so badly injured. In hospital, this initial package of care would consume at least three doctors and a team of nurses and support staff. I was on my own.

Come on, where the hell is Jenny?

I applied an oxygen mask and rapidly established venous access, which is a preparation for delivering drugs and fluids to the system. Again, the thought: *where the hell is Jenny?*

I started assisted manual ventilation with a hand-held ambubag to pre-oxygenate the boy. This elevates oxygen levels in the blood and buys some time when delivering a general anaesthetic, should we encounter difficulties getting the tube into the windpipe during intubation. The crowd were not impressed yet, and I could hear some murmurings. Some of them even started to heckle me. The general tone was that Billy wasn't better and he was still lying on the ground – why wasn't he going to hospital? I was starting to realise that if this patient died right here and now I'd have serious problems getting out of the crowd unharmed.

I glanced up to see if Jenny was on her way. No Jenny. Bollocks. I decided I had to crack on by myself and deliver the anaesthetic and get on top of Billy's deranged physiology. I went into hyperactive, super-focused mode and got the kit ready with the help of my two new biker friends. What could possibly go wrong? Emergency anaesthesia is a team sport and you need that second trained pair of hands even for a straight-forward patient. In this case, due to the massive facial injuries, I was expecting a problem.

Where the fuck is Jenny?

Okay, I thought, let's do it, no time to waste. I had to go for what we call 'crash induction'. The drugs first: thiopentone *in*... suxamethonium *in*... fluids open for drug delivery. Billy twitching as the paralysing agent kicks in. This is normal, every-thing is proceeding to plan. Open his mouth and suction out the blood, snot and gore. *In* with the laryngoscope blade... push the tongue over to the left... find the epiglottis and lift. There are the vocal cords – push the tube through the cords under direct vision. Laryngoscope out... inflate tube cuff... connect to capnograph to confirm position. Connect to venti-lator and he can breathe again. (And so can I.)

I waited for my adrenaline surge to subside and settle, and then turned my attention to the next steps. The patient was in a much better situation now. And so was I, now that the crowd of bikers had backed off a little.

I'd just about stopped thinking 'Where the hell is Jenny?' when she arrived, out of breath from the dash from the landing site. I was so relieved to see her. After I gave her a brief summary of events, she kicked into action. We worked efficiently together to finish the job of getting the young man ready for his flight to hospital. Billy's physiology stabilised, giving his brain the best chance of recovery.

In this case, jumping out of the helicopter in the hover position had saved a life. No doubt about it. And this time I hadn't ended up flat on my back seeing stars... Though I knew the bikers would have remedied this if things hadn't gone so well with Billy.

Back at base the Bat Phone rang. Derek answered and nearly choked on his energy drink as he repeated the job being relayed to him by Ambulance Control – 'Man injured by rampant llama!'

'Really? How do they know it's rampant?' I asked as Derek rang off.

'How the fuck would I know? Probably because it's just beaten up a guy with its two-foot cock!' he said as he pulled on his flying helmet, leaving only the ever-present porn-star moustache visible beneath the visor.

You know the joke about the definition of a farmer being a man who's outstanding in his field? Well, this guy just happened to be out standing in a field when a big fucking llama had run all over him. Not quite as unlucky as it sounds because it was, apparently, a llama farm and he was one of the workers there. Now if it had been a potato farm, that *would* have been bad luck.

I wasn't looking forward to this job at all as I had an uneasy relationship with large animals, dogs and cows in particular. Dogs I could cope with if they were of the 'hot' variety and lying in a bun covered in mustard and onions, and cows were fine so long as it was portions of them lying in gravy next to Yorkshire puddings.

I'd only ever encountered llamas, however, in a zoo. I remember that they smelled bad and looked like an incomplete camel. Also, I remembered that Michael Jackson had owned one as a pet, which I only took to be a very bad sign.

We eventually landed at the llama farm, scene of the llama harm. The llama farmer (who wasn't a farmer as such but we liked the sound of it) had sustained quite nasty injuries after receiving a good kicking from a rampant male llama whose romantic desires to get to a female llama had been thwarted by the worker. Why he had wanted to get between a hot lady llama and a six-foot tall, 400-pound randy male llama with a hard on, God only knows, but he must have had his reasons. Maybe they hadn't yet been properly introduced.

The man said he'd eventually managed to get Romeo into a locked barn before calling for help. I told him that he'd done well to even do that, considering the llama had given him some broken ribs and a nasty gash to his leg. During the attack, adrenaline and fear had obviously taken over and allowed him to move through the pain. Now, in the aftermath, the pain was really kicking in; but fortunately so too were our drugs.

While we worked on the llama farmer, we could hear the frantic efforts of the horny llama trying to kick down the barn door and get back to the females. As I administered the drugs and dressed and splinted our patient's leg, we made sure we kept the barn door in our peripheral vision. We kept turning to it, watching it straining against its hinges every time the llama kicked it violently. Somehow we managed to get the patient drugged, splinted up and on the aircraft in the nick of time before the barn doors flew open and the beast on heat burst out.

I thought that if the tabloid press got hold of the story, I could easily visualise the headline – 'GRIEVOUS BODILY LLAMA!'

Our man had got off quite lightly, considering that if the beast hadn't been able to get to the females it might have turned its randy intentions on our patient, I reckoned. And I know NHS nurses have supposedly seen *everything*, but you definitely don't want to be taken into an A & E department after having conjugal relations with a llama…

CHAPTER 7

Tin and Booty Shaking

Air ambulances in England are funded by charity. Although operationally an integral part of the NHS, they started out as local initiatives and spread so that they now cover the whole country. There are more than 25 helicopter units, flying 365 days of the year and averaging a take off every 10 minutes.

The early units found that the public very much liked giving money to Air Ambulances; it was all a bit heroic and seemed such a worthy cause, and highly visible. You couldn't exactly miss a bright red or yellow helicopter whacker-whackering overhead and not understand exactly where it was going and what it was doing.

So the charities did well, and this was the problem: Air Ambulances became a victim of their own success. The units funded themselves and therefore the NHS didn't need to support them.

Our Helimed unit was a new charity and like many others, we started life in the red. The contract we had with the company who owned and leased the aircraft to us and the pilots cost over a million pounds a year. Our medical equipment was also very pricey. The pilots were salaried by the aircraft company, the paramedics were paid by the Ambulance Service.

The charity set up to run our unit appointed a board of trustees; all people of a very high calibre. They understood the value of good PR and promptly decided to send us off to a number of public events. We'd spend many long days standing around the aircraft shaking collecting tins at steam engine meets, country fairs, school fêtes, open-air concerts, race tracks and just about any event that the charity could get us into. Events that were, funnily enough, exactly the kind of accident-prone locations we were often called out to.

But the reality was that shaking a tin all afternoon could only raise a few hundred pounds at best. And every hour of flying cost the charity a whopping £1,200. So it didn't make sense. Every time the Agusta's engines were even started, it cost a few hundred quid.

Raising serious money for an Air Ambulance unit is a serious business and needs a corporate, aggressive businesslike approach. Shaking tins raises awareness and some cash but doesn't fund the service. So the charity appointed a chief executive, Adrian Wilmott, who had the nous to run it as business. Adrian went on to develop the charity as a hugely successful business entity. He went for big donations and legacies but, in a clever move, also regular small donations from many thousands of people on a standing order from their salary. This turned out to be tremendously successful. At the same time, me and the chaps still had to turn out and attend events and play our part in the PR machine. Some of these occasions were more worthwhile than others.

One evening, I was sent to the annual dinner of a community group. We were their chosen charity of the year and they were going to present us with a cheque. I was met by a gracious elderly lady, who led me into the banqueting hall, where there were another 100 or so pensioners. I sat at my table and during the long dinner explained all about the Air Ambulance Service. Then the dinner seemed to get an awful lot longer because, as I was a doctor, they all took it in turns to ask me about their medical problems. I gave advice on haemorrhoids, keeping fit in old age, dryness (don't ask), their grandchildren's asthma, acid reflux, dodgy hips, chapped lips, irritable bowels and irritable husbands.

After the dinner, there were more speeches. Long speeches. Mostly about missing friends who had passed away over the last year. There were lots of tears.

And eventually, I was introduced. The attentive audience were told that the group had raised money for the new Air Ambulance Service and that one of the doctors – me – had come to represent the unit and pick up the cheque. After I was handed a white envelope, I made a gushing speech, thanking them. They then took photographs, I got a round of applause and returned to my table.

I opened the envelope discreetly under the table, and I had to smile to myself. Bless them – they had raised the grand sum of 50 quid. Well, I thought to myself, every little helps. And getting the word out is important. Still, 50 quid… the catering alone would have cost more than that!

A few weeks later, we received what seemed like a strange request from the charity's PR machine. Could we attend a dance studio after the shift in helmets and flying suits? Turns out the charity had got us a slot in the town hall in front of several hundred women, many of whom were seen as potential benefactors. And we were going to perform a Chippendale-style dance routine in front of them later that week.

My instinctive response to whether or not I wanted to be part of a Helimed *Full Monty* revival show was 'No'. As a rule, I don't dance – ever. Not even at weddings. And only rarely at funerals. But SKM, our RAF doc, was happy to be involved and thought it could be fun. Porky, unsurprisingly, thought so too. Bugger. That meant that I had to do it.

When I described it all to Jacqui I got the usual bemused roll of the eyes at what I was prepared to do in the name of medicine, and there were great groans of horror and embarrassment from the kids. David actually thought it was quite amusing but to the girls, and Laura in particular, it was unthinkable! I tended to agree, but it was too late to back out now.

Wasting no time – probably so we didn't have time to change our minds – later that evening, most of us were in a dance studio being instructed in the art of dirty dancing by a professional teacher. To the sound of the song 'Sexy' by the Black Eyed Peas, she had us enter the stage, not walking but strutting, and then had us put our helmets on the floor in a cheeky, bending-over-and-pouting sort of way; a way that none of us (I'm assuming) had ever done before.

Trained professionals that we were, with two doctorates and a commercial pilot's licence between us, we perfected our struts, our bends and our pouts, and dutifully learned our *Dirty Dancing* Chippendale routine.

Giving us even less time to think about it and back out, the following night we were in the town hall. On the way in we saw hordes of middle-aged women queuing to get in. I thought, this can't be happening, I'm a *doctor*.

We were the third act of the evening. I don't know what the other two acts were; I was too nervous to pay any attention – it could have been a talking dog that juggled gerbils and a trans-gender nun blowing ping-pong balls out of her chuff for all I cared! I just knew the sound from the crowd was getting louder and more unrestrained.

Suddenly, the mood and the lighting changed in the building. The sounds of 'Sexy' filled the hall. When I looked down the line at the boys ready to strut their stuff, it suddenly struck me how sarcastic the song sounded when applied to us: we were more like *The Half Monty*.

As we came on stage right through the curtain to start our routine, I was momentarily stunned by row upon row of middle-aged women gazing at us intently, most of them seemingly mesmerised. As soon as we appeared they began baying, and when we 'cheekily' bent over to put our flying helmets on the floor, the place went mad. Taking off a flying suit in an erotic way isn't particularly easy, especially if you haven't had the practice but the crowd just got louder as we became more exposed. Too late to bottle it now. So, with our flying suits shamelessly unzipped and underwear fully on show (along with a bit of middle-aged spread), we strutted, thrust and gyrated for all we were worth.

Any initial embarrassment or nerves had quickly evaporated in the heat of the theatre and the screams of support from the ladies. Only partially dazzled by the lights, we slipped automatically into our routine (all the practice had left us well drilled) and really started to enjoy it, feeding off the enthusiastic whoops, cat-calls and delighted laughter of hundreds of women. For those few moments, we really did feel like Chippendale dancers.

At the end of the routine, when Porky bent over to take a bow, I thought, I'll never *ever* look at that man in the same way again! And, hopefully, never again from this angle.

Afterwards we went down the aisles to give the women the chance to throw money into our flying helmets. One lady suddenly pulled me towards her, grabbed my crotch, shoved a piece of paper into my hand and said, 'Call me, naughty!' I glanced across the aisle and saw that SKM was taking his duties as a dancing doctor very, *very* seriously. I extracted myself from the lady's large bosom with a sucking sound and, as I walked around, I was prodded, pinched, plucked and slapped more times than a Christmas turkey, although I just managed to avoid being stuffed. But it didn't end there: I was groped and probed all the way down and back up the aisle (that's a medical term).

If I'd thought that the Chippendales' experience was bad, pain of an entirely different nature was ahead of me in the name of PR and fundraising. We had been flown to the base of the helicopter company, to meet two local MPs. The whole of the charity PR team was there   very corporate, very businesslike.

A new lady on the PR team introduced herself and said that she wanted to put an Air Ambulance team into the famous 'Tough Guy' competition held near Wolverhampton in the middle of winter. I had seen this Tough Guy event on TV. It was an extreme, hard-core eight-mile cross-country run followed by nearly 30 obstacles that included climbing, wading through deep mud, receiving electric shocks, running through fire, crawling through narrow tunnels and swimming through freezing and filthy water. Basically, it was an obstacle course for masochists, men who liked wearing wetsuits and those who for some reason wanted to give themselves an early heart attack.

'No way,' I said to her, 'It's not happening. No thanks.'

The PR woman smiled, turned and went over to Porky. There was a conversation between them, followed by a loud laugh from Porky. I thought, what the bloody hell is he saying to her? The PR came over to me again and said, 'He said *he'll* do it if *you'll* do it.'

I thought, well, that one's easily solved.

'Tell him to fuck off,' I said. She laughed.

She did some more shuttle diplomacy, playing us off against each other, probably grossly misrepresenting what each other said (which would have been the smart thing to do), and within 10 minutes Porky and I had unwillingly committed to entering the 'Tough Guy' competition. SKM and three of our paramedics agreed to join our group (one of these, Chris Wrekin, was an ex-marine). We had five months to prepare. I immediately lit a fag and downed an energy drink as I contemplated this new challenge.

Our entire group, except me, went for daily runs. Instead I went to the gym and started a diet to lose the excess five kilograms or so that I was carrying. At the gym I got into a routine and saw some progress with my fitness. I had not faced a challenge like this since my time in the military, all those years ago.

The competition was held in late January, in the deepest part of winter. All the better to pull a muscle, tear a tendon and for your frozen balls to clang together like steel conkers. Some browsing on the internet informed me that several people had indeed died during the 'Tough Guy' competition. So I lit up another fag, had a drink and watched the 'Tough Guy' videos on YouTube. I decided that I needed a strategy.

So I bought a short wetsuit and chose layers of clothing that I could put on or discard at various parts of the race. I was very concerned about finishing an eight-mile run and then being immersed in freezing water. Cold shock can kill middle-aged men. Not to mention scaring your testicles so far back up into your body you'd need Angelina Jolie in a thong to coax them back out.

I chose light canvas boots lined with plastic bags and a light rain jacket for my top layer. I put some energy drinks, Mars bars and a single cigarette and waterproof matches sealed in a plastic bag into the pockets of the rain jacket. No point in dying unhappy. If I was going to peg it, I wanted to lie on my back as I croaked and blow smoke into the face of one of the bastards who had organised this thing as they leant over me.

And how rubbish would this look on a gravestone: 'TONY BLEETMAN. FATHER, PHYSICIAN, FUCKING IDIOT'? Dying in a wetsuit isn't a good look, is it?

On the morning, the Helimed team of athletes assembled at my house for a high-carb breakfast of pancakes and maple syrup. They were in high spirits; I was quietly terrified. It didn't help that all my kids were genuinely impressed by me entering the 'Tough Guy' competition, which meant if *they* were impressed, it *must* be dangerous.

We piled into the family people carrier and set off towards Wolverhampton. I drove. On the way, to try and make myself feel better about the good we were doing, I asked how much money we had raised in sponsorship. There was a brief silence, then Porky burst out laughing. Not a good sign. Then he said, 'Nothing, Tone. Not a single penny. We thought the charity was doing the sponsorship fundraising and *they* thought *we* were doing it! We're getting absolutely bugger all.'

We were all pretty embarrassed about this but Porky said that the charity was going to make the best of a bad job and make full use of our participation in the event for PR purposes. Now we just had to not spoil things by dropping dead.

When we got there it was very cold and very wet. And I couldn't see Angelina Jolie anywhere. We joined the other thousands of people taking part and queued to have our entrant number drawn on our foreheads in indelible black marker by one of the race marshals. An easy way to identify the dead, I supposed.

We were all put in the 'newbies' group and that meant we had to wait until the real athletes and veterans had started out, I guess so they didn't have to jump over our gasping, cardiac-arrested bodies if we'd set off first. Some participants were treating it like the London Marathon and were dressed as Vikings or super heroes; others wore thongs and there were even two blokes wearing black dinner suits and bow ties. That was reassuring – at least I knew that if I didn't make it, there were people here who still looked bigger twats than me. Result.

There was actually a lot of excitement in the air. We decided to stay together but acknowledged that our ex-marine colleague, Chris, could do his own thing. We tried to pass this off as a generous acknowledgement of his superior fitness, but in reality we just didn't want to kill ourselves trying to keep up.

The race started with a blast of a horn. Former Royal Marine Chris took off, and we soon lost sight of him in the distance. The rest of us entered into our running rhythm and for the first few miles I thought it was going rather well. I felt okay. At the end of the cross-country section came The Slalom. You had to run up and down a steep hill six times on a slalom course. After ascent number five, I was in trouble. My legs hurt and I had run out of energy. A track marshal came over to me and said, 'You're tired, if you can't run this last bit, I'll have to take you out of the race.' That was not going to happen. I picked up the pace again and reverted to what I had learned in the Israeli Army: concentrate on putting one foot after the other, again and again and again. Depersonalise the pain. Externalise the tiredness. Internalise the strength. Vow to kill Porky. (It's good to have goals.)

The slalom section mercifully came to an end and there was a delay for us to get on to the obstacles ahead. Porky collapsed and started doing an impression of a traffic light – that is, his face went red, yellow, green. Irish Barry said… *something*. Time to regroup.

I drank two cans of the energy drink and ate the Mars bars – a Helimed 999 health snack. I sat down and felt good. As a reward, I enjoyed the single cigarette. I had a warm glow now and a new lease of life. I put on the rest of my layers; the aerobic workload would be less now but I still needed protection from the freezing water that lay ahead.

The obstacle course went on for ever and was clearly designed by some crazed psychopath who hated humanity. We climbed, jumped, fell, slid down ropes, got an electric shock or two, walked through fire, crawled through long dark tunnels and, worst of all, had to wade and swim through trenches of filthy, freezing water. It was like *I'm A Celebrity… Get me Out of Here!* crossed with the D-Day Landings.

My strategy worked well. I withstood the cold shock of the water. After the last of the water sections, I discarded my outer layers and, finally, made it to the finish line. A marshal took my number and put a medal around my neck. At that moment, it felt better than any graduation ceremony I had ever been through.

Later, we even received 'Tough Guy' cloth badges and sewed them onto our flying suits. Tough guy? Hell, yeah! Never doubted it for a second. (I did prick my finger sewing the badge on, though, and that hurt quite a bit.)

We started the day with pancakes and syrup at my house, so we ended it back there too – with a curry. I crowed about our success in the competition and showed off the medal, which even the kids respected. In fact, Rachel said she was thinking about doing it with me the following year. However, I knew how fiercely competitive she was and wondered how it would look for me to be beaten by a 12-year-old girl.

Apart from funding, another problem during the early days of the unit was that we didn't have enough doctors to put one on the aircraft every day. Some shifts had to be covered by two paramedics. While these guys were trained to a much higher level than a regular paramedic, they were not authorised to practise their critical care skills without one of our doctors present. So without a doctor, Helimed 999 functioned much like any other Air Ambulance – flying a patient to hospital; and not as a HEMS unit – flying the intensive care unit to the patient. That was the whole reason for our existence. And also what we wanted to help roll out across the country.

There were, however, ways around the non-availability of doctors for every shift…

I loved my little Beagle Pup, the last of the great British aerobatic trainers. It was a hot day and I was in the hangar, tinkering with my toy. Being glorious sunny weather, I was wearing open sandals, Bermuda shorts and a Hawaiian shirt so loud it should have had a volume button.

As I tried to secure the screws onto a new panel-mounted intercom box, my mobile phone rang in my pocket. It was Porky. He had seen my Sierra Wicked parked in the flying club car park as he drove to the base gate a couple of hundred yards further down the road.

'Tony, I saw your car, what you doing?' he asked, in a slightly ominous way.

'Tinkering with my aeroplane,' I said proudly.

He ignored me and without missing a beat, got straight to the point: 'I was hoping you'd be available to fly HEMS. We've got no doctor today,' he said.

'Sorry, mate, got a rare day off and I'm playing with my toy.'

He continued to cajole to get me to fly the HEMS shift but I really wanted a little time to myself. Eventually he gave up and said, 'Fair enough, we'll come over after the shift and take a look.'

I was looking forward to that. I guessed we'd end up flying the Pup and as always, I was eager to pick up some flying tips from Porky, who was one of the best pilots I'd ever flown with.

I finished securing the intercom box on the panel, and had moved on to sorting out my maps and other odds and ends that a pilot needs in the cockpit, when my mobile phone rang again. It was Porky and he was in full flow in his excited, animated voice.

'*Job!* Tony, we got a job and we need you!'

'Are you fucking mad?' I responded. 'Do you know what I'm wearing? A Hawaiian shirt, Bermuda shorts and open sandals. No flying kit, nothing!'

However, I was torn. If a job had been telephoned in then it meant that someone out there was having a pretty bad day, and might be critically ill. I knew our response could be the difference between a quick flight to intensive care or a slow drive to the undertaker's. I hesitated just for a second and that was all Porky needed; he jumped head-first into the hesitation with the words 'I'll bring a helmet!' and then he rang off before I could argue.

I opened the hangar doors that faced the runway. I heard the Agusta start up in the distance from its parking area outside the fire station and readied myself for another adventure. About a minute later, amidst a flurry of freshly-cut grass cuttings and engine noise it landed outside the flying club hangar. Barry approached me smiling, as if to say 'We knew we'd get you', and tossed me a flying helmet, which I needed to wear before boarding. I pulled it on and fastened it. Porky looked at me and gave me the thumbs up to approach the aircraft under the running rotors. Once he clocked my clothes and sandals, his face contorted with laughter.

I clambered aboard, strapped myself in and connected my communications cable.

Barry and Porky were rattling through the checklist and we lifted. Already Barry had the map work done for the job – an overturned car in a field a few miles to the south.

As we flew towards the car crash, Porky and Barry in the front decided to take the piss out of my choice of clothing.

'So before we rudely interrupted you, where exactly were you planning on flying to – Bermuda for more shorts? Or bloody Hawaii for more shirts? Nice Jesus flip-flops, too. *Very* fetching. You look like fucking Gandhi on a Club 18–30 holiday!'

If there was someone out there with their face embedded in the windscreen of a mangled car, I doubted very much whether they'd give two flying fucks if I turned up in a pink tutu and hobnail boots.

We landed in a field near the B-road that was the crash scene. A boy racer had rolled his little souped-up Honda onto its roof on a bend, obviously forgetting that this was real life and not a video game. I pulled on the rucksack and handed Barry the cardiac monitor. I'd just about forgotten my attire as my head was already in HEMS mode.

As we surveyed the scene, my mind was racing ahead, considering the best rescue approach and access to the occupant of the car. The Fire Service and police were already in attendance. I was reminded that I wasn't really dressed for the job when my right foot in its open sandal made uncomfortable contact with a tall thistle emerging from the long grass. Then my shins got shredded as I climbed over a wire fence. And then little stones from the road got into my sandals and under my feet and made walking very uncomfortable.

I fished out the stones and then looked up to set about approaching the job. Fire officers and traffic police were looking back at me in stunned silence. What was it about my outfit that had shocked them – the yellow/green Hawaiian shirt with pineapples and palm trees? Perhaps the checked Bermuda shorts or the Jesus creepers? Or maybe the fact that the whole ensemble was topped off with a flying helmet.

I got a quick glance at the boy racer, who looked fine and not a time-critical case. A land ambulance crew had covered all the paramedic stuff with collars and oxygen. Barry and I introduced ourselves and hung back; it would be fine to let the fire crew hoist him out of the wreck. We could look at him afterwards.

As we were waiting for the fire crew to do their stuff, the police traffic officer and the fire officer came over together and started delivering me with a severe ticking-off for turning up looking like a surfer at an accident scene. Well, if that's the thanks I get for giving up a day off, I thought. But I didn't say anything. They weren't to know, and I couldn't be arsed explaining. Though considering how I was dressed, I thought how appropriate it was that I should be getting a dressing down. As we flew back to base, Porky's voice came through the headphones. 'Right, *dude*, we better get you back home before the other Beach Boys start worrying!'

Porky and Barry's laughter crackled down the line. Surf's up, indeed!

CHAPTER 8

A Nice Quiet English Sunday Trauma

I love HEMS work in the summer. Rural England has retained its rustic charm. Our missions took us to many quaint locations and beautiful spots, lots of lovely places and stunning scenes... quite a few of them, by the time we got there, spattered with blood.

We attended riding schools, fox hunts, beer festivals, county fairs, dog shows, classic car rallies, Morris dancing competitions and quiet village fêtes... most of which we flattened with the downdraft of a digital turbine-engined helicopter as I jumped out with a medical pack. You haven't lived until you've seen the full contents of a home-made cake stall elevate, rotate and spiral off into a duck pond. Who'd have thought a sponge cake could fly that high?

For some reason, we seemed to get called to a fair amount of narrowboats on the canals. Probably because water, the age of the owners and the canals' proximity to pubs made for a deadly brew. The first we attended was an unfortunate lady who had fallen between the boat and its mooring. As she tried to get out of the water, the boat had crushed her chest against the concrete quayside. She was quite unwell when we got to her. We managed to carefully prise her out and, after draining her crushed chest, airlift her to recovery in hospital.

Wasp and bee stings are rife in summer but we'd only be called out to serious cases of extreme allergic reaction and potentially fatal anaphylactic shock – these cases can be incredibly time sensitive regarding the delivery of medicine and referral for hospital treatment. And, of course, on the basis that if something can happen it will, we even got a call-out to a summer double whammy – a combined canal boat/wasp incident. And no, it wasn't a wasp that had got trapped between a canal boat and a wall. It was a poor family who had been attacked by a black cloud of wasps while they were cruising the canals. The boat looked as if it had been dive-bombed by these killer wasps and most of the family members were badly stung. We dealt with the family on the boat. I guess you'd never think when you went out on a daytrip that something like that would happen, but once it did, the family were sort of trapped out there on the water with nowhere to go. Honestly, just when you thought it was safe to go canal boating…

One glorious summer afternoon we were called to a narrowboat in the middle of Oxfordshire. A woman had fallen down the stairs from the rear deck into the cabin and sustained a nasty head injury. Apparently she had been drinking.

Porky was flying us. Derek's Bitch was the paramedic and we had Jenny with us in the observer seat. Jenny had by now finished her critical care training but was accompanied by an experienced paramedic until she gained some more practical experience and performed independently to the required standard. On the way to the job, she dealt with navigation and radio communications very well. She had clearly got this part of the role sorted.

As we approached the canal, a man waved to us frantically from one of the narrowboats. Distress is quite easy to spot from the air. With experience, it is possible to instantly read body language. You also learn to 'read' the whole scene and work out how serious the job is likely to be. You can assess damage to vehicles quite easily but there are indicators in people that can be interpreted by the experienced HEMS crewmember. This man was clearly very worried. His whole demeanour and movements spelt deep distress.

Jenny had identified a potential landing site close to the boat but as we approached she called out, 'Abort! Abort!' Porky heaved back on the power and we whirled around. The man below looked even more worried now.

We had aborted the landing for a number of reasons that didn't become obvious until the final approach. There were lots of obstacles and loose items on the selected landing site. Just as importantly, there were horses in the surrounding fields that had started to buck around and run on our approach, startled and terrified by the noise and wind generated by the Agusta's rotor blades. We had been badly burned by angry horse owners and equestrians before and so we were extremely wary about landing anywhere near them. Even though we did our best to avoid literally scaring the horses, in the end, as with our encounter with allotment chickens, the patient had to come first.

Because of the compromised landing site, we landed some 400 yards away from the narrowboat. It was a long trek across a couple of fields and over a couple of electrified fences to get to the job. It was a hot day and the four of us lugged all the kit. As we walked, the Bitch briefed Jenny.

'I want you to lead on this job, Jen. Work with Tony, assess it, come up with a plan together and get it done. Tell me what you're planning to do and how you're going to do it.'

She was a superb teacher. Jenny looked confident and seemed keen to impress us all. I was already very impressed.

We clambered aboard the rear deck of the boat and squeezed through the narrow door and into the cabin via a few steep steps. A tall middle-aged lady was lying face down on the floor. There was a pool of blood ballooning out next to her head. She was breathing but not moving or talking. Her anxious husband explained that she had consumed a few glasses of wine with lunch and had fallen down the steps from the rear deck into the cabin, striking her head on the floor. She hadn't moved since. I stepped back and let Jenny take the lead, as we had planned. While she engaged with the anxious husband and then assessed our patient, I looked around. It's always interesting to see how people live, what they had for lunch and what books they have on their shelves. Already I had quickly worked out what we needed to do. I just needed to wait for Jenny to reach the same conclusion.

She conducted a good assessment and established that this lady needed to 'go to sleep' prior to packaging and transportation to a hospital that could offer us emergency CT scanning on a Sunday afternoon. From my perspective, this job was the ideal training opportunity for Jenny to deliver a general anaesthetic: it was not a time-critical job, there was good lighting and adequate room to work in.

Until only fairly recently, delivering an anaesthetic would only happen in a hospital and would only be delivered by an anaesthetist. Anaesthetists are very skilled at delivering anaesthetics for patients undergoing surgery but often have little experience in providing an anaesthetic in emergencies. This is a totally different situation. You need different drugs and different techniques. Our patients were not prepared for what happened to them so would often have a full stomach, or they might have been drinking alcohol, and their medical history is usually unknown. This is very different to the more controlled situation in hospital. We therefore used a skill set referred to as Rapid Sequence Induction (RSI). It involves giving powerful drugs to 'send the patient to sleep' and then paralyse them so they stop breathing. This is important as it is impossible to intubate them – that is, pass a tube through their vocal cords and on into their windpipe – if they're still breathing. We have to stop them breathing first in order to help them start to breathe better and take over their physiology.

RSI also allows us to control important aspects of their physiology by controlling what they breathe and the depth and rate of ventilation. But having said all that, the moment in your clinical career when you first deliberately stop another human being from breathing is an anxious and ominous one. In hospital you develop this skill under close supervision and there are numerous reserve parachutes available if it all goes horribly wrong.

The drugs used for RSI are also very potent and can have significant side effects, particularly in emergency situations. On top of all that, the final potential minefield is the process of getting the tube into their windpipe (the intubation). Usually this is straightforward but on occasion, the tube doesn't go in easily or ends up in the gullet. This is when things can get extremely dangerous and we start to use well-rehearsed emergency routines to get us out of trouble. If we can't get the tube down fairly smartly or find a viable alternative to get air into the lungs, our patient will die. So we practised RSI a lot. We trained in it and rehearsed our drills frequently to cope with failed intubations and, in that case, to cope with failed alternative methods of ventilating paralysed patients.

In that worst-case scenario, the final rescue intervention for this dreaded double-whammy of 'can't intubate/can't ventilate' situation is a tracheotomy – simply put, cutting a hole in the windpipe to put a tube in that the patient can breathe through. It's a procedure often shown in films because of the inherent drama and last-ditch nature of it; I've even seen it depicted where the clear plastic body of a biro is stuck into the windpipe hole as the breathing tube. In reality though, it's actually quite simple but it can be scary.

We felt we were fairly slick at all aspects of RSI as we had trained in it so often and so well. But today we encountered a new RSI complication that we hadn't predicted.

Jenny was working with the Bitch to set up for the RSI on the lady. All was going well. I sat on an armchair in the boat and watched. They laid the equipment out beautifully. The patient had been prepared exactly as we had trained: the monitoring was attached; the drugs had been discussed, calculated, checked and agreed with me. The syringes were labelled; a bag of fluids was running slowly into a vein for drug delivery. This was the perfect operational training opportunity. Jenny decided that she wanted to intubate and asked me to undertake the other role – drug delivery and patient monitoring. Porky sat on another armchair behind us, taking it all in. I briefed the unconscious woman's anxious husband about what he would see so he'd be prepared: 'Your wife will be given drugs to make her sleep. She will twitch for a short time as the drugs take effect. This is normal and of no concern. Then we're going to pass a tube into her windpipe and breathe for her using this bag, which is called an ambubag. Once we're in the aircraft, we'll put her onto a mechanical ventilator until we get her to hospital. We're doing this because it's important to take over these functions to reduce the risk of brain damage and make it safer to get her to hospital.' He seemed reassured, to a degree.

This was going well. Textbook perfect so far. Jenny gave the order to start. I checked the monitor and gave the drugs. Our patient twitched and stopped moving, as expected. Jenny intubated with confidence. She reached over and picked up the ambubag to connect to the tube. This went very smoothly. She connected the carbon dioxide detector that would confirm she had intubated the windpipe and not the gullet by taking a reading of CO_2 exiting the lungs. As Jenny squeezed the ambubag to ventilate our lady, the bag's valve and its housing simply came apart and the component parts scattered across the floor. Slightly stunned, we all paused. We now had a real problem; we could not ventilate this lady without an ambubag. We needed a new one to replace the defective one that had just disintegrated in Jenny's hands but we carried some spares on the aircraft.

'Porky, get back to the aircraft. We need a replacement ambubag. It's in the drawer on the right underneath the cot. Be quick,' I ordered, trying to keep any potentially alarming urgency out of my voice for the sake of the husband. Porky got to his feet, ran off. I guessed he would be at least a few minutes as he had to get back over the electrified fences, find the kit and return to us, covering a round trip of about 800 yards in the process.

Bitch and Jenny and me were now lying parallel to each other on the floor, at the head of our intubated lady. We knew that one of us would have to manually ventilate her by physically putting our lips around the tube coming out of her mouth and breathe down it as she had been paralysed by our drugs and could not breathe for herself. It was a game of chicken. Which one of us would bite the bullet and breathe into the tube while we waited for Porky to return? The husband looked anxious again. I made eye contact and said, 'It's all going *very well*. She's asleep and we just need another item of equipment before we move her to hospital.' He seemed a little unsure.

We all stared at the monitor and slowly and predictably her oxygen saturation began to drop, indicating that she needed someone to breathe for her. The three of us shuffled uncomfortably. We said nothing but we all knew that one of us would have to do this. I broke first and calmly put the end of the tube in my mouth and exhaled into it. Her chest inflated accordingly and within a few seconds her oxygen saturation had returned to a reasonable value. The taste and smell of stale alcohol was overwhelming and made me retch. Between breaths and gulps and gagging I looked up and smiled then told the husband, 'It's all going... very well.'

He said nothing. Bitch and Jenny were starting to exhibit the tell-tale signs of trying to hide the first barely contained bubbles of amusement. Which is a weird contradictory thing that can occur during moments of high stress: when you sometimes feel the compulsion to do the one thing that you know is most inappropriate – and knowing that makes it even worse. You just cannot burst out laughing when someone is potentially dying. Obviously. Despite whatever beneficial release it might provide, it would tend to undermine one's professionalism.

Bitch saw that I was in trouble and she eventually piped up, 'She's doing fine; we're just checking that the tube is in the right place. We'll get her connected to the equipment in a minute and get her to hospital.' The husband seemed reassured and seemed to relax a little. Jenny also got involved, 'You might want to pack some things for her while we have some time.'

That was brilliant! She'd got him occupied doing something. That was better for us all, including him. He busied himself looking for his wife's nightgown and toothbrush.

After several very uncomfortable minutes of me breathing down the tube, a very out-of-breath Porky finally clattered down the narrowboat's steps into the cabin clutching a new ambubag. Brilliant. But then my heart sank. He'd brought the tiny ambubag used for newborn babies. 'Er, Porky, I need the *adult* one,' trying to explain more specifically which one it was. For a split second, I almost felt sorry for him. I spent another few long and lonely minutes blowing down the tube while the Bitch and Jenny dealt with the husband. Porky looked extremely rough when he returned. His face was apple red and he was very out-of-breath. He was sweating profusely and wasn't happy – I thought for a second I was going to have to use the ambubag on him. After all, without a pilot, we were screwed anyway. This time he had, however, brought the right ambubag.

By this time, I was feeling light-headed from having to breathe so hard for the previous 10 minutes down the tube into our lady's lungs, as well as inhaling her alcoholic fumes.

We finally connected her to the ambubag and everything began to take shape. There was just the small issue of getting this paralysed, anaesthetised and quite tall woman up the narrow steps and onto the deck of the boat, then onto the canal bank before trekking through a couple of fields, up a slope, over a couple of electrified fences and onto the aircraft. All the while constantly ventilating our patient with the ambubag and lugging our medical kit and supplies. It was like the 'Tough Guy' obstacle course all over again but with the extra burden of having to carry an unconscious, paralysed, five-foot ten-inch tall woman, and all while I still had a lungful of second-hand red wine fumes.

What could possibly go wrong?

Well, we could drop her in the drink. Which we almost did. At the critical moment when we were carrying her across from the boat to the canal bank, the boat shifted a few inches and the gap between the boat and the mooring suddenly widened. Porky was on the canal bank holding her head and shoulders, we were on the boat holding her torso and legs. As the gap widened scarily, for one horrifying second it looked as if the poor lady might end up head first in the dark water.

Fifteen minutes later, as we flew at a rapid pace to hospital, Porky, who was by now in an unusually contemplative mood, turned to me and asked, 'Tony, if she'd gone into the water, could we have still ventilated her with the ambubag?'

'Er… probably not, Porky, no,' I responded.

'Ooh, I *see*. Well then, that could have been *rather* nasty,' he replied.

I agreed.

CHAPTER 9

Her Majesty's Pleasure, but not ours...

There was a high security prison about four minutes' flight time from the base. We had occasion to go there fairly often; as you might imagine, prisons are places where 'accidents' often happen.

The call that came through sounded a little bizarre. A prisoner with a severe allergy to brown sauce had deliberately poured it all over his fried chicken at lunch and had subsequently become unwell. We were given very clear instructions to land in the car park outside the prison, where prison officers would secure the site and lead us into the exercise yard, where our patient was reportedly in a collapsed state.

We got airborne, and were soon approaching the prison. I could see three prison officers waiting for us in the car park, standing next to a car. We could also see a man on the ground in the exercise yard surrounded by prison officers and a nurse. Several dozen prisoners were standing on the other side of the yard. The exercise yard was a good few hundred yards from the car park.

The pilot that day began his approach. I heard him mumble an ominous, 'It's going to be a bloody long walk from the car park... ' Me and the paramedic thought it was just a general observation, but it became obvious from the angle of his approach that we were not going to land in the car park after all – we were heading directly towards the exercise yard.

I looked at Jenny, our newly qualified critical care paramedic. She looked at me. This was bad. First, there was the obvious problem of ignoring strict and explicit instructions from the prison authorities. Then there was also the minor issue of breaking the strictest aviation laws relating to helicopters and prisons. As an amateur pilot, even I knew that you couldn't fly a helicopter within 2,000 feet of a prison. You didn't have to be a genius to work out the sum of a possible equation: helicopter + prison landing + long-term inmates that haven't had a shag in 10 years = bloody good reason for them to try and hijack our craft.

A whole basket of butterflies was suddenly let loose in my stomach at the thought of flying into an exercise yard filled with high-risk category prisoners. I just hoped none of them wanted a joyride in an Agusta 109 – I didn't fancy being thrown out the helicopter mid-hijack and ending up a big puddle of jam on the street.

As we began our descent, the officers in the car park waved frantically, pointing to their feet. They were making it as clear as they could that we were to land in front of them, in the yard. The pilot pressed on with his approach over the car park and then over the high-security wall and towards the exercise yard.

After much discussion about small things like aviation laws vs. patient care, to my surprise, we ended up landing in the exercise yard in a spiralling cloud of dust kicked up by the downdraft from the rotors. Prisoners and prison staff were clearly stunned. Through the dust I could see their shirts and trouser legs fluttering furiously in the wind. And the blanket that was covering our patient was quickly blown away by the helicopter's downdraft. I could also see two men in suits start to gingerly approach the aircraft. I assumed they were probably prison governors. They looked angry and incredulous. And dusty.

I decided it was time to quickly engage with the patient and leave the pilot to his fate with the prison authorities.

Anaphylaxis, or what most people call anaphylactic shock, can be potentially fatal. What happens is that the body wrongly perceives the allergen (for example, a particular food or wasp sting) as a threat and so the immune system reacts badly. It can lead to low blood pressure, loss of consciousness, airway obstruction and respiratory and heart failure. Because of the potential for it to kill, we always have to treat it as an emergency. An adrenaline shot is given as soon as the reaction is diagnosed as serious, which is why people with food allergies carry things like Epipens for self-administering adrenaline.

I knelt down beside our patient, but he immediately puzzled me. On the face of it, he looked quite unwell. He was wheezy and his skin was all blotchy but it didn't quite add up. We administered steroids, anti-histamines, ranitidine, nebulisers and adrenaline. His numbers on the monitor were fine. For a moment as we stood around him, we discussed treating him in the prison and waiting to see how he got on. But as we stood next to him and discussed our options, he seemed to get worse. I decided that we should probably take him to hospital.

I don't think the prison service had ever encountered this situation before: a sick category 'A' prisoner who needed helicopter transport to hospital being airlifted directly out of the prison.

There was only one spare seat on the aircraft. A small female prison officer was tasked with escorting this rather tall and heavily-built prisoner to hospital. I wasn't convinced that she could offer us complete security in the aircraft. Even unwell, he looked like he could have picked her up with one hand and thrown her like a dart. On top of that, she didn't even handcuff him, but sat with a little sports bag containing her prisoner transport equipment. I asked if she was not going to cuff him. She said she was not allowed to chain a prisoner without there being *two* prison officers present. I was staggered by this particularly brilliant Home Office regulation, probably dreamt up by some Health & Safety jobsworth.

So it was unsafe to shackle a prisoner if there was only one prison officer but safe to do it if there were two of them. I think that's what the Americans call ass-backwards. If it was up to me, I'd have restrained him, but I suppose the prison officer was more shackled by regulations than the inmate would have been by handcuffs.

During the flight to hospital, our prisoner seemed fine. In fact, he appeared to get better, and even sat up to look out the window as we flew along. It didn't take long for the realisation to sink in: we had been severely duped by this guy and we were probably about to enter a whole world of trouble with a strong, healthy escapee. I accepted that he had some form of allergy that made his skin a bit blotchy, which is obviously why he'd had the brown sauce with his lunch and then eaten just enough to give him some convincing physiological symptoms. But the wheezing and 'collapse' must have largely been feigned or at the very least, greatly exaggerated. So that meant he was still at full strength, and we were about to land at an unsecured helideck in the middle of a big city.

It became increasingly obvious that this bloke was obviously planning to make a break for it as soon as we landed. For the first time, I noticed that he had four faded blue-black letters tattooed across the knuckles of his right hand – A. C. A. B. (Or 'All Coppers Are Bastards'.) Oh, good, that was reassuring. At least he didn't have H.D.M.D (Helicopter Doctors Must Die) across his other hand.

I decided it was the right time to get assertive with our pilot, who I knew was totally oblivious to the situation. Our prisoner had no headset so was not be able to hear any conversations on the intercom over the engine noise in the cabin.

'Listen up,' I said to the pilot. 'This guy has been pulling our chain. He's not that sick. I think he's going to make a break for it and get us onto the evening news. And if it goes badly enough, we might even make first bong on *News at Ten*.' We'd often made the local news for some rescue or other that we'd been involved in but I'd never planned on being the lead story because I'd been on a team that effected a jail break from a high-security prison.

'Gosh,' he replied.

'Yes, exactly, fucking "gosh". Look, I need you to arrange for the police to meet us when we land. I don't fancy taking on a guy two feet taller than me and one foot wider. And I definitely don't fancy chasing him across rooftops.'

I was beginning to really regret the prisoner not being handcuffed; I knew he'd be difficult to subdue. We had a slim chance that he might tire himself out beating me to death, but outside that, not much hope. Funny how you never have brown sauce on you when you need some.

As we landed, our conman con seemed to perk up considerably, and even more so as he was pushed on a trolley by hospital porters down the exit ramp. Our little prison officer trotted behind, clutching her prisoner transport bag. If the police aren't here right now, all hell's going to break loose, I thought.

We banged through the doors of the Emergency Department and our prisoner suddenly became very alert and started to sit up and look around… just in time to see that we were about to be met by four strapping police officers. I wouldn't say they exactly matched the description across Brown Sauce Boy's knuckles, but they certainly didn't look like fluffy bunnies.

So, finally, our prisoner was at last securely handcuffed by the police, prior to us handing him over to the hospital team.

Back at base, the pilot received several severe, eye-watering spankings over landing us slap-bang in the middle of the prison yard. The prison, the Home Office, our PR company, the helicopter company and Porky each gave him a piece of their mind. It had been outrageously risky to turn the prison yard into our landing site. Thankfully, we'd managed to get away with it without being taken on an impromptu flight to Cuba. However, the next prison job was to be even more outlandish.

Before that, however, these recent run-ins with criminals made me think first of my father and then of myself as a child: my father because as an optician he had served Britain's most famous villains, the Kray twins; and myself as a child because from early childhood, I had three ambitions in life. I wanted to be a doctor, a pilot and a gangster. Strange, I know. I achieved the first two but thankfully shied away from the last. My fascination with organised crime grew from my father's early association with the Krays.

My father had an optical practice in Bethnal Green Road in east London. In the early 1960s, all the Kray brothers – Ronnie, Reggie and Charlie – had eye tests and bought their glasses from him. They'd grown up on Vallance Road, about a quarter of a mile down the road from my father's shop. At that time, the Krays were the most well-known and feared gangsters in London, but after their arrest in 1968 they became the most famous villains in the country.

Having these men as customers was not without repercussions. My father was called as a witness for the defence at the

Old Bailey trial of the twins, on behalf of Ronnie Kray. In 1966, Ronnie had shot the rival gangster George Cornell through the forehead with a 9mm Mauser in the Blind Beggar pub. Thankfully, my father wasn't in the pub at the time, but he was called to give evidence about Ronnie Kray's ability to see at distance without glasses as he hadn't been wearing any when he shot Cornell. The fact that he wasn't wearing the glasses my father had prescribed for him obviously hadn't made much difference to Ronnie's aim.

My father later told me that he found the entire episode of giving evidence at the murder trial quite terrifying. I was only seven years old at the time and it was this reality check that destroyed any illusions of glamour I had surrounding crime and made me realise that perhaps medicine was the better option.

Another crime-cum-Helimed connection I dwelt on is that the Krays used to eat at a now-famous café in Bethnal Green Road called Pellicci's, a lovely family-run business that hasn't changed over the years. Pellicci's had known me since I was a kid as my father used to take me there. As well as being still packed out with real East End characters, it now often hosts big chaps in orange flight suits from the London HEMS.

The funny thing is, my father says that the Krays still owe him money for their glasses because they were arrested before they paid. He would never have guessed that I would also end up in and out of prison, albeit onboard a bright yellow Agusta 109 helicopter.

*

Soon after the Brown Sauce Man mission, we had another call-out to a high-security prison. A category 'A' prisoner had been stabbed in the chest by another inmate. He was very sick, possibly near death from the sound of things. On this occasion, Porky was flying us, so I had high hopes that we wouldn't land on top of the prison governor's desk.

We scrambled double-quick, got airborne and were soon at the Agusta's top cruising speed, clipping along at 200mph. I thought about how many stabbings I'd seen and dealt with over the years. When I was a very junior doctor at Glasgow Royal Infirmary in the early 1990s, a well-known local gangster was brought into the hospital. He had been shot in the chest, and was dying. He was in such a bad way that a thoracotomy – a surgical opening of the chest – was done right there in the Emergency Department. Being a new doctor – and certainly new to seeing a man's chest cut open and lifted off like a lid to reveal every internal organ glistening under the strip lights – I was quite shocked at witnessing the event. The guy had a bullet hole in the heart, resulting in devastating damage. He didn't survive. So I'd left the resuscitation room a little stunned to find that the attending police officers had all gathered outside. This gangster was obviously a big local player and the police wanted to know the state of play. A police inspector stepped forward and asked me how the guy was and I said that he was dead. He immediately replied, 'Thank *fuck* for that!'

That was the first thoracotomy that I'd ever seen. Since then I'd seen, and also carried out, several more open-chest procedures. A young Asian woman, stabbed repeatedly in the chest, was dead on arrival at hospital, but after we opened her chest, plugged the hole in her heart, gave her open heart massage (along with fluids) and got her heart restarted, she survived. A young man in his early twenties, stabbed twice, was delivered in near-cardiac arrest on arrival, so we opened his chest, evacuated blood from the pericardium, identified the hole, repaired it, gave him open heart massage and restarted his heart. He was eventually closed up down in the operating theatre, and he survived. Another guy in his early twenties, stabbed multiple times, was delivered to the hospital losing blood pressure and consciousness, so we opened him up, found major bleeding from the intercostal artery, tied off the bleeding and restored his blood pressure with blood units. He was taken to theatre for closure of the chest, and survived.

Don't get me wrong, we did lose people. But as we were now clipping along at a rate of knots through the sky, back towards the prison and another stabbing victim (and another possible thoracotomy), I didn't want to dwell too much on the losses.

This time we dropped down into the prison car park, as instructed. No theatrics. We jumped out the aircraft, threw our kit into the back of the waiting car, and were rushed at speed through a series of gates into the prison exercise yard. Our patient, a stocky man in his late thirties, was lying lifeless on the ground with a single stab wound to the front of his chest. His shirt had been opened, revealing a one-inch wound to the left of his breastbone with a small pool of blood on his left side. Clearly most of the bleeding was internal and, as I was soon to discover, most of the blood loss was into the chest cavity from the stab wound to his heart. I couldn't give him a blood transfusion – we can't carry blood on the aircraft because of the problem of refrigeration – but I could increase blood volume by infusing just enough saline solution to maintain a pulse. If we infused large volumes of fluid in an attempt to increase blood pressure, we would just cause more bleeding. The solution is to fix the hole, arrest the bleeding, maintain a pulse and get the patient to hospital as soon as possible.

'How long has he been like this?' I asked a terrified-looking prison nurse.

'He stopped breathing a moment ago,' she said.

I thought, well, if this nurse hangs around she's going to end up a great deal more terrified (as I was in Glasgow) because, as I'd suspected, this patient was a perfect candidate for a thoracotomy – we'd got there right on the tail of the loss of cardiac output. If I could get into the chest quickly, evacuate blood from around the heart, plug and stitch up the tear in the heart (or clamp the bleeding vessel), the outcome might be favourable.

I'd use what is called the clamshell approach, where the breastbone is cut and the chest opened like the bonnet of a car. It's an extreme approach, but gives almost complete exposure and access to the thoracic cavities. But – and there's no way around it – it is brutal and bloody.

Thoracotomy is a team activity. Someone needs to open the chest; someone else needs to hold up the top half of the opened chest to expose the organs and allow the operator to get into the chest to rapidly identify and manage the injury. A third person will usually be required to pass instruments and generally assist.

Assisted by our trained HEMS paramedic, Jenny, I rolled our patient onto his back and we took his arms out to the sides. Porky, our pilot, who at urgent times like this was also drafted in, had already found and unwrapped a sterilised scalpel for me. First, I made an incision beneath our patient's left armpit. I drew the blade down in a seeping arc, slicing across his chest and beneath his left nipple, then across the chest midline, under the right nipple and up steeply towards the right armpit – leaving a long incision like an opening zip across the chest, pulping out with yellow-white subcutaneous tissue. I then cut the muscle between the ribs. All the fingers of my blue surgical gloves were now slimed red. The breastbone was to be dealt with next. Jenny passed me the Tuff-cuts, the large heavyweight trauma scissors useful for cutting bone. I worked through the sternum, snipping and crushing the bone until it separated. The used equipment I passed over to Jenny, who passed it back to Porky. Once the bone was successfully divided, I slid both hands into the incision, feeling the warmth from inside the body, and lifted our man's severed breast towards his head. Jenny got her hands underneath it and took it from me: another pair of hands lifting away this part of our man's body. His chest was now open, exposed, internal organs glistening. The pericardium, the sac around the heart, was now visible. I cut through it longitudinally, taking care not to also cut the phrenic nerves that make the diaphragm work and are essential for breathing. Now I'd exposed the non-beating heart. I found the stab hole in the heart and plugged it with a finger to arrest the bleeding. Then I took the heart in my hands and squeezed it gently to try and encourage a spontaneous heartbeat.

We got nowhere. I knew we'd lost our man: the damage had been too great. We couldn't save him.

I looked up for the first time and saw the row of horrified faces of prison officers and the prison nurse, all wide-eyed and silent. Our patient, and their prisoner, was dead. We covered him with a sheet, rolled off our sticky latex gloves, and started to do the paperwork.

By this time the police had arrived. They were a little over-whelmed by what they saw after removing the sheet: the body of a ghost-white corpse lying on the ground with its arms outstretched, its chest cavity wide open and displaying all the reds, pinks, purples, whites and yellows of the organs inside – like a grotesquely bloody human fruit salad.

That's enough to stop anyone in their tracks, even the most hardened copper.

We sat down – me, Jen and Porky – calmly completing our required forms. As I did so, I was vaguely aware that we were covered in human blood, darkening as it dried. I was practically wearing red sleeves of it. Already I could feel it tighten on my skin. I thought about how some people described getting into this work for 'the juice', meaning the adrenaline rush, but what they didn't tell you about was all the other juices you got as well – the blood, mud, snot, grot, spit, shit and piss, engine oil, aviation fuel and general filth that were all part of the job. But it didn't bother us. We'd go home, have a shower and hot-wash all that 'juice' off our flight suits, ready for the next shift.

Just as we were finishing our paperwork, one of the police officers suddenly went into officious crime-scene-preservation mode. 'Right, don't touch anything,' he ordered. He had his brown paper evidence bags and was judiciously labelling them after he packed them with items retrieved from around the scene. He then noticed that the three of us – the happy band of Helimed 999 – had liberal amounts of blood spattered on our orange flight suits and boots. I saw him thinking about it for a minute, and then said, 'Right, I'm seizing your flight suits and boots as evidence from a murder scene. Please take them off and put them into these bags, which I will give you. I need each of your names as I call you forward.'

Porky laughed loudly and looked at me. Then he looked back at the copper and realised that our policeman was entirely serious. He then took on a more considered approach.

'Are you seriously suggesting that we fly our helicopter back to base in our Y-fronts?' he asked.

'I'm sorry?' responded the policeman.

'I said, do you want us to fly back in our Y-fronts? I mean, do I look like bloody Superman!'

The copper gamely soldiered on, 'But your clothing and boots are being seized as evidence in a murder.'

Porky thought for a second and calmly went into chief pilot mode. 'Aviation law, supported by the Civil Aviation Authority, mandates that all aircrew must wear fire-resistant flight suits and protective footwear. If you seize our clothing, you will be forcing me to break the law and I will need to report that.' He went on. 'If you continue with your actions, you will deprive a large part of England of its frontline Air Ambulance unit.'

The policeman persisted, albeit a little more reticently. Porky brought the conversation to a close with a quick and hearty, 'Right. Fuck off, it's not happening.'

The policeman recoiled a little and seemed bewildered – after all, he'd probably never before been told to *fuck off* at a murder scene by a blood-smeared, pissed-off pilot. He then noticed me removing bloodstains from my beloved Breitling watch, using an alcohol wipe.

'Doctor, is that blood you're removing from your watch?' he asked.

'Probably,' I answered truthfully, 'I've been up to my elbows in his chest.'

'I'll need to seize your watch then,' he continued.

I saw that Porky had got further with the short-sharp-shock technique, so I responded with, 'You're not seizing my Breitling – fuck off!'

The policeman backed off. We were then escorted back to the aircraft by several prison officers. During the flight back to base we chuckled all the way. Porky was on form. 'So he wanted us to fly back to base in our underwear? What a cock! I think he just wanted to see you, Jen, with your kit off! Bloody cheek!'

'Well, if you'd got your kit off, Porky,' I offered, 'we definitely would have seen too much cheek!'

This kind of banter was a much-needed psychological release after seeing a man die in such a brutal way. We could have flown back in silence and felt worse, or kept the darker thoughts at bay by letting in some light with a few gags. It may have only been whistling in the dark but it's one way to let each other know that we're all in this together.

This would be another job too traumatic to take home and share with the family, so they'd never know that I'd been in prison, albeit briefly. Like most emergency service workers I didn't take the job home unless the story was funny or there was something amusingly weird about an incident.

In retrospect, I thought that back at the prison we were quite close to getting arrested. We had played chicken with a policeman and had won, this time. Or at least we thought so until the police came to visit us on the base later that afternoon for a debrief. The interviews didn't go that well. But Derek, our big boss saviour, was ready and waiting. He had heard about the job and made his way to the base, correctly predicting what was going to happen. Derek was a past master at causing trouble so he recognised it on the horizon when he saw it. And he got us out of trouble again. Our debt to him was increasing all the time.

CHAPTER 10

Critical Transfers & In-Flight Terror

Within a year of starting the unit, we had accumulated well over 1,000 missions. We were by now the busiest Air Ambulance unit in the country, so we started to measure our quality and effectiveness. Derek had designed and introduced a clinical database that we had to complete for each job. He produced monthly activity reports and we were able to look in detail at the safety and effectiveness of the advanced procedures that we delivered. We linked up with local hospitals to follow up on our patients to see where we had made a difference and also to identify where our practice needed improvement.

Clinical and operational audits were undertaken and most of the crew gathered every month for governance meetings at which we shared audit results and learning points from the hundreds of missions that we had flown. We were now very good at what we did. The doctor–paramedic HEMS partnership worked and was much more effective than the traditional paramedic-only Air Ambulance model. Quickly and directly, we were getting intensive care to critically ill people on the ground where they lay.

The charity also recognised that there was money to be made by helping to provide another service – flying critically ill patients between hospitals. These critical care transfers between intensive care units happen a lot in the NHS. Typically, after initial stabilisation at a peripheral hospital, the patients are transferred to larger or regional specialist centres. In Air Ambulance work, we often started the intensive care level of advanced intervention *before* we got to hospital. We were good at starting the intensive care process, but maintaining patients in this state can be very, very challenging and not for the occasional hobbyist. For the paramedics and non-intensive care doctors on the service, this was a little outside of their comfort zone. It was certainly outside of mine.

So, not wanting to be left behind, I attended a two-day simulation course on critical care transfers in Bristol. It was one of those rare life-changing courses. The realism of the simulation was unbelievable. We had to push a 'patient' with all the associated monitors, ventilator and drug delivery pumps across a busy main road from one hospital building to another. Halfway across the pedestrian crossing, our patient developed a heart problem and we had to deal with it. Another simulated scenario took place in the back of a real ambulance driving through real Bristol streets. The patient got into difficulties and when I ordered the driver to divert and get us to the nearest hospital, he activated real lights and sirens to get us there through the real traffic. The realism of these simulations really got the adrenaline uncorked and the brain shifting up through the gears.

The course helped me to identify and learn a few additional things in the transfer process that I hadn't considered before and this would come in extremely useful when we were back in the air.

Transferring a critical care patient had to be planned down to the smallest detail. Before accepting the transfer, we had to know everything about the patient by talking to the referring intensive care unit. We had to know the numbers on the monitors and their trends; we needed to understand the array and complexity of drugs that were keeping them alive. Then we had to speak with the receiving hospital to tie things up there as well. After all of this, we had to work with the pilot on flight planning: weight, fuel, weather and possible interference of the medical equipment with the aircraft systems all had to be considered carefully.

Receiving a critical care patient should always be done in a careful handover with the referring intensive care unit. It can take some time to get it right and keep the patient safe. Before you set off, you need to calculate medical gas volumes and drugs required for the journey. Electrical power, batteries and backups for the equipment all need to be worked through very carefully. All the equipment and spares must be checked. You need to review the case notes, documents and charts, and make sure you have the scans and test results. And you need to personally check every tube, line and lead for yourself. Only then would you consider a careful move to your vehicle or aircraft. Once in the aircraft, all checks need to be made again before starting the engines and flying off.

Once on the move, you need to observe by the second every number on the monitors, drug pumps and ventilator. This requires total concentration, vigilance and situational awareness. In critical care transfers we would be transporting the human equivalent of a highly damaged and delicate item of precious china that had been very carefully pieced back together again but still hadn't yet set.

For air transfers there is also the added complexity of selecting a landing site and planning a secondary transfer by land ambulance if you can't land in the receiving hospital. The pilot and crew will be very interested in the weather, fuel endurance and weight and balance calculations.

As a team we threw ourselves into this new area of critical transfers with our usual gusto. You couldn't say we didn't love a challenge. And by the time I had already successfully undertaken a handful of these critical care transfers on the aircraft, I was beginning to gain some confidence in my ability to safely deliver a complex critically ill patient to a receiving unit. This was a new test for me and I began to look forward to the next one with a degree of both trepidation and anticipation. In other words, with excitement. (Unusually, we also got paid for these critical transfers, which helped.)

With the growing confidence that I had in my ability to take on these critical transfers, I was happy when Porky called me at home late one afternoon. 'Are you available for a transfer to Manchester?' he said. I asked when it would be.

'Now,' he replied.

'Should be okay,' I said. 'Do I get any details?'

'We'll all brief you once I pick you up.'

'Pick me up? Are you planning on flying to my house?'

'No, you twat, I'll pick you up from your hospital! I'll be there in 20 minutes.'

This was suddenly becoming a potentially interesting job. I was going to be picked up from my hospital workplace, which meant loads of people would see it. Cool!

I put on my flying suit, took my flying helmet with me and drove in to work. I called ahead to the hospital and mobilised the helideck fire team. When I was there we waited on the helideck for a few minutes before we heard the familiar drone of the approaching aircraft. The drone and clatter got louder as Porky landed and kept the rotors running, beckoning me to get on board. I climbed into my familiar seat in the back of the aircraft and strapped myself in. I was surprised to see Irish Barry sitting in the paramedic's seat – I'd thought this was just a pick up to take me to the base where we would plan the flight. I knew then that there was a good chance I wasn't going to have the opportunity to do this transfer by the book.

'Where are we going?' I asked.

'We're flying a burns patient to the burns unit in Manchester – it's the very last burns bed available in the UK, apparently,' advised Barry through the intercom.

Then Porky advised, 'I've got his height and weight. We've got enough fuel to get there and just enough for an alternate, if we can't get in. We're expecting shitty weather over Manchester in a couple of hours but we should just make it before it turns nasty.'

Fuck. I knew if we got caught up in the air in that shit storm then the weather wouldn't be the only thing turning nasty. I tried to protest: 'Er... Porky, I really need a structured medical handover here, and I'll have medical stuff to do before we launch...'

'No problem – do your medical stuff when we get to the first hospital. But don't take too long. We've got to get him there tonight otherwise they'll lose that last available burns bed. We've got about a two-hour window until the bad weather comes in.'

By the time we were hovering down towards the hospital's landing zone, I was stunned to see a team of intensive care staff in their surgical scrubs already pushing an intensive care bed towards their designated landing site as we approached. This was bad. I knew in this situation I had no chance of receiving even a half-decent clinical handover and little chance of working out gas, battery and drug requirements on a patch of concrete on a playing field next to the hospital. I didn't even know what drugs were keeping this patient asleep and, more importantly, what drugs and ventilator settings were keeping him alive.

I quickly looked around our aircraft. It had only our regular equipment designed for primary HEMS work, not any additional kit for a critical care transfer.

After we landed and the rotors stopped, a young-looking doctor gave me a hurried handover and said, 'I've told the burns unit that you'll be there in an hour. And I've brought you some extra propofol (anaesthetic). Here's his paperwork. We got the last burns bed in the country, you know.'

I knew. It had been mentioned twice already. I wondered if the panic about losing this last burns bed was getting in the way of making an accurate assessment of whether or not we should fly. I was now close to subdued panic – this all felt like carefully controlled chaos.

I knew I should have turned down the transfer right there and then, but when I saw the state of this patient, I felt I couldn't refuse: the only parts of him that weren't wrapped up like a Mummy were burnt scabrous and black. This boy really needed that burns unit bed, especially if it was the last one in the country. It looked like we were going to have a desperate 140-mile race against the deteriorating condition of the weather *and* the patient. But, in my personal opinion, this was the best thing for the patient. I hated to think of the alternative.We manoeuvred our man into the aircraft and I tried to work out the lines, tubes, pump and ventilator settings as best I could; all of my training on 'what to do when things go wrong' instinctively kicked in. We'd been rigorously trained in just about every worst-case scenario you can imagine. I laid out the drugs and fluids that I thought I would need. I placed his observation chart on the spare seat and checked oxygen supplies on the aircraft. If we got there within an hour, we'd probably just about make it on the oxygen reserves left on the aircraft, I thought.

I got into the groove and focused on the numbers I needed to calculate and maintain the patient as the Agusta's engines whined into life. The blades began to whip up to speed and, finally, we lifted. Wheels left the ground; I was only half aware of the familiar feeling of the aircraft tilting forward just before we surged up into the sky. Ignoring the idle chat coming from the front, I concentrated on every number and setting on the monitor, ventilator and drug pumps. I recorded them on the chart and looked for trends, just as I had been (only fairly recently) taught.

After about half an hour in the air, Porky piped up: 'Our ground speed is only 100 knots; we're flying into a hell of a headwind.' I looked up, not just because of his ominous announcement, but because at the same time I noticed that the cabin had suddenly become very dark and gloomy. Porky and Barry were just dark silhouettes against a darkening sky. I immediately looked out of the side window – I could see only dark grey clouds billowing expansively and quick flashes of jagged strips of lightning that looked like white-hot lines of barbed wire.

The Agusta suddenly lurched and bucked in turbulence; my neatly arranged supply of labelled drugs scattered and rolled all over the floor. I tried to retrieve them. The aircraft dropped sickeningly, then lurched upwards. Dropped again. Some of the meds jumped vertically out my hands. I managed to catch them as they dropped.

I knew we were now flying between violent thunderstorms. That was the good news – that there was space between them.

But the bad news hit me straight away – when these thunderstorms grew and joined together, as they were doing, and became one vast black storm, there would be no space left for us at all. We'd be flying through the heart of an immense collision of air pressures and violent electricity. At that moment I imagined that from the outside, what we thought of as our mighty Agusta 109 must right now look like a trembling bee flying into satanic mushroom cloud.

The idle chat in the front had stopped. That was a worrying sign. Porky was focused; this scared me. He was never quiet. Even worse, Barry was silent too. Christ, I thought, it must be bad. Then there was a blip of light and an implied blank, and I did a double take as I saw our patient's monitor screen go dead – its battery had expired. We carried a reserve. I quickly changed the batteries and breathed a sigh of relief when the screen lit up again. The numbers remained stable. But the battery bar on the right side of the screen indicated only two little bars out of the five. I figured that was about half an hour at best. Not good. At the same time, two of the five drug syringes in the pumps were nearly empty. I used my last reserve ampoules from the standard HEMS kit. But now the oxygen cylinder was also getting low. Then it started to rain, heavily, lashing the windows.

I had a growing knot of tension in my belly as Porky eventually announced, 'The GPS says we're over the hospital landing site! But I can't see anything and I daren't get any lower! I'm going around and we'll try again.' I looked out the window again and we were in thick, thick cloud. We were still bucking around. The ship was shaking. For all the sophistication and power of this aircraft, right now it was moaning and bucking like an old galleon on rough seas. Porky dropped us down towards where the GPS indicated the landing site should be with all his skill fighting against the buffeting air currents, but it was just too much. He declared a missed approach, aborted the second landing attempt and quickly announced, 'Let's try Leeds! Just got enough fuel. I think... '

The knot of tension in my belly was by now double-tied. I knew that even if we managed to get in to Leeds without being forced down, we would need to road transfer our patient all the way back to Manchester after landing.

I checked over our man again and he was fine and stable; he was definitely the least worried out of any of us. Then I returned to my charts, desperately working through our options.

'Barry! I need some help. Please radio the Ambulance Service at Leeds. I need a blue-light ambulance to go to the nearest hospital and pick up a list of drugs, which I will write down and give to you. I also need some *charged batteries* for the Propaq. They need to meet us *immediately* after we land at Leeds!'

Barry said something in his heavy accent (I felt too uneasy to even make the usual joke). I detected an 'okay' and a couple of alarmed 'fucks'. I wrote down the list of drugs and passed it forwards. While aware of some radio traffic from the front, I was too focused on my patient to listen. Barry was using the phonetic alphabet to tell control precisely what we needed. He was good and seemed to have developed some insight into the difficulties of other people understanding him.

Every inch and angle of the sky seen out the windows was now ominous blacks and greys. What was that seventies disaster film – *Terror at Ten Thousand Feet!* or something? I'd gone from once watching it to now being in it.

I also realised I was now out of some of the drugs and was making do by using alternatives from the HEMS drugs bag. The patient remained stable and the numbers were still all fine.

The cockpit remained silent; we were all tense. Porky announced as quietly as he could for us to still hear, 'Okay, boys, I'm close to declaring a fuel emergency. I reckon we've got another 12 minutes max to get into Leeds – if we can – and maybe 20 minutes of fuel tops before the big fan above stops. That's it. Sorry.'

No one said anything after that. We flew on, bucking around in the storm. I noticed that even the raindrops were juddering and taking crazy paths down the window glass. I also knew that this was the kind of heightened clarity of detail that one only experiences at times of high stress and great risk: the human brain and eye opening themselves wide to suck up the danger signs. Millions of years of evolutionary fight or flight instincts to the fore. Well, we certainly had the flight, it just remained to see if we had the fight.

Gamely, Porky flew on and, as a pilot myself, I knew he'd have to make an 'instrument approach' to Leeds Bradford

International Airport. Instrument approach is a way of trying to land an aircraft in bad weather and low-visibility flying by following the instruments on the panel.

Finally, desperately low on fuel, and all out of empty prayers, Porky followed the ILS towards the runway. We peered through the muck outside looking for any hint of runway lights as we flew down the glide slope. If we came out of the cloud and mist too low we'd miss the decision height – this is the minimum height to be able to abort the landing and pull the craft back out of descent without running the risk of smacking into terrain or masts, or whatever the fuck was down there waiting to kill us. And as we bucked through the darkness I wished I didn't have all that information because it meant I knew just how grim and risky things were. And I knew we must be nearing the point of no return when suddenly the runway came into view – just before the decision height to abort.

We'd no sooner touched down than my relief that the flight was over evaporated and transformed into our next worry: the land transfer. I had nearly run out of drugs, oxygen and batteries. An airport fire engine pulled up next to us as the Agusta's engines wound down. An eager fire officer opened the door and announced, 'I'm a trained first aider!' Barry and I looked at each other, not sure what to do with this information. The officer continued, 'You declared a medical emergency, didn't you?'

At that point I released some of the incredible build-up of tension and said, 'Great, this man's got 70 per cent burns and is running on propofol, noradrenaline, rocuronium and fentanyl. His vent settings are fine and he's been stable. You take over for a few minutes, I need a break.' He looked stunned. I realised he was only trying to help and I immediately regretted opening my mouth. I brushed my comment aside as a poor attempt at humour and genuinely thanked him. He seemed fine with that.

'Listen, we requested a blue-light ambulance with some kit for us. Please make sure airport security don't cause any delays. I need that ambulance here, right now!'

The fire officer shot off to sort it out. A couple of minutes later an ambulance duly arrived. The crew approached with the desperately needed replacement drugs, batteries and oxygen. I spent the next 10 minutes sorting out our patient's needs and the equipment's requirements. My stress dissipated a little.

We loaded our man into the ambulance and I asked the crew how long it would take to get to Manchester on blue lights and sirens.

'Manchester?' the driver said. 'No one said anything about Manchester. We can take you to the hospital here in Leeds, if you like.' I was momentarily at a loss as this wasn't what we expected. Barry jumped in and quickly intervened. I got lost somewhere between the Irish and Northern accents being bandied about, but eventually the crew agreed to contact control and, having done so, were officially tasked to travel to the burns unit in Manchester. They advised us that they would have to refuel on the way. We set off on blue lights and bells.

Unbelievably, we stopped at a petrol station a few miles down the road, switching off the emergency lights as we stopped at a petrol pump. Porky had already recovered from our terror flight and was back on form: 'Anyone want a Diet Coke and a Mars bar?' he asked. I'd run out of my stash of chocolate so I ordered three jumbo Kit Kats, an energy drink and a copy of *Viz* magazine, if they had one. Scant reward for that flight, but it would have to do.

As a portrait of the sometimes surreal realities of the job, this scene would take some beating. An out-of-fuel land ambulance on a night-time petrol station forecourt with a desperately ill patient in the back; a whistling ambulance crewmember stood at the pump, clocking up the fuel; one pilot, one doctor and one paramedic in orange flight suits, all coming down from recent flight terrors and industrial amounts of adrenaline by guzzling pop and chomping through chocolate bars for the sugar hit and the comfort; and all while parked under the sickly yellow lights of the forecourt and next to a souped up hatch back full of teenagers, fresh out of a nightclub and with club-volume levels of dance music booming out the car. You could practically see the window glass bend out with the pressure.

We went one better when we screeched out the petrol station and hit the siren and blue lights. Beat that, club kids!

Thankfully, the journey by road was mercifully uneventful and we had an easy handover at the burns unit. The receiving medical and nursing team seemed happy. Our patient had been stable throughout and was doing as well as could be expected. They wheeled him away and we all semi-collapsed and sat slumped silently in the corridor, every one of us looking washed out under the hospital strip lighting. Faint tendrils of steam were coming off our rain-wet flight suits.

We blagged a ride back to Leeds with the ambulance crew. Porky then broke it to us that we wouldn't be flying home as he had used up all of his flying duty hours, the limits of which the Civil Aviation Authority rigidly enforced. He knew it was a career-threatening issue to flaunt these rules and besides, the weather was still far too bad to fly. It was a huge relief. As much as we loved the old girl, none of us wanted to get back into the aircraft that night.

Surreal image of the night, number two: the ambulance crew dropped us off slap-bang in Leeds' rainy town centre. As the ambulance pulled away with an acknowledging blip of its lights, we stood there on the pavement in our bright orange flying suits, all dressed up and nowhere to go, each one of us dripping wet in the pouring rain. I was now very conscious of big drops of it running coldly down the back of my neck. Another booming car full of clubbers sped past and sounded its horn at us. Talk about going from hero to zero.

'Now what?' I asked of no one in particular.

'Erm… okay boys, anyone got any money or a credit card?' Porky asked.

We had nothing. Zero. Zilch. We set off traipsing towards a nearby hotel, whose illuminated sign we could see blurrily through the rain. As we squelched into the foyer, the foreign-looking gent behind reception looked at us with a mixture of puzzlement and concern. He looked like he thought we were some new form of drug-addled urban nightlife high on horse pills and desperate to ram-raid the hotel-room mini bars.

Porky squelched off into a corner and made some calls on his mobile phone. We stood in the foyer, dripping. I looked down at our feet and idly thought, wow, we're making quite a puddle. Then the phone rang at reception. The man answered. Then he looked across at me and Barry. Me and Barry looked at each other, then back at the man. He looked back at us. Then he hung up, and nodded at us. Me and Barry exchanged silent frowns.

Porky returned a minute later with a beaming smile: 'We're staying here! The helicopter company have sorted it. Have anything you want from the restaurant and bar!'

We had a drink and a steak on the company's account, still wearing our orange flying suits, which were now pulled down to the waist. The hot meal was fantastic, but now I had another problem. I had to start work at 8 a.m. the following morning and as I was always bollocking junior staff about being late for work, I could not possibly show up hours late for my own shift.

'Relax, mate,' Porky said in a reassuring tone. 'I'll get you there on time.'

And so he did. He flew me into work the next morning, lowering us down onto the helipad in our trusty, rain-battered, windswept Agusta 109. For a short while, it added to my kudos at work.

We would complete many critical care transfers after our terror flight to the North but none would be quite so hair-whitening. My experience on the flight emphasised why these transfers need to be undertaken with caution, forethought and careful planning.

Yeah. That was the very last time I wanted to run out of jumbo Kit Kats.

CHAPTER 11

Fighting Fire with Fire

None of us liked late jobs. They came in just as sunset approached and we were about to go offline and put the aircraft into the hangar for the night. The late jobs often left you with residual tension and lingering images that dogged you into the night. They laid out a bit more tiredness in your marrow. And the late jobs stopped us all from doing what we usually did at that time: going for an end-of-day drink at the flying club bar.

The club bar was a nice place to sit, chat and enjoy each other's company; to offload some of the tension, dial down some of the emotions, and to try and dim the light on the projector that sometimes flickers images of the day on the screen in your mind. These chill-out times were as essential to us as fuel for the Agusta or drugs in the syringe for the patient. It strengthened us as a unit.

On the best summer evenings, I would sometimes pull my little blue and white Beagle Pup aircraft out of the flying club hangar beneath us, and take a paramedic or one of the pilots out for a relaxing flight and some gentle aerobatics over the countryside. Smoothly turning the lightweight plane upside down at 4,000 feet as the inverting sky flamed orange was a great way to end the day. It was a great way of feeling free. Very often, it was the perfect finale to a less than perfect day.

And if none of us liked late jobs then what, would you imagine, would be the worst ever late job? That's right: a late call-out on New Year's Eve. No one could be that unlucky, could they?

This particular New Year's Eve Chris, Barry and I had enjoyed a really good day. We had flown several good missions, where we had worked well together and felt we'd done something useful for humanity. Barry got up, looked at the clock and said something that we understood meant it was probably time to pack up for the day. I was looking forward to a session in the flying club bar with my pals. Chris was seeing a new potential alimony claimant and I was keen to hear all about her.

We were minutes away from a clean getaway when the Bat Phone rang. Job on. Chris immediately ran out towards the helicopter. Barry's face was unusually serious as he took the call; he made some unintelligible noises but his expression was one of urgency. He had scribbled details down on his knee-board and which I read as he pulled the toy helicopter far over to the eastern extreme of the map to calculate distance and flight time. He had written, *'Car vs tree – female trapped – V serious injuries'*.

After the usual pre-flight checks, we lifted. It was a relatively long flight for us, almost 15 minutes. When we arrived we landed in the middle of a remote country road. Already a fire engine and an ambulance were in attendance. But there was not the usual coordinated and professional buzz that, having worked with fire crews at hundreds of jobs, we had become accustomed to. To me, this job felt scrappy and disorganised straight away.

When attending a scene of this nature, we always liaised with the fire boss to plan the rescue. We would assess the scene from a medical perspective and decide whether or not it was time-critical. Our assessment influenced the fire team's approach to the rescue. In time critical situations, they would sometimes get us into the vehicle to start work on our patient while they cut bits of the car away from around us. We would agree the measures to keep us safe inside the car while they smashed glass and used power tools to slice the A and B posts and remove the roof, the doors or even execute a 'dashboard roll', where hydraulic rams were used to push, or 'roll', the dashboard, peeling open the front of the car like a sardine can to free trapped occupants.

Usually, I liked working in teams on these precarious situations and dangerous jobs; it was exciting and challenging. This scene, however, was noisy and messy. There were lots of orders being shouted with no one really responding. The fire crew did not look as slick as other fire teams that I had previously worked with. Then I realised that this was a retained crew of volunteers, not regulars.

Even above the shouting and the racket of the generator used to power the cutting gear, I could hear that awful, familiar wet snoring noise of a partially obstructed human airway. It was slow and getting slower. Barry and I approached the smashed car, crunching over glass, and saw a young woman in a really shocking state. She was unconscious, very pale and gasping for air. Her face was a mask of blood. She was pinned tightly by the impacted dashboard across her chest. Her car had hit a tree hard, and been massively deformed. Trees are one of the most unforgiving objects to hit: they're deeply rooted, they don't give. The force had crumpled her car like a cigarette packet. On both sides the doors were corrugated, as was the roof. The smashed radiator was hissing and bleeding.

It was obvious to both Barry and I that this was extremely time-critical. The poor girl was about to die. Just then, a middle-aged man wearing a suit and tie partially covered by a fluorescent coat with BASICS DOCTOR on the back approached. I quickly searched for the fire boss, but he was too occupied in barking orders to his crew to engage with me. So I went into assertive mode: 'Chief, this lady is dying. I need her *out of the car now* – or me *in the car now*. This is time-critical.' He seemed unsure how to respond but after a few seconds he replied, 'Once we've stabilised the car and dealt with glass management, we will snip the roof off. I reckon another 15 minutes.'

'No, listen,' I said, a little louder. 'This really *is* time-critical. I need you to get her out *now* or get me in there *now*, or this rescue will become a body recovery.'

He turned away to bark some more orders. Fuck it.

I ran back to the car and saw the BASICS doctor injecting a drug into a cannula that he had inserted into the lady's exposed right arm. So I quickly introduced myself: 'What have you just given her?' I enquired, hoping to get some handle on how to plan our medical approach to this situation.

'Ten milligrams of midazolam,' he said.

Fuck it, Part II. This was a big heart-sinking moment. Midazolam would 'calm her' but would also likely eliminate any of her residual breathing effort that she had left. It would calm her gently into suffocation. This had now escalated from a time-critical problem to an immediate do-or-die situation.

Barry and I now knew that we had to get into the car straight away. The rear windscreen was shattered but still in place. Barry kicked it right in. I scrambled through the hole and fell head first onto the rear seat of the car, which was sugared with safety glass. Our girl was now only making the occasional rattle; she was approaching death. I crawled between the front seats and wedged myself there. Now I could get to her head and open her airway with my hands. This didn't help much as she wasn't really breathing any more (the midazolam had kicked in). But Barry was (as always) at least two steps ahead of me. He thrust our airway pouch into the car. I put the ambubag over her face. I could just about hand ventilate her and get her chest to move a little. But this wouldn't last for the 15 minutes that the fire boss had estimated. I also knew that he had no chance of getting us out in 15 minutes. It was going to be a very long job. Then I overheard a firefighter outside say, 'He's sending me back to the station to get the hydraulic ram. Our one's knackered.'

Fuck it, Part III.

That comment confirmed to me that the 15-minute plan was screwed – the fire boss had obviously worked out that snipping the A and B posts and removing the car roof could not possibly work without levering the dashboard off our lady's chest. This was helpful because it meant the decision was made for me.

'Barry – we're going to RSI her *now*. Let's go with ketamine and suxamethonium – 150 milligrams of the ket. I can't get a second line in her as I can't get to her left arm. Give the drugs into the cannula that we've already got.'

We had to stop breathing to start breathing, meaning, we had to paralyse the patient to give us the freedom to intubate her – to clear her airways and get a tube into her trachea. Barry passed me the intubation kit. This was going to be hard, if not impossible. Jammed between two seats, I was not in a good position to get the breathing tube into her. By now we had given her anaesthetic drugs that would lead to paralysis and stop all breathing efforts (without paralysing patients you can't get the tube in). So it was a high-risk procedure if I did it, almost certain death for her if I didn't. And we didn't have much of a Plan B if it all went tits up.

I managed to attach a monitor to our patient as Barry sorted out the drugs. The numbers on the monitor screen were appalling: this girl was nearly dead. It is good practice to improve this sort of situation by providing high-flow oxygen for several minutes before giving the anaesthetic drugs; this gives your patient a fighting chance if you couldn't get the tube down first time. This 'pre-oxygenation' bought us valuable time to re-position and try something else if it went wrong. But I knew I couldn't even pre-oxygenate this patient as I couldn't ventilate her adequately in that position, and she had no respiratory effort of her own. The midazolam had really terminated her struggling efforts to breathe for herself.

Fuck it, Part IV.

I told Barry to give the drugs so I could start with the RSI. He administered and our girl twitched, went floppy and stopped breathing – completely as expected. I'd already wriggled around and approached her from a cocked sideways position and, with great difficulty, I could *just* visualise her vocal cords with the light from my laryngoscope. I started efforts to get the tube past her vocal cords. First attempt no. Second attempt... no. Next one, again... *no*. Finally, the tube eventually went through into the windpipe and I quickly started to ventilate her to get her oxygen levels into a range that would be compatible with life. Her skin soon pinked-up and the numbers on the monitor screen improved a little. I quickly attached the tubing into our portable ventilator.

I knew we could possibly win now. I was a little more relaxed as Barry gave the drugs that would keep her asleep and paralysed. It was now time to think: I couldn't really access her chest from where I was, so I didn't know if there was a problem there, but given the mechanism of the crash, it seemed quite likely there was damage to her chest wall and lungs. I knew she had lost blood – her pulse was very weak – and I couldn't get the monitor to pick up a blood pressure.

'Barry – try a bolus of 250 ml of fluid and we'll reassess.'

At that point, the alarm on the ventilator shrilled, indicating pressure. I immediately replaced the ventilator with a hand-driven ambubag so I could feel the degree of resistance for myself. There was huge pressure, and it was preventing me from ventilating her chest. It had to be a huge air leak around one of her lungs causing the lung to collapse – the resultant build-up of pressure in the chest flattens the lung and stops it from inflating. It can be fatal if not relieved quickly. I felt for the position of her windpipe and it was where it should be. The windpipe can be shunted sideways, away from the side of the collapsed lung. So this didn't give me any clue which lung had collapsed. I couldn't use a stethoscope because of my position in the car, lack of access and also because it was too noisy to hear.

'Barry, can you get to the right side of her chest?' I asked. 'They've managed to clear the right door and I can get to some of it.'

A few seconds later he said something that sounded like, 'Jesus, chest tight as a drum – splinted – no air entry. I'll needle it!'

'Fine, but we're going to be here a while. We'll need a chest drain.' I reconnected the ventilator and clambered back out through the car's rear window. We were setting up for a chest incision to drain the pressure, to re-inflate her lung and to get her breathing properly. Just then a firefighter came over to me and said, 'I thought you said this was time-critical. You're in the way. If you want her out quickly, you'll have to stand aside and let us get on.'

I briefly tried to explain what we were doing and why we were doing it now. He looked at me blankly and repeated his demand for me to step aside. Ignoring him, I clambered back into the car and pushed a scalpel into our patient's chest and got the drain through the incision. Straight away there was the sound of air hissing out from the drain hole in her chest. This was very reassuring; we had got it right. Things were improving.

Just as we were working on securing our girl's chest drain with a couple of large sutures, the firefighter came back over again and again he tried to get us to move. This was idiotic. My response included the words 'piss' and 'off' and 'you' and 'clown'. In roughly that order. I shooed him away.

In desperate situations like these you can get very protective of your patient and extremely resistant to anyone or any thing that puts them in peril, even if that thing is someone trying to help. At moments like these, time can grind down and shudder to a halt. In the sudden calm and clarity of the moment, you realise that there is a very, very thin curtain dividing two states: between the soul of this human being beginning its journey to wherever it is we go when we die, or it staying lightly tethered enough to the body to remain right here. Our job was to get it to stay, to stop that journey beginning. To help that curtain remain as the divide.

So, in that context, 'Piss off, you clown' was, I thought, actually pretty restrained.

Once the chest drain was in and our patient was breathing normally again, Barry and I cleared out of the way and let the crew continue with cutting up the car. I got back up and climbed back into the car through the smashed rear windscreen to reassess our patient. Her numbers on the monitor screen were far more encouraging. Pulse and oxygen saturation were reasonable; the CO_2 reading confirmed that the tube was in the windpipe and we were ventilating well.

At this point, the Fire Boss came over to me. 'You've upset one of my firefighters. Why did you call him a clown and tell him to piss off?'

I explained the urgency of what we had undertaken and why the firefighter's behaviour had frustrated efforts to save our patient's life and that I shouldn't have needed to repeatedly explain to him our methods. However, the Chief was in no mood to hear any of this and continued laying into me. I decided to fight fire with fire (which is okay for a doctor but, if you think about it, a bloody silly thing for a firefighter to do) and promptly called him a prick. He stormed off in a huff; Barry and I cracked on.

The rescue attempt went on, but painfully slowly. Over an hour later, Barry and I were still in the car, contorted into painful positions to try and maintain our girl's precarious health. But she'd been in this awful position for just too long: she was becoming very unstable and we were increasingly desperate. We needed to get her to a hospital and some trauma surgeons, pronto. The fire team were still struggling to cut the roof off the car. Barry was agitated. He got out the car and picked up a heavy oxygen cylinder. His idea was to use it to hammer a crease into the roof, as the firefighters were struggling to peel it back. It was a good idea – and it worked – but I wished he had given me some warning: all I heard was a massive BANG inches above my head as I sat inside the car. For a second I thought that something had exploded and we were all done for.

Finally, enough of the crushed vehicle was cut off or bent back, or peeled away for everyone to be extricated from the car.

As we wheeled our patient down to the helicopter, I got another tap on the shoulder. I turned this time to see the Big Fire Boss, who was possibly, it occurred to me, the County Fire Chief. His timing was about as good as the other two because he started to fire orders at me about having a debrief to smooth the ruffled feathers of his officers. I told him quite clearly that this was a bad time as our lady was still in critical condition. He didn't get it, and carried on barking. I snapped – and to my growing list of the day's expletives, I added the word 'cock-sucker'. In my defence, we had exchanged reruns of *Top Gear* for *The Sopranos* back at base and it seemed as good a word as any. The Big Chief just looked at me, speechless.

We loaded the aircraft and got set up for the flight to hospital. As the rotors were whirring up to speed, Barry called in the hospital alert and got the receiving trauma team mobilised. We heaved up into the air. The power and speed of the Agusta had never felt more needed. And with good reason: several minutes into the flight, our patient lost her pulse. Out loud, I said, 'Oh no you don't, lady!' I increased the fluid infusion rate and also gave adrenaline. I performed a few chest compressions and she was back with us... But not for long. This was one of three times that our patient would die during the flight. Fortunately, each time I managed to revive her.

One very, very quick clatter across the sky later and we got her to hospital alive. We kept in touch with the hospital for updates and learnt that our lady was in a coma for a week, had to have a leg amputated and then had to endure several major operations. But we eventually found out that after many months of recuperation and rehabilitation, she made a very good recovery.

When I got home that night, I went straight to my computer and wrote my letter of complaint to the Fire Service. They, apparently, had done exactly the same thing about me. Apparently calling the Fire Boss a 'cocksucker' was offensive. No surprises there. My complaint was that they had made an already stressful and life-threatening situation worse; that by trying to follow protocol they had slowed me down and put the life of a young woman into even more jeopardy than it already was and, in my humble opinion, getting called a 'cocksucker' was the least of what they deserved.

I was so focused on what I was about to do – type a furious letter of complaint – that I ignored the New Year's Eve family gathering in the house as I furiously typed away. Knowing that I'd pulled the New Year's Eve shift, they were already resigned to my not being there. But even when I'd returned home, Jacqui could see I was still intent on something to do with the day's work and knew enough not to ask me about it.

After I'd written the letter, the internal fireworks gradually blew themselves out. Happily, if exhaustedly, I eventually returned downstairs. Jacqui could see how tired I was and helped prise off my boots, get me out of my dirty flying suit and carefully steer me towards the shower. The steaming hot water had never felt so good.

This particular episode went down in HEMS folklore as the 'cocksucker' job. A lesson in diplomacy and tact for generations to come.

Weeks later, after our respective service bosses had talked, it was agreed that I and one of our HEMS paramedics would attend a fire officers' training day to conduct a formal debrief on the mission. Barry was away on holiday so I went with one of our chaps, Neil Vickers, who was available that day. We visited Fire Service HQ and were met by about 50 firefighters, all sitting in silence with their arms folded. So, a nice easy gig then.

Fortunately, Chris, our pilot on the day, had taken lots of pictures of the scene and the rescue. In preparation for this, we had put together a slide show. Never underestimate the power of a slide show. As the pictures were projected onto the screen,

I explained our priorities from the medical perspective; how there was no point in prioritising the removal of the car roof if the time it took to do that just gave us better access to a dead body; how our aim was the preservation of life first, before anything else. Otherwise, what's the point?

A few minutes into the talk we had a breakthrough when they understood the immediate threats to our patient's life. The atmosphere thawed. By the end of the meeting, we were all best friends and, on later jobs, we got on an awful lot better and worked much closer together.

Amazingly, the 'cocksucker' job got us a nominated for the National Life Saver Award for bravery. This entailed a trip to 10 Downing Street to meet the then Prime Minister, Tony Blair, and also an attendance at the Awards dinner.

I wouldn't have called this job particularly heroic. There were plenty of other jobs where we had taken much greater physical risks to our safety to save a life, but this particular adventure and the outcome of this job had captured the imagination. And it was great publicity for the unit.

We had an amazing time in London. The night before we met the Prime Minister, we attended the awards dinner at the Café Royal. I took my wife Jacqui and my parents – and they, like David, Laura, Rachel and Mim, were all quietly proud of me for being given the Award.

We met a few celebrities in attendance to add some glitz to the proceedings: model Nell McAndrew, actor Martin Kemp, the singer Annie Lennox and Gary Lineker. As Martin Kemp had played Ronnie Kray in the film *The Krays*, my father enjoyed regaling him with his own involvement with the twins and being a witness at their murder trial. But the one person that I got excited about meeting was former Flight Lieutenant John Nichol, the RAF navigator who, with pilot John Peters, was in a Tornado jet that was shot down by a heat-seeking missile in Iraq during the Gulf War. He was tortured in Abu Ghraib prison and, famously, appeared on TV news around the world when his captors filmed him and a badly beaten John Peters, and then released the footage to news networks.

I'd also thoroughly enjoyed watching John's aviation programmes on the Discovery Wings channel. I was thrilled to be able to chat to a man who I had avidly watched on television talking about flying and aircraft. And a brave soldier too. He was very engaging. He congratulated us on being given a Bravery Award. I asked him how our exploits could possibly be called brave by a man who had ejected from a burning jet over hostile territory and endured beatings and torture at the hands of his Iraqi captors. But he just smiled and said he hadn't felt particularly brave at the time either. Top bloke.

The next day, when meeting the Prime Minister, Tony Blair, our Barry got to show off his sense of humour. Barry manoeuvred himself so he was standing just behind Blair for a group photograph. When the PM asked the photographer, 'Do you want me to stand here?', Barry, who was just behind the PM's left shoulder, suddenly barked in his very heavy Irish accent, 'You're the Prime Minister! You can stand anywhere you bloody well like!'

I saw Blair jump a little and a brief flash of alarm cross his face at hearing a booming Irish accent in his left ear. Luckily for us, the Prime Minister seemed to be in good enough health to survive the shock. So we didn't have to break out the defibrillator to jump-start his heart.

Mind you, that could have led to another Life Saver Award.

CHAPTER 12

Media Stardom

The charity was going from strength to strength. Our finances were in good order and there was talk of establishing a second Air Ambulance unit. A key part of the charity's success was the power of the PR machine. We had all done our fair share of publicity events, some small and others very big. Some events, such as our dance and Chippendales routine, required more courage than others.

For sums of more than £10,000, we would fly to the donor's event. For £1,000, we would show the donor around the base and the helicopter. This happened most days. We developed a little patter and our guided tours became quite slick.

Not infrequently, our former patients also came to the base to thank us. These meetings were occasionally a little emotional for them. Sometimes we would remember the job, especially the more dramatic or touch-and-go jobs, but by now we were dealing with so many incidents that we couldn't recall each face and circumstance. But it was gratifying to see the results of our work and to see people putting back together lives that had seemed hopelessly damaged, or even close to ending. Seeing these patients was a salutary reminder that getting to the scene quickly to deliver advanced hospital skills did make the crucial difference. Our lady from the infamous 'cocksucker' job visited a few times and kept telling me that she remembered my voice. Which, considering some of the language I'd used, made me wonder *exactly* what she heard. I hoped it was my words of consolation.

The charity had negotiated a deal with a television company to produce a TV series – we were going to be on the small screen, and hopefully this would help raise awareness and funds for our service.

The TV company put cameras everywhere. We had pencil cameras fitted to our shoulder epaulettes and a microphone clipped to our flying suits, a microphone box went into a pocket on our flying suits and two small cameras were fitted inside the Agusta's cockpit. We were told just to be ourselves and to ignore the cameras. That turned out to be easier said than done.

During filming, a woman from the TV company accompanied us in the aircraft's observer seat with a handheld camera so she could run beside us (or, more often, behind us) to the jobs and film us from the perspective of a bystander. The training room was turned into an editing suite so we could watch the footage at the end of each day.

Unless this show was going to go out under an '18' certificate, we knew we had to clean up our act for the camera. Which, again, was easier said than done. Those first couple of minutes of flight were usually very pressured, as we tried to find the right maps and mark our position, route and destination. We also had to look for electricity lines and other obstacles while maintaining a visual lookout for other aircraft and birds, while managing the radio calls. The pilot had to call up Air Traffic Control if our route took us through controlled airspace. This part of the mission was very busy as we had maybe two minutes to get ourselves sorted – and we were moving over the ground at speeds well in excess of 150mph at low level – which meant that the language in the cockpit could be a bit ripe. Then, once at the accident scene, there was the issue of finding a safe and suitable landing site, getting in there safely and keeping the area secure until the aircraft had shut down. Again, this could all lead to language that was… overcooked.

So, for the TV we decided to try and make ourselves sound more professional and less profane. We even practised. Derek adopted a posh accent and instead of the usual 'Where the bloody hell are we, you fucking muppet?' he tried out a more restrained, 'Tony, please could you locate and mark the map for this accident. Thank you.'

I responded with, 'Certainly, Derek, I believe it's on land ranger map 116. Here it is. I have marked the grid reference. There are wires running east to west, two miles ahead.'

'Thank you, Tony. Most helpful,' he replied. 'Thanks so much.'

And so it went on. We did it for the first mission and when we brought the tape back and watched it in the editing suite, it sounded ludicrous on the playback, like a Sunday afternoon

Radio 4 play. The producer told us just to be ourselves. So we did just that.

We started to behave as we normally did and ignored the cameras. The footage, even with the occasional expletive, looked and sounded very slick on the playback in the editing room. At first, it was strange to have a camerawoman follow us everywhere and at intervals ask for a brief summary of what was happening. Usually you would only have an internal mono-logue going, describing and logging the events; but now we had to immediately externalise that and, essentially, become commentators on our own lives, as if it was some kind of sport-ing event. But soon she got us to feel comfortable and to talk in layman's terms when explaining things to the camera.

For the first few missions, we were very aware that we were being followed everywhere. After a while, we lost the self-awareness that every comment and every action was being recorded and every movement filmed.

Fortunately, the cameras weren't with us the following week when me and Porky learnt about the dangers of an 'open mic' when we went out on a job. As an amateur pilot, I have a limited knowledge of air law. When flying my little Pup, or indeed any other small aircraft, my call sign was simply the aircraft's registration, which I'd call out in phonetic alphabet letters – Golf Alpha Whisky Whisky Echo. And it made me wonder how Helimed 999 was allowed to use that call sign. So I asked Porky. He looked up from his *Nuts* magazine and thought for a second or two before advising me.

'I think you make a request to some bureaucrat in Brussels or Strasbourg and you pay some money and then you get it.'

I thought for a minute. 'Is that it? So I could ask for "Tony 101", or "Airdoc 1", could I? Like getting a personalised number plate?'

Porky pondered, 'I think so.'

There was silence for a minute or two and then he followed up with, 'Or you could get "Motherfucker 17" or "Cocksucker 11".' This banter went on for a while as we went through the possible funny call signs we could get. It was interrupted when the Bat Phone went off.

After the usual scramble to the craft and pre-takeoff checks and departure, we flew off to a job. On the way we decided that our favourite imaginary call sign from Brussels or Strasbourg, or wherever the hell you got them from, would be 'Motherfucker 17'. We liked the sound of that and it fitted in with our regular viewing of *The Sopranos* at base.

Porky had to get zone clearance for our flight so he got on the radio, opened the airways and clear as day he said, 'Kidlington, this is Motherfucker 17 for zone transit.' I could hardly believe my ears and started chuckling uncontrollably. I knew he hadn't meant to say it, but 'Motherfucker 17' was just in his head when he pushed the transmit button.

'You said that out loud,' I advised him.

'Oh fuck,' Porky responded.

'Er... sorry? Say again call sign...?' came the hesitant response from the tower.

'Apologies, this is *Helimed 999* for zone transit,' Porky responded professionally.

He turned around to me, half horrified, half amused. 'Jesus Christ! I can't believe I said that out loud.'

'Well, you fucking well did, you moron!'

In the end, the filming went on for months. There was the expectation of a pilot show followed by two eight-part series.

One lovely summer's day, we were sent to a road crash on a remote section of a country road. It was quite a bad smash. The car was badly crumpled at the front but the doors opened easily. There were two patients, both women. One was quite large and it was tricky getting her out on the spinal board. I considered discharging them both from the scene as they seemed to have sustained only modest whiplash injuries. However, given the obvious magnitude of the impact and their neck pain, we decided it would be prudent to package them in collars and blocks, and strap them down onto spinal boards so they could be assessed more thoroughly in hospital.

Derek decided to fly one of the ladies to hospital and leave the other at the scene with me as we couldn't fly both together due to the TV lady taking the spare seat on the return flight and also due to the large size of one of our patients. With Derek taking the first one to hospital, I knew I would be there with the second patient for at least half an hour. I had completely forgotten about the TV programme's camerawoman, who had already wandered off to film footage of the wrecked cars.

As it was a hot day, Derek and I decided to put our boarded lady on some grass at the side of the road underneath a tree for shade. Derek then flew off with the first patient. I sat next to our boarded lady on the grass and reassured her that all would be fine. It's sometimes too easy to forget that these moments, even when the injury is not serious, can be traumatic for patients. Sometimes psychological shock kicks in and they are left suddenly feeling quite disturbed. Events that we see every day, they only experience perhaps once in a lifetime. So a few softly spoken reassurances always went a long way, and a psychologically eased patient went some way towards being a physiologically steadied one.

As I engaged her in idle conversation, I noticed that even on this country lane, the traffic, which had been stopped and blocked either side of the accident, had now built up quite badly. No one had thought to get it moving again. The car wreck was only blocking one lane, so there was no reason why we couldn't get the traffic moving. There were stationary cars sitting idly in both directions running as far as the eye could see. The attending police officer was busy with the car wreck and then he had to get the details from our patient, who was doing absolutely fine.

While he was doing so I decided to help out by getting the traffic moving. After making sure the patient was safe and secure, I excused myself and walked quickly back to the road block and removed all the traffic cones that had been put out to stop the traffic. I put them around the wrecked car but left the other lane open. This was going to be fun: I was to play traffic cop! We've all seen cops do this in films – usually wearing white gloves – and how hard could it be? What could possibly go wrong?

I put out my hand with the palm facing forwards – in a 'talk to the hand' sort of gesture – towards the first car on the west-bound side of the road. I made sure I got eye contact with the driver and once I felt confident he understood that I wanted him to stay there, I looked towards the first car on the east-bound side of the road and made a beckoning motion. The traffic started. It worked. Cool!

After a minute of traffic flow – and of successfully not directing anyone into a tree – I pointed to the driver of a car in the slow-moving traffic and made the 'stop' gesture. He duly stopped. I could now get the westbound traffic going again. The traffic queues started to get a little shorter. Amazing what you can do with a little confidence and lot of cheek.

I glanced over towards our lady under the tree and the policeman was still chatting away to her. They seemed fine and happy in each other's company. So I continued with my amateur traffic management. I also started to add some flour-ishes to my hand signals as I had seen the Italian police do on TV – we are supposed to be European now, after all – and also threw in a few extra movements and fancy flicks. Then some deeply disturbed part of me unlocked the part of my brain that had hidden away the awful dance moves we'd done during our Chippendales' strip routine, and I started to throw a few of those shapes too.

I was having great fun.

Several minutes later, I was brought back to reality by the sound of the helicopter returning. I had to stop the traffic one last time. But it turned out that this wasn't a simple undertaking as I had to leave a 40-metre gap on the road for our aircraft to land. Bugger, I hadn't considered that! And as the Agusta got nearer and nearer, and lower and lower, I could make out Derek's increasingly puzzled expression as he stared through the glass at me – he might as well have had 'WHAT THE *FU*—?' stamped across his forehead. And I really didn't want to end up with 'BLEETMAN, YOU MUPPET!' stamped across mine.

Guiding in or, as we call it, 'marshalling' the aircraft was a necessary and potentially risky part of the job. We'd trained how after being dropped off in the hover, or when repositioning the aircraft on the ground for a pick up, one of us would clear the selected landing area and use a number of hand signals that we had been taught: signs for Approach, Hover, Move Left/Right, Abort, and Fly Away. Our pilot, Crewe, had really got us going on this. And with his 'whites of the eyes' technique. We'd had a couple of close shaves with the Agusta ending up uncomfortably close to trees and wires. Crewe told us that while he did pay attention to our marshalling hand signals, he looked more at the whites of our eyes – because when our eyes widened to reveal more of the white, he knew he was getting too close to an obstacle!

I had this in mind as I knew I'd have not one but *two* different hand signalling jobs ahead of me – stopping the oncoming cars, and guiding Porky and Derek in to land. I started gesturing ever more frantically to get the oncoming traffic to stop, even running towards the car at the head of the line to try and get it to halt quicker. I stopped it just in time, and preserved the space in the road with only seconds to spare, before the big Agusta suddenly loomed over us. Turning quickly, I made a few cursory marshalling signals to Porky.

The Agusta's blades became a deafening blur of huge power carefully contained, the noisy clatter blowing away birds, cow herds, large animals, small stones, every speck of dust and blade of grass, and even obliterating human thought. You couldn't think about anything else.

There is something about the imminent approach and the descent and landing of a helicopter that is irresistibly compelling; I've never *not* seen anyone and everyone nearby stop and stare. It's impossible not to. People are mesmerised by it, and much more so than watching a plane land. It fascinates me, but I think I know why it is.

With an aeroplane, the forward motion of it is familiar and explicable; our cars move forward, and if they went fast enough and managed the air pressure correctly, they could take off (and, hopefully, also land!). After all, a Bugatti Veyron goes fast enough to take off, so why doesn't it? Only because the air pressure it generates is carefully managed to press *down* and not *up*.

But the behaviour of a helicopter has none of this, what we might call, motion familiarity – so the vertical takeoff and vertical landing is still a fundamentally bizarre thing to see. It looks unnatural. And the vertical descent means that, unlike a plane, we can get very, very close to a helicopter landing – it's one of the rare occasions when we can be in that close a proximity to such a huge amount of power. Combine all that with the immense violence of those rotor blades slicing through the air at approximately 200mph – and also how much catastrophic damage we know they would do if they suddenly worked loose and span off our way – and you have a riveting and heady recipe for human wonder and awe.

Porky flew helicopters and fixed-wing aircraft. He described how both types of aircraft are very similar, with only one key difference: 'In a helicopter you have to stop and then land. In a fixed-wing aircraft you have to land and then stop! If you remember that you'll be fine, if you fuck it up, someone's going to get hurt!'

Derek, however, was somewhat less than overflowing with human wonder and awe for my impromptu performance as a traffic cop. He was somewhere between extremely bewildered and amused – let's call it bemused, then.

'You fucking muppet! I leave you for half an hour with one patient. All you had was a simple babysitting job. That's all, nothing else, just chat and be nice. I come back and the patient's with a bloody policeman and you're playing dancing traffic cops!'

Worse was to come. During the entire episode, I had completely forgotten about the TV camerawoman who was located over by the crashed vehicles. She hadn't forgotten me, though, and she had filmed the whole traffic-directing episode.

The problem with filming Air Ambulance work is that the television company could not broadcast anything too gory or show any dead people. They also need written consent from the patients to put them on TV. So the 'big jobs', the ones where we made a difference, never got on to TV. Those patients were usually traumatised, anaesthetised and smashed up. Television was restricted to showing only the less exciting jobs.

So, desperate for all they could use, the television company made a real meal out of the traffic directing episode. They selected the highlights and screened it to the soundtrack of a song called 'Tony's Theme' by the American band, Pixies. So when the series aired on TV screens across the nation the song provided the soundtrack to images of some silly sod in an orange flying suit directing traffic. The audience even got a glimpse of the policeman sitting under a tree with our patient. My humiliation was complete.

We went on to make several series of the programme. It was cheap-to-make TV; all you need are a few cameras pointing towards a bunch of clowns in a helicopter and the patience to wade through hours of dull footage and pick out the interesting scenes that aren't covered in too much blood and snot.

Unusually, the Bleetman clan thought my exploits on TV were fantastic and they sat at home with their mates watching Dad on the telly: David, of course, was interested in the clinical and procedural side of things; Laura, Rachel and Mim just wanted to see me on the box. A sign of the times, I suppose, that it wasn't until I'd made it onto a reality TV show that I was thought to have achieved something!

We were often met at big PR events by Jonny Riff, our friendly radio DJ. He would line us up centre stage at any event and 'big us up' before asking us to say a few words into the microphone. 'So, Tony, you're a hospital consultant and you give your time for free. Why do you do that?'

'Well, Jon, we can deliver hospital-level medical care to people that need us. It's a privilege to be able to do that.'

He would end each interview with, 'Ladies and gentlemen, I give you the crew of Helimed 999, YOUR *very* own Air Ambulance!' The crowds loved it.

Our roaming DJ was very good. We were at a steam rally somewhere and had just done our chat in front of several thousand people. We were sitting on the grass, licking some blagged ice cream cones. I asked him about his job and he explained how he delivered the patter. He gave examples of different pitch and rhythm of speech for different parts of his classic rock radio show.

I tried to impress him with my best imitation of a DJ voice: 'It's five to one! Coming up to the news *on the hour*, we've got time for just *one more track*. Competition coming up *after the news* – great prizes including a dinner date with Saddam Hussein. Who remembers this *classic* Hollies' hit from 1967?'

'Not bad,' Jon offered.

I told him I wanted to do a radio show and he invited me to come to the studio. So I turned up and joined him for his four-hour drive time show. Between little bursts of DJ activity, he showed me the computer monitors and how the tracks were lined up. It was largely computerised and scripted almost down to the last second.

At the start of the show I was introduced: 'We have a special guest today. Dr Tony Bleetman from the Air Ambulance will be hosting part of this show.' After complimenting the unit, he faded out the song and asked me a few questions on air – all the better to promote our work; you never knew if potential new sponsors and benefactors were listening.

During the news he showed me how to operate the machines. When the screen had this black line going across it, you could talk; when it went red, you shut up. You had a 10-second warning before the colour changed to red. This screen also showed you the tracks lined up to go. 'Okay,' he said, 'the next one is "Sgt. Pepper's Lonely Hearts Club Band". Watch your language. You can say *crap* but not *shit*. *Bugger* is not allowed. And definitely no *eff* or *cee* words.' I wondered why he thought it necessary to tell me to watch my language.

'What about *motherfucker*?' I joked.

He scowled. I knew I could do this. How difficult could it be? I was a man who had directed traffic, for Christ's sake. The screen duly went black after the news and I started my very short-lived career as a radio DJ.

'1326, Classic Rock AM. Welcome back, Tony Bleetman here, your Air Ambulance doctor, standing in for Jonny Riff this afternoon. You may have seen us last week at the steam rally in Tickington – it was a great show and raised lots of money to keep us flying. Thanks to all of you that helped us. We hope you had a great day out, the crew of Helimed 999 certainly did.'

The 10-second warning came on the screen.

I continued. 'Who remembers this classic Beatles' track from 1967, the Summer of Love? It's "Sgt. Pepper's Lonely Hearts Club Band".'

After the second hour of alternating the DJ duties, Jon put me back in the driving seat and I got on with the radio show under his watchful eye. Then he got up and left the small studio. I was alone in charge of a radio station! For a few seconds, some mischievous thoughts flashed through my brain, but I restrained myself and just introduced a couple of tracks and read out a traffic alert.

By the time the first filmed pilot show was 'in the can' it had a working title of *Sky Doctors*. Porky somehow arranged for it to be shown at a local cinema. We donned our rented tuxedos and took our wives wearing their posh frocks to the grotty little cinema for the premiere of the TV show. Porky had even managed to blag some free catering. It was a genuinely joyous event as our two kinds of families – our wives and kids, and our Helimed extended family, all gathered together, watching ourselves on the big screen. We couldn't believe we were seeing ourselves up in a cinema. Cheers, critical comments, whistles and thrown popcorn filled the air.

We got involved with other media enterprises, too. Often we did pieces for the newspapers. Exciting jobs were reported to our PR company and they got us column inches to maintain the high profile of our operation and keep the money we needed rolling in.

Then Channel 5 got in touch and said that for a new series called *Britain's Bravest* with Dermot Murnaghan they wanted to reconstruct the car crash rescue that had led to our awards and to meeting Tony Blair. The reconstruction was to be a much bigger affair than any of the other filmed events, more like a mini film set, in fact. They had sourced a wrecked car and actors to play the role of the casualties and patients, but they had some difficulty in getting a fire engine and a fire crew to demonstrate how the crews cut people out of a car wreck. Our paramedic, Sean told the producers not to worry and said that he would sort it.

We assembled with the TV production team at the allocated time on a freezing country lane at the crack of dawn, all set for a day's filming. We were there in our official capacity as medical and technical advisors, but as it was so bloody cold and we were so bloody bored, we quickly adopted our unofficial roles of being the ones in charge of chatting up the shivering young aspiring actress who was about to play a near-dead person in a car wreck. The anxious producer was pacing up and down and beginning to curse about the non-arrival of the all-important fire engine. Suddenly, out of the early-morning mist, we heard the brief burst of a siren and then saw a red fire engine appear with Sean at the wheel and some uniformed firefighter pals along for the ride.

Because we'd been through the real thing – with all the adrenaline, stress, tension, arguments, jeopardy and elation that came with it – when it came to a mocked-up reconstruction, we were slightly underwhelmed. Especially when in order to film it we had to go out *even earlier in the day* than we'd had to do for the real event.

We were pretty much all agreed: give me the real thing any day.

CHAPTER 13

Two Families

In my second year of working for the Cowboys, David, my eldest, had turned 16. His early interest in medicine had carried on and as he was a good studier and curious, I thought he might continue to medical school. Laura, the next eldest, had no interest in medicine at all. It was strange how they were both so different and yet like me because they both represented two different sides of myself: the analytical and sober, and the thrill-seeker and risk-taker.

A perfect example of this was on the occasions when David and Laura came along on blue lights and siren rides in my own car when responding to call-outs for the Ambulance Service. Laura liked the fast driving but wasn't really interested in what we did in terms of on-scene medical work once we got there. On the other hand, David wasn't keen on the fast driving but he was fascinated by the real-life application of medical procedures on patients at the scene. Similarly, he wasn't too keen on flying – when I took him up for a spin in my little Beagle Pup, he said, 'Dad, even your hobbies are stressful!' – but Laura hollered and whooped with excitement when we flew together. There was no fear with her, just delight at the experience and the pints of adrenaline.

It was kind of weird, and pleasing, to see such a perfect delineation between the two personality types – as if my personality had split in two like a lopped apple and each half was represented by a different child.

One day, Laura, who was 11 by this time, was alone with me at home on a Sunday morning. I got an emergency call asking to attend a crash on the M42 motorway, where a car had left the road at very high speed and had come to rest, bizarrely, high up in a large tree on the embankment, wedged there with the driver still in the vehicle.

We sped off on blue lights and sirens and got there quickly. Laura did her whooping with pure pleasure routine as we weaved in and out of the motorway traffic at very high speed. Nothing fazed her. In David, when younger, I had seen a potential doctor; in Laura, I saw the first female Formula One champion.

I stopped on the hard shoulder behind the other emergency service vehicles and told Laura to stay in the car. The scene looked even stranger in reality: a large car jammed high into a tree, stuck there as if a giant had thrown it like a dart. It had actually got there through a combination of the immense speed and the angle of take-off when the driver had lost control and the car sheered straight through the motorway barrier. Beneath the tree were pools of hot oil and petrol and still-steaming water. I got out my car, put on my high-visibility clothing and got involved with the scene.

Towards the end of the rescue, a police officer came over to me and asked me to look at a girl he had seen standing near the crash scene, assuming she had been one of the passengers. I looked around – it was Laura. Again, without any fear, she had come closer to take a look. The police officer was initially incredulous and then angry. I explained that she had come with me as we had been alone when the call from the Ambulance Service came in.

So, Laura loved the ride but had no interest in the event. David was no fan of the blues-and-twos high-speed driving but was fascinated by the drama at the scene. And though he would eventually grow taller than me courtesy of his maternal grandfather's genes, at this stage he was just about big enough for me to put him into a high-visibility jacket to pass as someone involved in proceedings.

We did a few jobs together and I noticed quite early on that he was calm under pressure and not unduly fazed by blood and gore. He also began to express an interest in pre-hospital care and medicine. This was interesting to see. I saw the glimmer and light of the first sparks flashing within him that I'd felt inside myself as the flint of fascination for medicine was struck.

One day, like most schoolkids of his age, he was asked by the school to arrange some work experience. In recent times it has become virtually impossible to arrange work experience in hospitals for schoolchildren because of issues with patient confidentiality and health and safety. But for David, I had a brainwave: I could arrange a six-week summer holiday attachment to the HEMS unit. Derek readily agreed and decided that

David could come along as an 'assistant stores operative' to help with base administration and stores.

David spent the first couple of days drinking in the atmosphere on the base while he checked stock levels of drugs and equipment against a list on a clipboard. He assisted in packing and restocking the response bags on the aircraft after the crew returned from a mission. In one inspired moment, he suggested that we could use laminated sheets of photos to check the contents of the bag and went on to produce them. Daily bag checks became easier and Derek seemed impressed by this little innovation. The folder of laminated photos went on to the aircraft and the crew found them very useful.

David went off to the base every day for six weeks and seemed to be enjoying it. He heard the flight stories of Porky, the tales of spiritualism from Chris, reminiscences of girls from John, funny medical tales from arse doctor Steven, was mothered and looked after by the Bitch and, of course, he really enjoyed seeing us all getting the occasional shouty bollocking from Derek. And not being old enough to have watched the show as a child, he had to ask – 'Dad, what's a muppet?'

One Monday, David called from the base and told me that Porky was going to fly the aircraft to the airfield where the maintenance company conducted weekly servicing and had asked him if he wanted to come along. He wanted to know whether I could pick him up from the airfield, which was about an hour from home. I was happy to go and pick him up as I knew what he was about to experience: Porky would give him

202 | CONFESSIONS OF AN AIR AMBULANCE DOCTOR

the flight of his life. But as David was none too keen on the wild stuff I didn't worry him in advance.

An hour later, after they had landed, when I picked David up from the airfield, he was sitting next to Porky in the bar and still had some residual exhilaration gleaming in his eyes. Porky turned around to me, beaming, as if to say 'Beat that, Doc'. I knew I'd have difficulty topping that experience. On the way home, David told me that they had rolled, stall-turned and flown other aerobatic manoeuvres on the way to the mainte- nance base. I knew what that felt like, it was unforgettable.

There was some anxiety about taking David out to live jobs during his work experience. Even though he had fitted into the unit well, the crews were aware that taking a schoolkid on oper- ational flights might carry some risk.

On a hot summer afternoon, I was working on the unit. David was working in the stores. We had been dispatched to reports of a crash and as the job was very close to the base we used one of our cars. I was working with Derek. With David with us, we quickly arrived at the scene of the crash. Two cars, head-on, leaking fluids and pools of liquid all over. Steam from the engines still in the air. Glass everywhere. Concertinaed metal. Dashboards pressed into human laps.

Derek and I ran over to the scene. After a few minutes' working, during which we stabilised the trapped passenger, and as we waited for the last few seconds for the fire crew to cut off the car roof, I turned and looked back. I saw that David was stood out of the car, its doors still wide open from where we'd jumped out. He looked back at us in the middle of the accident scene, and he was composed, interested, not at all fazed. Fascinated. I could see that he was dying to come nearer for a closer look and I knew then that he had what it took to enter medicine: my little 'doctor'. Now all I had to do was get Laura to focus her sense of adventure on flying and we might even have a pilot too.

I also thought that if David decided to pursue and to seek out again that feeling of excitement in flying that I'd seen Porky put in his eyes through the esprit de corps and aerobatics, then future Helimed units might be in the hands of another Bleetman.

Being in the middle of a hot summer, me and Jacqui held a barbecue at the house for the crew – and about 20 showed up. I'd learnt the value of relaxing with people and bonding over good food through Jewish culture, and through the way I saw it work in groups – in the Army, for example, when Jacqui's amazing traditional Jewish dishes had made me very popular.

It was always good for the camaraderie of a crew for them to hang out together and build a family spirit. And it was good to get my two families together – the Bleetmans and the Helimedders. David felt like one of the boys, hanging out with his buddies from the airbase.

Of course Jacqui and the kids loved Derek, Porky and the rest of the squad. We adults all got a little drunk and the boys started to talk about guns. I mentioned I had an air rifle and before you knew it, I'd got it out and Porky decided to demonstrate his skill by shooting out the wick of a lit candle. Much to everyone's amusement he missed repeatedly and hit the fence behind. To the neighbour's *un*amusement, the pellets went straight through the fence and took out one of his windows so that led to a bill for the glass and soured relations for a while.

The way-to-a-man's heart routine had continued when I started HEMS work. We'd get hungry by midday and there was no opportunity to go and buy any food as we were stuck on base for the entire shift. So being typical of the kind of men who specialise in self-neglect, we snacked on free crisps and chocolate. Some people occasionally brought sandwiches. Within a short time, Jacqui suggested she prepare some food and we talked about the Israeli Air Force days when I would bring food before sociometric assessments. Jacqui thought it would be a really good idea to feed the crew as she is a typical Jewish mother figure. The usual fare was chicken breast fried in breadcrumbs. She took one of my daughter's picnic baskets and filled it with freshly fried chicken breasts (schnitzels), fried fish, pitta bread, a jar of mustard and a tub of hummus. There would be lamb that was considered so good that Barry, in his near-unintelligible Irish accent, said, '*Nothing* this good could possibly be legal.' There would also be some fruit and chocolate for afternoon tea. Always there was enough food to feed the crew of three or four.

When the time was right and we had a chance, I heated the pitta bread and schnitzels in the microwave. A layer of hummus went into the pitta bread, the hot schnitzel was packed in and a thin layer of mustard applied. The crew loved it. It knocked a bag of crisps and a Mars bar into a cocked hat.

The lunch in the picnic basket became a regular feature of my HEMS work. Crews would come in without their sandwiches when my name was on the roster as they knew they could expect lunch. Providing good food for work colleagues makes you extremely popular.

There was an expectation on base that everyone would share in the washing up of mugs after a round of tea. I would present the food to the crew at lunchtime and announce that free food was available but I would expect an exemption from base-cleaning duties. The offer was always accepted and I was let off washing up and cleaning duties. Everyone was a winner.

Jacqui, or 'Mrs B', became the unit's unseen culinary goddess behind the scenes. The crew would talk about her in reverental tones: 'Please pass on our thanks to Mrs B'. On rare occasions when she would phone or pop in to the base, the crew almost doffed a cap to her; something that she found a little strange.

One of the reality TV show episodes that we did went out with a scene where I can be seen getting out of my car, trying to look super cool in my Aviator sunglasses and flying suit, conveniently forgetting that I'm carrying a schoolgirl's picnic basket covered with a pink gingham tea towel. Never saw that in *Top Gun*.

Having my own family made the call-outs we got to deal with children extra difficult. About a quarter of all Helimed work involves children. We're all a little apprehensive about managing severely injured or ill children. It starts with understanding their physiology, anatomical differences and injury patterns. The technical skills are far more challenging than dealing with adults. Managing their airway was terrifying for some. And then there were further challenges with venous access and drug calculations. Beyond all of these challenges was the emotional toll that these cases took on us. We had to work alongside terrified parents, schoolteachers and family members. Children can be robust in many ways and yet so fragile in others. We also needed a completely different set of communication skills to manage the children and their parents. No amount of training can prepare you for breaking the worst news to parents of a young child. But there were some situations that seemed worse than the death of a youngster.

We were scrambled to a primary school amid reports of a collapsed child in the playground. Jenny was our paramedic, and we had a relief pilot flying us. We got there to find a seven-year-old in full cardiac arrest. Children rarely suffer cardiac arrest and when they do it is usually for different reasons than adults. An adult's heart stops following heart attacks and other diseases caused by ageing and poor lifestyle. Most cardiac arrests in children are caused by lack of oxygen due to respiratory conditions. A significant number suffer cardiac arrest after drowning or injury.

We approached the lightly-built boy who was lying on his back, completely lifeless. A distraught teacher was doing her best with CPR. Another teacher was trying to marshal away the rest of the children in the playground. Many of the children were bewildered, upset and crying. One young boy was more excited by the arrival of the helicopter in the school than the condition of his classmate.

We quickly got to work on the child. The heart monitor identified some random electrical activity in the heart, which might be amenable to electric shocks. It was, and after several minutes his heart was beating normally and he had a reasonable blood pressure. But he wasn't breathing and was tolerating the tube in his windpipe without resistance. His pupils were dilated and responded poorly to a bright light shone into them. This was all rather ominous. All the indicators were that this little boy had suffered brain damage from the lack of oxygen to his brain during the time that his heart was not beating. This was not a good place to be. The cause of his cardiac arrest remained unclear at the scene, though later it transpired that the boy had been born with a heart defect that had not previously been detected.

Jenny got quite attached to this case. She phoned the hospital at least once a day to keep track of his progress. For the first few days, he was on a ventilator in intensive care with little sign of useful brain activity. It seemed that he had indeed suffered overwhelming brain injury. However, day by day, his condition improved. Within a week, he was breathing for himself. A few days later, he opened his eyes. By week three, he started to look around. But I think deep down, we all knew that the best outcome for this child would still be very difficult.

Months later, Jenny announced that the little boy was about to be discharged from hospital and the family wanted to bring him to the base to meet the crew. She busied herself tidying the base before the family were due to arrive. After much manoeuvring, the boy was wheeled in by his parents. He had a vacant stare through a deviated gaze to the right and his head was propped up on a pillow.

The boy's mother was very chatty. She described in detail the progress with physiotherapy and speech therapy; the little milestones of recovery. All the time she directed her comments to her now profoundly disabled son. The father pushing the boy's wheelchair said nothing throughout. There is nothing stronger than a mother's love for a child. She was totally immersed in caring for their son, which was a humbling, profound thing to witness.

When we got a call-out, it was difficult to predict which way a job would go, especially with child cases. Towards the end of the summer we got a job that seemed to combine the worst of our fears – a shooting incident with a child.

We were sent to a firearms incident on an illegal travellers' trailer site. In accordance with police instructions, we landed at a designated rendezvous point to meet the firearms officers. There were reports of a shooting within the trailer park. The police were out in large numbers. There were roadblocks, police dogs and armed police; all engaged in securing the scene and planning the operation. It was like they'd heard that Porky had got hold of my air rifle again and was planning on trying to shoot out another candle.

The plan here was for the police to enter the trailer park and secure the area, find the gunman and ensure that the area was safe and sterile prior to sending us in to deal with the shooting victim.

It took quite a while for the police to sweep the place and secure it to their satisfaction but eventually we were escorted into the park. The trailers were in fact more like pre-fab buildings, beautifully adorned and decorated.

We were guided into one of the trailers and ushered into the bedroom of our shooting victim. In the room was a tremendously overweight boy of about 12. Taller than me, he was twice as wide. He was standing up and had obviously been crying. In all the excitement, he seemed to have been largely ignored, and was alone. We introduced ourselves and asked what had happened. He opened his hand and showed us an airgun pellet in his palm. 'Some bastard shot me with this!' he explained.

'Okay, where did it hit you?' I asked.

'Here,' he said, and then he pulled down his shorts to show me a very small graze over a very ample right buttock.

I tried hard to suppress a smile and felt my shoulders start to tremble slightly.

'I see,' I said thoughtfully, actually very pleased that there was nothing worse to see. 'Are you up to date with your tetanus injections?' I asked.

He confirmed that he was.

At this point, his massively-built father burst in, blocking out all the light from the doorway and a significant amount from the windows too. In the gloom I could make out armfuls of dragon tattoos.

'What are you going to do about this, then? He's been shot!'

I knew I had to carefully contemplate my response as I pulled out an alcohol wipe from my pocket. 'I'm going to clean his wound with this wipe,' I said flatly, 'and then I'm going to put a sticky plaster on it. It should be fine, but if it goes red and gets sore then you should take him to see his doctor.'

The father was not impressed. But nor were the fully armed and mobilised police SWAT team poised outside. And I was especially unimpressed at us being called out to this incident. I also imagined that, should it come to it, the local GP would be none too impressed at having this child's large spotty bottom repeatedly shown to him in the near future.

So maybe we got off lightly.

CHAPTER 14

Death by Golf

People will have you believe that snowboarding, bungee jumping, skydiving and skiing are dangerous sports. And they are. Especially if when you're snowboarding, a skydiving bungee jumper on skis drops out of the sky and kills you. Which would also put you into the two categories of 'Bloody Unlucky' and 'Bad Holiday Companion'.

But those are not the most dangerous sports. The most dangerous sport – even more risky than playing darts with blind alcoholics – is golf. It's said that the worse thing golf leads to is an appalling dress sense. And, personally, I wouldn't be seen dead wearing golfing clothes. Unfortunately, a lot of golfers are: golf is the sport with the highest mortality rate of all.

People think that the greatest risk is of being struck by lightning – and that is something that does happen, and when it does it can be very nasty: it can lead to serious burns, lesions, kidney failure, bone destruction, cardiac arrest, respiratory function paralysis, frazzled hair and severely singed underpants. But, outside of lightning, most deaths by golf are due to good old-fashioned heart attacks. An awful lot of retired men die on the golf course.

It's not that golf in itself is dangerous, it's because the recently retired 'type A' personalities who engage in golf are heart attacks waiting to happen. Years of overindulgence and a sedentary executive lifestyle have clogged up their coronary arteries. The increase in exercise required to get round 18 holes just sometimes pushes them over the edge and they collapse with a heart attack, which often leads to cardiac arrest.

The sad thing is that they all looked very similar, lying lifeless in the middle of the fairway, often still clutching a golf club in one hand. I suppose it is of some comfort that they died doing what they love.

Working on a golf course could often be a very unpleasant experience and cardiac arrests on golf courses caused us a number of problems. Attending to a cardiac arrest in an open and public space is not particularly dignified for us, or the patient. We also had to deal with other golfers, who could be surprisingly impatient and irate as our medical activity stopped them from proceeding around the golf course. Often these retired businessmen took their Alan Sugar-esque boardroom manners into retirement and out on to the golf course. And they seemed oblivious to the fact that getting themselves worked up about their game being stopped because of a corpse on the course was actually bringing them a bit closer to joining it.

We also had problems with the golf clubs themselves. Golf clubs, like any other venture, have to be run as businesses. We found that officers of golf clubs would sometimes pressure us to load our cardiac arrest patients into the helicopter and fly away so they could continue to operate the golf club and not lose revenue or risk upsetting their members. On occasion, golf clubs were nice to us. We would sometimes be given a free drink or perhaps even a snack as we sat in the clubhouse completing paperwork and dealing with a recently bereaved widow. But some people can be very self-centred and obnoxious in the extreme in certain environments, even when someone's life is at stake. I well remember working on a collapsed patient in a casino. Gamblers quite nonchalantly stepped over us and the body of the soon-to-be deceased as they migrated between gambling tables. To them, a dying man on the floor represented no more than a minor obstacle that they needed to negotiate between placing bets. This was very different to attending to a cardiac arrest patient in, say, an allotment (probably the second most dangerous hobby after golfing in terms of mortality).

I don't think we ever successfully resuscitated a collapsed golfer. They all seemed to die where they fell. I guess the years of unhealthy lifestyles had eaten away at any meaningful physiological reserve. Their coronary arteries were shot. The thickening blood, labouring to chug through the thickening fat in the arteries, eventually got to the point where it said, 'Fuck it, I'm not going any further'. At which point: golfer meet heart attack, pleased to meet you.

Crewe had flown me and the Bitch to yet another golfer in cardiac arrest at a very prestigious golf course. He had collapsed on a long fairway and we found the job quite easily from the air – we saw the sun reflecting off the pale yellow jumper and white shoes. Crewe landed the aircraft very gently about 50 yards from the collapsed golfer. We spilled out of the doors, hit the ground running and launched into our cardiac arrest routine. Our golfer was overweight and had a ghastly blue complexion, his face was swollen and intubation quite difficult due to him having a small jaw and his neck being rather short and fat. We cannulated him and commenced CPR. The monitor showed a flat line and we all knew at that point that recovery was very unlikely. We went through our standard resuscitation protocols and after a generous 20 minutes, during which time there had been no improvement, we decided to stop.

I stood up and looked down on the poor old bugger.

The Bitch went off to find a club official. I got on the phone to Ambulance Control to arrange a land ambulance to come and recover the body. We were obliged to recover the body from a public place. This was an often unpleasant part of our job but it was something we had to do. We just couldn't leave a corpse out in full view. As a crew we found it a little irritating to have to spend time doing this because, like any medical crew that wants to preserve life, we considered too much time spent with the dead as time that we might have more fruitfully spent attending to the still living.

While on the phone to Ambulance Control, I became aware of a party of golfers who were waiting for us to clear the scene and remove the helicopter from where it stood on the fairway. This was of little concern to us. We were there to do a job and we wouldn't leave until it was over. This involved removing the corpse to a land ambulance, completing paperwork and probably breaking the bad news to the golfer's widow.

I began to sense that the group of golfers was becoming impatient. I finished my phone call to Ambulance Control, having arranged for an ambulance to meet us and recover the body to the local hospital mortuary. With nothing further of use to do at the time, Crewe and I stood by the helicopter and idly chatted. Crewe lit a little cigar. We had managed to cover the deceased with a blanket. Suddenly, as we chatted, we heard something whizz past us at very high speed. A golf ball had been driven towards the hole by one of the golfing party behind us. I know golfers call this 'playing through', when they catch up to a slower party and play past them.

'Can you fucking believe this?' I said to Crewe. 'They're actually trying to play through, over this poor guy.'

We were both shocked by this overt lack of respect for the recently deceased golfer and, indeed, ourselves as emergency crew. But we were also rather surprised that any golfer, no matter how serious he might have been about his game, could have prioritised it over our safety. Instinctively, we dipped our heads as more golf balls hummed past on their flight over us and the helicopter and the blanket-covered body.

I had seen Crewe irritated at times but nothing could have prepared me for the sudden anger that took hold of him. The craggy features of his face reddened and he drew his lips tightly across his teeth. He strode off decisively towards the golfers and I quickly followed, thinking 'Oh boy, this is gonna be good...'

'Which one of you clowns did that?' he said.

Now, up to this point, a profuse apology from any of them would likely have defused the situation, but they were in no mood to apologise – they had an important round of golf to play.

A rotund golfer wearing a striped jersey stepped forward. 'Listen, laddie, I have been a member of this golf club for 29 years and the rather exorbitant fees we pay here allow me to play golf *whenever* and *wherever* I please. I'm sure your work is important to you but my golf is very important to me! I think we have been more than patient, waiting for you and your first aiders to do whatever you do. I am here to play golf and you and your helicopter are in my way. Now kindly leave.'

I couldn't begin to comprehend the arrogance and callousness of this man in the face of the death of another human being. And another golfer at that. Maybe he just saw it as the elimination of a competitor.

Crewe took a deep breath, his eyes narrowed. 'You have just driven a golf ball at high speed within inches of a four-million pound helicopter. Not only that, but the ball passed within inches of our heads. And not only *that* but you drove the ball within a couple of feet of a dead golfer.'

'Yes, perfect drive!' he chortled.

Crewe remained motionless – partly, I think, with shock at what was being said, and partly at trying hard to restrain himself from tee-ing off with a five iron on this guy's fat head.

The golfer inflated his chest. 'Listen, over the 29 years that I have been playing golf, I have learned to drive very accurately. You've parked that bloody helicopter in the middle of the fairway for more than an hour and I have been more than patient. I intend to get round this course as my membership allows me.'

I saw Crewe visibly stiffen at this. He clenched his fists by his side and escalated things in the only way he safely and legally could. 'As captain of the aircraft, I am now concerned that your golf ball might have caused damage to our helicopter and I am unwilling to fly it until it has been checked over by our engineers. This may take several days.'

It was time to intervene. I stood between the two of them and turned towards the golfer. 'With respect, your behaviour is unhelpful. I don't think we are going to achieve much standing here arguing the rights and wrongs of your golf club membership. Please do not strike any more golf balls within a hundred yards of our aircraft.'

I then turned towards Crewe. 'We need to disengage. We can take this up with the golf club later on. We've got to get the corpse off the golf course now.'

Crewe reluctantly disengaged and, after taking the corpse to the ambulance, we walked back towards the aircraft. He lit another cigar on the way, leaving a trail of blue smoke in our wake. I could hear him muttering violently under his breath and managed to pick up 'cheeky fucker', 'selfish bastard' and 'fat fucking golfing prick'. And I'm pretty sure there was the odd 'twat' thrown in there for good measure.

We flew back to base feeling a little empty and dissatisfied. At least we'd learned the deceased golfer's name – Jim. That put some colour to him, made him alive in the imagination in some way. You could picture things like his mother probably only calling him James when he was a kid in trouble. I wondered what Jim would have thought of the idiot golfers trying to play over him. And wondered if he would have done the same. I decided I'd prefer to think he would have liked Crewe lighting up a cigar on the fairway.

CHAPTER 15

When Flying Goes Wrong

We were flying back to base after a big job: a lorry had smashed into the back of another on the motorway and one driver was in a sorry state. We'd got there quickly, done our critical care stuff, stabilised the patient and got him air-lifted to hospital for his on-going care. The handover at hospital had also run to plan. We looked good, created some new admirers in a new hospital and most importantly, saved a life. The job had gone well and there was a buzz in the cockpit about it; we knew we'd made a difference today.

Porky too was elated. From his perspective, the piloting had been fun: he had got us into a tight site near the crash and had been very helpful in the medical support role. The result – he was in one of his elated, boisterous moods.

One of the problems about big jobs is that the kit gets trashed. On this particular job, the equipment and drugs bags were in a mess, depleted of content and filthy with blood, wet mud and remnants of the lorry driver's clothing. Pouches, bags and individual equipment packs had been thrown into the back of the aircraft just before we lifted on the transfer to hospital. With the equipment in this state we were non-operational. We were keen to get back to base to replace the equipment and clean and re-stock the kit.

Usually we tried to start the tidying up process while returning to base from hospital. We would try to reassemble the bags and identify which items needed to be replaced. To do this, you have to unstrap and clamber around the cabin retrieving items and repacking the bags.

I surveyed the back of the aircraft; it was a mess. 'Unstrapping,' I advised Porky.

'That's fine,' he chirped back. As I started to retrieve and repack what I could in the cabin, I was vaguely aware of some muffled giggling in the front. The nose of the aircraft started to rise and continued to rise some more. I began to roll towards the back of the cabin. Then Porky pushed the cyclic control firmly forwards so that we dropped out of the sky at zero G. We were weightless. For a few seconds I was floating in mid-air in the back of the aircraft with bits of kit floating around me. As positive G came on again I descended down to the floor rather sharply.

After a split second of panic and surprise, I had a feeling of exhilaration. We laughed. Between outbursts of laughter, Porky said, 'Your face – you should have seen it! Astronaut Bleetman!'

At times, when we were returning to base and all strapped in, Porky would sometimes engage in some well-executed aerobatics. The first time this happened took me entirely by surprise. The aircraft dived and very quickly picked up speed. There was no 'Mayday!' call from the cockpit – only some excited *Top Gun* style yee-haa whooping – so I knew this was another flying stunt and not an aircraft malfunction. Either that or Porky had just flipped out. As we dived, the ground completely filled the windscreen, items of loose kit rolled forwards. So that's what it looks like to die in an aircraft crash, I thought. Then Porky pulled hard on the cyclic. We rose sharply, climbing steeply into the first half of a loop; everything that had rolled forward now rolled back. We carried on rising, slowing. The helicopter soared to the loop's high point and then inverted. Everything not nailed down fell, hitting the now upside-down roof of the craft. We tipped over the top of the loop, and Porky rolled us out of it. We were the right way up again but our stomachs were still catching up and our eyeballs still wobbling back to centre like spirit-level bubbles.

After my initial reaction of 'You fucker' for not warning us, my next favourite reaction was to pretend that nothing at all had happened.

'So, Porky,' I said casually, 'any plans for tonight?'

He laughed, knowing what I was doing.

'Yeah,' he replied, 'I thought I might go to Alton Towers. Good roller coasters, I hear.'

But we always felt safe with Porky's aerobatics and most of us thoroughly enjoyed it. The problem was that not all the crew liked aerobatic rides in the Air Ambulance. Other doctors and paramedics who were exposed to moments of aerobatic exhilaration went into these upside-down manoeuvres and screaming dives with, let's say, a certain amount of trepidation, some green faces and an awful lot of white knuckles.

People began to talk about the aerobatic Air Ambulance. These rumours spread to the rather conservative and traditional circles of North Central Ambulance, our neighbouring and rival Air Ambulance Service. Once too often we had heard that we were being labelled as cowboys by our colleagues at North Central. So we reclaimed the 'Cowboys' name and adopted it – not in the way that means amateurs, because we certainly weren't that, but in the spirit of a Wild West frontiersman who knows how to tame a wild horse.

As an Air Ambulance doctor I liked to be flown by skilled, professional pilots. This is a very different type of flying to my recreational flying and I was happy to be a crewmember on high-performance and sophisticated helicopters flown by experienced and talented HEMS pilots. It took me almost a day to plan a flight to France in my little aeroplane; it takes a HEMS pilot a couple of minutes to fly an unprepared route through busy airspace on a mission in marginal weather. They earned my respect and I trusted them with my life.

Most accidents are caused by pilots doing things that they are not trained or qualified to do. Aeroplanes rarely catch fire or break apart. Aircraft engines rarely fail and, even if they do, you turn into a large but manageable glider. I practised forced landing techniques in the hope that if it ever happened to me I would be able to deal with it.

I didn't talk about the flying accident attendances at home. Oddly enough, Jacqui felt safer with me in a plane than in a car. She always said that I was better at flying than driving. So, when we went off to France or Spain for a break, I always made sure that I flew us there, rather than drove.

My biggest concern in flying is that of hitting something in the sky: another aircraft, a flock of birds, a parachutist, a glider or whatever else out there that could hit me. On HEMS missions we had the benefit of three pairs of eyes keeping a good lookout. Even with this support we still had the occasional near-miss with a big bird, a glider or a light aircraft. We tended to fly a lot lower than light aircraft and so largely kept out of their way.

However, when flying along at 1,000 feet we were slap-bang in the band of sky used by military jets. It was almost impossible to see them coming. Every so often we would be startled by a Harrier Jump Jet or a Tornado screaming past us at extreme velocities – so quick that Derek rarely had the chance to even shout *'Muppet!'* – and sometimes frighteningly close by. They'd *BOOM* out of an even clear blue sky without warning. This terrified even us. I learned very quickly that military jets tend to fly in pairs so that after a near-collision with one there will almost certainly be a near-collision with another.

The other big killers of pilots are pushing the boundaries too far in terms of weather conditions and aircraft handling. Occasionally, we responded to flying accidents that were caused in this way. Witnessing the total misery and overwhelming suffering caused by aircraft accidents made me much more cautious about my own recreational flying.

My first encounter with an air crash was during my first summer on Helimed 999. We were dispatched to reports of a light aircraft spinning into the ground. Porky got us there very quickly and we commenced a search. The radio was alive with updates on the possible location of the crash as more 999 calls came in to Ambulance Control. We were aware that RAF Search and Rescue had also been scrambled. The atmosphere in the helicopter was tense as we all looked out, scouring every field and hedgerow for the downed aircraft. After a few minutes, Jenny spotted the wreck: 'Ten o'clock, half a mile, in the middle of the brown field.' Porky banked us hard over to the left and confirmed the sighting.

'Looks like a Grumman. It hasn't broken up,' he said.

As we flew the approach I could see that there were two occupants in the crashed plane. The canopy had separated from the broken cockpit and was lying about 10 yards away from the fuselage. The occupant of the left-hand seat was slumped over to the left, the occupant of the righthand seat was sitting upright and I thought I could see him move a little, probably responding to the noise and blast generated by the Agusta as we approached. We jumped out of the aircraft as soon as the wheels touched and ran over to them. Being in a rural and remote location, we were first on the scene. Porky would give our position to Ambulance Control and the RAF.

The little broken aircraft was largely intact. Both main undercarriage wheels had sheared off, lying on either side of the aircraft like broken legs. The aircraft's spine was snapped, its tail was twisted. I could smell aviation fuel and I became concerned that this could turn into a big fireball. The occupant in the left-hand seat was lifeless; his body slumped over to the left with a small trickle of blood dribbling from the side of his mouth and from his nose. From the way he was sitting it was clear to me that his neck was broken and his chest had been crushed. I quickly felt for a pulse and found none: this man was very dead. The occupant of the right seat was breathing slowly and his eyes flickered open from time to time. Clearly, this flyer was still alive.

I leant into the cockpit, 'Are you okay? Can you hear me?' He opened his eyes and as soon as I looked into them I could sense his terror and pain. I offered some reassuring words, 'It's okay. Stay as you are, and we'll get you out and sort things out for you. Stick with me, fella, okay? Stay with me – I'm staying with you.'

Our first priority was to make the scene as safe as possible. I could see the fuel cock on the left side on the cockpit floor so I ran round to the other side of the aircraft, reached between the dead pilot's smashed legs and turned the fuel cock to the 'off' position. I then scoured the inside of the cockpit looking for the master switch and turned that off. The final thing to do to reduce the risk of fire was to disable the magnetos. In light aircraft this is often controlled by a key, which I found, and turned that off, too.

Jenny was talking to the survivor. She had attached a collar to his neck and applied an oxygen mask. Now she was busy putting a cannula in the back of his hand so that we could give him pain relief and start fluid resuscitation. As we worked with our survivor, two fire engines were slowly making their way across the rutted field towards us, the red vehicles rising and falling over the ruts in the field. When they got to us they worked quickly; they did not need us to tell them that this was a time-critical job.

Jenny and I infused 500ml of fluid into our patient just before the fire team lifted him out on a spinal board. We gave him some fluid volume because we had learned over the years that severely injured patients can drop their blood pressure as they are straightened out and lifted vertically from wrecks. This strategy worked and our downed airman stayed fairly conscious during the extrication.

The fire crew put him on an ambulance trolley and we assessed him in more detail. His chest seemed okay but we were very concerned that he might have bled into his abdomen as it was tense and tender when I examined him. His limbs seemed intact but as we log-rolled him to get to his back, it was clear that he had sustained injuries to his spine. Beyond paralysing a patient, a spinal injury poses another challenge: damage to the spinal cord can cause a large drop in blood pressure as the sympathetic nervous system is disrupted, causing blood vessels to dilate. I knew that this complicated resuscitation attempts and we had to balance the risks of giving large volumes of fluid to maintain blood pressure in the face of massive internal bleeding against other clinical considerations. The human body is a thing of astounding and beautiful complexity and, when it is smashed this badly, it can seem like a 10,000-piece jigsaw puzzle, every piece painted white, which has been swept off the table.

Our downed airman was clearly very unwell. He looked up into my eyes with terror and at that moment he knew he was going to die. I knew it too. And I knew that he knew this. Thinking ahead to the helicopter transfer, I thought it would be better if we anaesthetised him and took over his physiology. It would also deal with his pain more effectively than the morphine and the ketamine that we were giving him.

I have often thought about what patients experience as we give them a general anaesthetic, particularly if they are going to die. The last thing that they will experience will be my face, my words of encouragement and comfort as they drift off to final sleep. It will be their last earthly experience, and I have spent many a sleepless night dwelling on this.

On this occasion, as I explained that I wanted to make him sleep so that we could help him, he knew that this would really be for him the moment of last light. The rapid sequence induction of anaesthetic went very smoothly. He drifted off to sleep and twitched a little as the paralysing drug took effect. His physiology stabilised for a short while, but after perhaps 10 minutes, as we prepared to load him into the helicopter, he had a catastrophic deterioration and died shortly afterwards.

Jenny and I sat next to him in silence for a few minutes. The whole scene had been extremely traumatic and we were both moved by being an intimate part of this man's last few minutes on earth.

We thanked the fire crew and trudged back to the aircraft. For a few minutes we sat in the cockpit in silence, digesting and processing the events of the last half hour. The sight of overwhelming horror and suffering, together with the emotional demise of the man had touched us. This was the kind of experience that made me take my own recreational flying safety very seriously. I did not want to die like that in a field.

The cause of the accident turned out to be a pilot flying outside his own capabilities and that of the aircraft. He had been seen performing aerobatics in the little Grumman. The aircraft had developed a flat spin and struck the ground at high speed. It was not just the pain of the injuries that these aviators would have suffered, but also the terror of that last minute or so while the pilot would have been desperately trying to get the aircraft out of the spin. At some point during the descent both of them must have realised that they were going to die and that it would hurt. I shuddered at the thought of this and I knew it would come to me whenever I flew.

Flying light aircraft is perceived by many to be unsafe. Beyond the risk of mid-air collisions and flying beyond your own capabilities, it is a relatively safe pastime. But this applies only to 'A to B' straight and level flying. Aerobatics introduces a completely different dimension to recreational flying.

This message was further reinforced when our crew attended a glider crash uncannily close to the crash site of the little Grumman. This job was particularly unpleasant as when we got there we found a 16-year-old boy on his first glider flight, dead alongside his instructor. It appeared that the glider had aerodynamically stalled during a manoeuvre that had been performed too close to the ground for the pilot to recover. We stood and looked at the lifeless bodies of the two occupants of the aircraft. I looked at the pale face of the poor 16-year-old, and it was unbearably sad to think of his exhilaration and excitement turning to terror.

We always felt uncomfortable when a rescue mission turned into a body recovery exercise. We felt obliged to assist in the removal of body parts, and tried to offer some silent comfort to the victims and probably also to ourselves in that we were doing something good for them: the last good thing that could be done. The badly broken bodies of both glider occupants looked human but were so badly deformed when we moved them. Limbs had turned into unstable blocks of flesh as the bones within them had been shattered.

But it's not the body destruction that haunts you so much, it's the snuffing out of the spirit of whatever it is that makes us alive. It's sobering how eyes alive with pain and awareness can, in an instant, suddenly still.

It wasn't only pilots who got into trouble. Sometimes passengers did, too. Helimed 999 was located at an airport from which 'no-frills' budget airlines operated. One day Jenny and I were called to await the arrival of a Boeing 737 from Malaga to reports of a female in a collapsed state. We stood on the tarmac as the holiday jet slowly taxied towards us.

As we entered the aircraft, the first thing that struck us was the smell of stale alcohol and vomit. The plane was full of partied-out youngsters in their twenties. The cabin crew looked fraught and exhausted. Our patient was slumped spread-eagled in a seat at the rear of the aircraft. She had a nice face but it was drizzled liberally with various shades and textures of vomit, and her mascara was running down into it. Her top seemed several sizes too small and a push-up bra was doing its best to heave her cleavage, which was also decorated with puke, out of her top. She had also vomited over the back of the seat in front of her and down onto and into her shoes. One was still on her foot, the other was off and filled with sick. The whole scene was like *The Exorcist*.

She reeked of stale alcohol. But she was breathing and her overall colour was reasonable; her pulse was strong. The flight attendant told us that along with many others she had been drinking constantly from the start of the flight. After coming out of the toilet she had projectile-vomited down the aisle, which must have been nice, and then became unconscious approximately 20 minutes before the plane landed.

I looked into her pupils and did not see any signs to suggest that she had taken heroin or opiates. Her blood sugar was in the normal range. It was difficult to say with any certainty why she had collapsed. The most likely cause – surprise, surprise – was alcohol poisoning. You can actually drink yourself to death.

Thanking God for latex gloves, we managed to manoeuvre her into the aisle as the cabin crew disembarked the passengers from the front of the aircraft. With the help of ground crew we got her down the aircraft steps and into an ambulance. Her blood pressure, pulse and respiratory rate were within normal limits and, although she remained deeply unconscious, we decided not to intervene further.

However, she was not to be denied, and on the way to hospital she came round just long enough to look up and smile, and to vomit all over again.

CHAPTER 16

35mg of 'shut-the-f**k-up'

One of the most satisfying things we can do as emergency physicians is to fix painful injuries and quickly make people better. I suppose the classic example is a shoulder dislocation. Large rugby player falls over in a scrum; there is sudden excruciating pain as his shoulder is wrenched out of its socket and, as the joint capsule remains stretched, the pain continues until it is pulled back into place. The problem is how to get the patient's muscles to relax to allow you to manoeuvre the joint back to where it belongs. Their muscles go into spasm due to the pain so you can't fix it – a vicious circle.

Or sometimes, when a joint has been disrupted and bent out of shape, it can shut off blood supply to a hand or a foot. The joints need to be reduced to a reasonable position to allow the blood to flow and save the limb. There are a number of ways of getting patients to relax. Most involve powerful drugs, although a boss of mine once taught me hypnosis, which can be useful sometimes.

In the HEMS world, we use the drug ketamine a lot. Ketamine is a powerful anaesthetic. It's not a new drug – one of its early uses was as a battlefield anaesthetic in Vietnam – but it is a drug with a bad reputation: you say ketamine and people think 'horse tranquilliser' and 'hallucinations'. That's because it's used not only by doctors, but also by vets for sedating and anaesthetising horses. It is also more popularly known by the drug-taking public and *Daily Mail* readers alike as the clubbing drug 'Special K'. Not to be confused with the breakfast cereal which, if snorted, would probably make your eyes water.

So, ketamine could be used to stun both horses *and* hallucinating ravers. Which was useful to know if we ever got called out to deal with a racehorse off its tits in a nightclub.

Joking aside, we did attend a horse-related incident that required us to use it on a person rather than the animal. We flew out to a farm, where a vet had been badly kicked by a horse she had been examining. She had a nasty open lower-leg fracture. Sitting against the wall of the stable, she was very stoical; medics, even animal doctors, are usually easy to deal with as they know the routine. I told her I wanted to reduce the fracture and get her in a decent splint before the flight to hospital. I said I was going to use ketamine and she smiled knowingly. We had a conversation about the drug, horses and hallucinations. I learnt from her something surprising: that the drug calculations I used for people were the same as she used for horses. So, before I gave her the shot, we calculated her dosage together – although it always seems impolite to ask a lady how much she weighs!

Ketamine is unique and predictable. If you know what you're doing, it works. Give a little and the patient's eyes flicker and they go quiet and become a little spaced out. However, they keep breathing and their blood pressure will not drop. Give a bit more and they will let you do anything and keep breathing, and their blood pressure will be fine. Give a full anaesthetic dose and they go to sleep but many will keep breathing until you give another drug to paralyse them. This is so useful in high-risk and desperately ill or injured patients. We all got slick with ketamine. We trained the paramedics to use it and we used it with children and adults. If you made sure your calculations were correct, you got the desired response (almost) every time so we did more with it than fixing broken wings. It was a very useful weapon in our armoury – a good arrow to have in your quiver. In fact, considering some of the crazy situations we had to use it in, a syringe of K taped to the end of an arrow would have been a handy way of delivering it to patients, though I wasn't convinced I'd get that idea past the General Medical Council.

Ketamine however, while being safe, predictable and short-acting, did on occasion cause adverse reactions. Some patients would get very agitated after it went in; others when it wore off. Some would say they really enjoyed the experience; others woke up and reported flights of terror. Almost all of them thought they had been flying in space.

Porky noticed that patients went quiet after we gave ketamine. Their pain and anxiety went away within seconds of squirting it into a vein. Five minutes later, they woke up from their short 'space flight' in a much better frame of mind and out of pain. He began to refer to ketamine as a syringe of 'shut-the-fuck-up'.

Here's an example of how well ketamine can work for us. We were called to a farmer on a remote hillside. He had been up a ladder cutting branches from a tree when he'd fallen hard onto his left leg and bone was sticking out. A perfect HEMS job. Remote location, difficult access and a requirement for some hospital-level care in the field. Our man was lying on his back, propped up on his elbows, and in obvious pain. Barry expertly slid a cannula into a prominent vein on his left forearm and administered some morphine.

The farmer's lower leg was badly angulated and a shard of white bone protruded through a hole in the skin. I removed his boot and sock, trying hard not to move his leg too much and cause him further pain. His foot was cold and there was no pulse in it. We had to straighten out his leg, get the bone inside where it belongs and hope that in doing so, we could restore his blood supply. I explained this to our man and told him all about ketamine. He resigned himself to his impending drug-induced flight into low earth orbit.

Ketamine did its thing, our man remained propped up on his elbows with a glassy stare in his eyes, detached from all proceedings here on earth. Barry irrigated the protruding bone and surrounding area with copious amounts of saline and Beta-dine solution. I used a scalpel to enlarge the opening in the skin while Barry pulled hard on the foot and the bone fragment slipped back into place as the leg was straightened and the foot pulse was restored. Within a minute or so, the foot became pink and warm. Throughout all of this, our man remained motionless and didn't even whimper. We gave some intravenous antibiotics, and dressed and then splinted his leg. He woke up on the stretcher.

'You okay?' I asked. 'Any pain?'

'A bit of an ache,' he replied. 'What happened?'

'Your leg's fine but you will need an operation,' I advised him. He seemed happy with that. Ketamine had done its thing again.

In the field, we didn't just deal with physical injuries, we also had to cope with patients with psychiatric illness too. Increasingly often we'd find ourselves having to try to treat mentally disturbed patients. Sometimes it was just a case of our drugs vs. their drugs. Our syringes of ketamine and naloxone against theirs of heroin and crack.

There is no reasoning with agitated psychiatric patients. Their behaviour often gets the police involved, then a pursuit and a fight ensues, followed by a restraint. Sometimes, these people die during that restraint. It is thought that a combination of psychiatric upset, powerful (legal or recreational) drugs, alcohol, exhaustion and restraint in which adequate breathing is impaired brought about such deaths. Sometimes, there might be an undiagnosed injury or medical problem that caused them to act in this way – diabetes, head injuries, sepsis and others. In the past, these poor people would often get carted off to a police cell only to be found dead there a few hours down the line – lots of high-profile cases about this have hit the news.

We believed that terminating the struggle early on might reduce the risk of death. There are several ways of doing this but first you need to get physical control. Before tasers solved this problem for the police, we had to work with them to get a safe restraint onto the patient to allow us to get close with a syringe-full of sedative. It helped, but only if you could get it in them.

In one situation, the police had called us out to a job when they worked out that their quarry was sick and not a criminal. He was holed up in his flat after threatening a neighbour, and they had entered but couldn't get near to subdue him. By the time we got there he was barricaded behind his upturned couch using a stash of objects from the flat as missiles.

He had just about thrown everything at us but the kitchen sink (and that was only because he wasn't in the kitchen). We had faced a barrage of various fruit, a telephone directory, sofa cushions and an ashtray. We quickly retreated to the doorway and found the two police officers stood there, smirking.

'Bit unlucky with that banana there, Doc,' one of them said. 'I would have thought that would've just boomeranged back to him.'

We peered around the door and immediately a TV remote control, some tangerines and a shoe were lobbed at us. I thought we could try to wait him out, but as ever my short attention span drove us to seek a more immediate solution. I turned around to discuss it with Barry, Porky and the police. Porky froze, slices of freshly peeled tangerine in his mouth and a look of 'What?' across his face.

This was a situation where a bow-and-arrow delivery of a syringe would have been very, very useful. Right now, I would have quite happily taken aim and made the shot. Instead, we agreed with the police that it would be in everyone's best interests to restrain him quickly and safely prior to administering a form of 'shut-the-fuck-up.'

We followed the police and ran back into the room, dodging more missiles. Eventually we all ended up rolling around on the floor until I managed to dart an arm and inject it. Luckily, out of the eight arms on offer I managed to get one of his two.

It wasn't really our month for drug-induced psychosis in tower blocks because a few weeks later we were called out to another. This time we had attended in one of our emergency response cars to a tower block in the middle of the city to support a land ambulance crew who had been dealing with a young black man, who had nearly died after overdosing on heroin. We approached the depressing tower block with some sense of dread and were met by a police officer, who told us that our man was on the 14th floor. He broke it to us gently that the lift was out of order and we would have to lug ourselves and our kit up to the job. Fuck! I wondered whether Porky back at base couldn't instead land the Agusta on the roof so we could walk *one* flight down, but that would never happen.

After 28 flights of stairs in dark, urine-smelling stairwells, we finally got to the flat. The place was in a very poor state – filthy with pizza boxes and assorted needles, syringes and foil wraps. A young black man was on the floor. He was huge, probably almost seven feet tall, and heavily-built. Already he was being ventilated via an endotracheal tube by the land ambulance crew. That was interesting; it is impossible to intubate anyone unless they've been totally anaesthetised. As ambulance crews don't have the training or drugs to do this, there could only be one conclusion – our man had overdosed to such an extent that he had in effect anaesthetised himself into a deep coma. That was handy for intubation.

He showed no attempt at breathing for himself; the ambulance crew were breathing for him using an ambubag. They had managed to package him on an aluminium scoop with straps, ready to go. He was connected to a monitor; all the numbers were good (reasonable blood pressure, pulse, oxygen saturations and end-tidal CO_2). The crew had done a superb job; the man had been beautifully resuscitated and packaged, ready to be taken to hospital. So I had to wonder, why had they called us? It was because there was the issue of getting down 14 floors without a lift, so they wanted us as extra muscle to get him down 28 flights of stairs. We weren't too pleased about that; or as Derek would have barked if he'd been there – '*NOT* happy!'

Even with us helping, it still wasn't going to happen. While we were thinking it through, our policeman arrived out of breath to tell us that a lift engineer had been summoned and was on his way. We adopted a holding pattern; we waited for what seemed a long time but there was no news of progress with the lift.

I decided that we could try something a little risky. We could give him naloxone, which should in theory reverse the heroin and wake him up. Our drug versus his drug.

Naloxone is a powerful opioid antagonist drug. It directly reverses the effects of morphine, heroin and other similar substances. Given into a vein, it works almost instantaneously, but also wears off very quickly. When treating heroin overdoses in hospital, we learned to give a big dose into a muscle before injecting into a vein. We found that when we gave it into the vein of a heroin addict who had overdosed, they would open their eyes almost immediately, tell us to *fuck off*, get up and run away, only to collapse again in the street a few hundred yards from the hospital as the naloxone wore off. If we gave it into a muscle, there was a half-decent chance that the slow release of the drug would keep them safe until the heroin was out of their system.

Assuming he hadn't sustained any hypoxic brain damage due to lack of oxygen, we could wake him up and possibly get him to walk down the stairs with some support. Much easier than carrying him down.

I gave the naloxone, first into muscle to give us the sustained effect and then some more into a vein for immediate effect. Within 30 seconds, he coughed and started to move.

We took out his endotracheal tube. He vomited, coughed and started to move around. After a couple of minutes, it became clear that we had made a bit of a mistake – we had turned a heavy 20-stone, seven-foot package that had only been a lifting and handling problem into a 20-stone, seven-foot and very irritable and confused wrestling opponent. We had effectively super-sized our problem. And so we wrestled with him trying to escape until he tired. We left him alone and he eventually rolled over and started to snooze. This wasn't going to work. We stood around waiting, feeling a bit foolish.

To our relief, the policeman announced that a lift engineer had arrived and said he could lower us slowly down in the lift. An ambulance man was sent down to fetch up a carry chair, which has wheels on the rear so you can tip backwards and transport the patient in that way. He returned 20 minutes later with it. We all struggled and lifted our man into the chair and strapped him in. His head was slumped forwards but he was breathing fine and no longer irritable and fighting. We got into the lift, and it was tiny – there was me, our paramedic Barry and this very large man. The lift started to drop but only six inches at a time as we were being manually lowered down the lift shaft by the invisible lift engineer. We were going painfully slowly, it was getting hot inside and I was starting to get very claustrophobic almost to the point of hyperventilating and panic. Just when I thought it couldn't get any worse, it did.

When we were several storeys down, the naloxone that we had given into his muscle started to kick in. Our man woke up angry, growled and strained against the straps across his chest holding him to the chair. He was very agitated and tried to escape. We had no room to move out of his way. I had not brought any drugs with me to take him back down to the Land of Nod. I had also cleverly not brought a radio with me. We were alone in there with 20 stone of confused aggression. As the weirdness of the situation he'd woken up to began to sink in, he started to thrash around violently. He straightened his legs and banged his head on the lift panelling, denting it. As he carried on thrashing, me and Barry were smacked, punched and kicked repeatedly as the lift dropped slowly through floor after painful floor, one at a time. Things got so violent in the tiny, confined space that I thought one of us would be killed. His shouts and threats grew louder. We tried to at least hold his massive arms so he couldn't club us with them.

At the bottom of the lift shaft, the doors at last slid open and we all fell out, collapsing in a gasping heap. I quickly retrieved the drugs bag from our rucksack that had thoughtfully been brought down by an ambulance technician. As we resedated our giant patient prior to loading him into an ambulance I said, 'If we get a call now, tell them that we went to the wrong flat and we've got to get this guy back up there!' Barry said something in Irish which ended with '… I'm fucking quitting.' 'It's half past two,' I replied.

There were other times when the patient's reaction to a barrel of some 'shut-the-fuck-up' was unexpected. One day, when I was back at the hospital, I was working on the case of a very sweet teenage girl, who was brought in with a dislocated elbow after a bad fall. She needed urgent reduction. Using ketamine would save her a general anaesthetic and she would be able to go home once her injury had been dealt with.

The girl's parents were with her and understandably anxious – I went through it with them a number of times before they signed the consent form. I gave the injection. The girl cried for a few seconds and then her eyes started to flicker and she became peaceful. She was transferred to a trolley in the resuscitation room and we attached all the monitoring equipment to keep her safe during the procedure. Afterwards, I reduced the joint, applied a plaster cast and left her with a nurse to watch over her and make sure that she recovered uneventfully.

At about that time, a female teacher was wheeled in with a badly fractured ankle. I noticed from her notes that this very prim-looking woman worked at the same school as the teenage girl attended. In the teacher's case, ketamine would also be my weapon of choice. After consenting the teacher for her sedation, I went back into the resuscitation room to see how the girl was doing and to have a few words with her parents. She remained deeply asleep. Her parents anxiously asked when she would wake up. 'It can take between 20 minutes and an hour or two,' I explained.

I then wheeled the teacher into the resuscitation room and into the bay next to the girl, drawing the cubicle curtains around us (I clocked the recognition in the parents' eyes when they saw their daughter's teacher). I cannulated the teacher, attached her to a monitor and checked all the emergency equipment in case we got into difficulties. Another nurse was ready with a plaster trolley to apply a cast once the swollen ankle had been reduced. I calculated the dose of ketamine in my head, administered the drug and watched with some satisfaction as Miss's eyes started to twitch. Then, from nowhere, she suddenly came to, tried to sit up and began screaming out at the top of her voice in a very posh, high-pitched shrill: 'OH, *FUCK* ME! *FUCK* ME AGAIN! *Fuck*-me-*fuck*-me-*fuck*-me!'

I stood frozen, transfixed by this insane but oddly fascinating transformation of a quietly spoken school teacher into a raging, full-on foul-mouthed porn star. I'd never seen *this* before. For a split-second it occurred to me that if you could cause this deliberately, and then sell the formula, you'd be on your way to making your first 10 billion – although the whole school system would be a bit of a mess.

Then I snapped out of it and realised that in the cubicle next door, separated only by a thin curtain, were the (I imagined extremely horrified) parents of the woman's pupil. God only knows what kind of treatment they thought I was giving out. I just hoped they weren't thinking that her reaction was a result of my bedside manner.

I panicked and pushed my head through the cubicle curtain. Bad idea. The girl's mother and father stared back at me in horror, clearly completely traumatised. I smiled and silently mouthed '*Sorry...*' through a rising chorus behind me of FUCKs, FUCK ITs and FUCK MEs – and one very sudden and unexpected 'YOU DIRTY, *DIRTY* BASTARD!'

I returned to her and acted fast, emptying more of the syringe of ketamine into our teacher's vein just as she was announcing to the world, 'OH, FUCK ME'! 'There, there,' I said quickly, 'There, there… '

Our porno teacher fell silent. I mentally said a quick prayer for the sudden silence: 'Oh, blessed syringe full of "shut-the-fuck-up", how we adore thee.'

The whole hospital now seemed deathly quiet. I considered another head-pop through the curtain and another mouthed 'sorry' to the parents, but thought better of it. Instead I decided to make full use of that innate quality of the British when faced with something acutely embarrassing… *act as if nothing has happened*. If *I* didn't mention the 'fuck'-shouting teacher, *they* wouldn't mention her.

The teacher's ankle reduced easily and was duly put into a cast. She recovered fine, came around from the sedation and was utterly oblivious to what had happened and everything that she had said; everything that she had very, very loudly said. I think she thought that everyone was smiling at her because we were all just so happy in our work. Which was true.

She described the feeling of being sedated as like an exciting flight into space with the sensation of floating around above her own body.

In the interests of keeping my sanity – and also because I feared bursting out laughing – I decided not to ask her what subject she'd most enjoyed teaching during her career, just in case she replied 'Sex education'.

CHAPTER 17

Casualties in the Class Wars

All this talk of chicken mass slaughter, obscenity-shouting teachers, heart-attack suffering golfers, stabbed prisoners, violent drug addicts, snapped limbs, cracked heads, amputated legs, throat openings, chest cavity piercings, collapsed lung re-inflations, outdoor open-chest surgeries, car crashes, motorbike smashes, airplane disasters, traumatic helicopter flights and all those death scenes that became the blood-guts-snot-and-shit parties to which we always got an invite might give you the wrong idea that it was all fun and games.

Sometimes it was actually serious.

And sometimes the threat to our lives came not from up in the air but from down on the ground.

We got a call-out on one hot summer afternoon – a report of a hanging. The job was very close to the base and as Derek and I had been out in the car anyway on another nearby call, we immediately went back out.

Derek drove us in the rally Seat on a skilful and obscenity-laden high-speed dash through the traffic and across the city centre. We arrived at a very run-down-looking housing estate. It was easy to identify the job from the crowd of people outside a small maisonette. The crowd was anxious and restless; everyone was smoking. I also worked out from their body language that this was a very serious job. Derek pulled up sharply outside the house. Some of the crowd immediately approached the car, while others were running in and out of the front door of the maisonette. We quickly got out and went to the rear of the car to get our kit from the boot. A tubby and heavily-tattooed man wearing a replica football shirt started to confront us. 'What are you fucking waiting for?' was his opening line.

We ignored him, grabbed our kit and ran into the house. The smell of cigarette smoke was overpowering and clouds of it came from another crowd of people in the hallway, blocking our way through the door off to the left leading into the lounge. We tried to negotiate our way through the mass of people in our path.

Derek's height enabled him to hack a route through and see what lay ahead. The first thing that we noticed when we entered the lounge was that the plasma screen was as big as the wall that it was hung on. It was showing music videos but with the sound turned down. Lying in front of it on the floor was a man in his thirties with a rope still around his neck. He looked lifeless. I caught Derek's eye and he seemed to be thinking it was as bad as I thought it looked.

Evidently, our patient had tried to hang himself. His girlfriend had gone out briefly after they'd had a fight. After buying some cigarettes, she had come back to find our patient hanging from a rope slung over the top of a door into the kitchen and attached to the handle on the other side. A moment of madness. Some suicide attempts are just an impulse reaction to a simple argument; out of character for the person and probably bitterly regretted even as the cord is tightening around the neck or the blood pulsing like party string from the wrist.

Someone had helpfully cut him down from the door but the rope was still tight around his neck. We removed the rope and rapidly established that our man was in full cardiac arrest. Derek caught my eye and diverted my gaze to our patient's right ankle, on which was attached a criminal tagging device. He leant forward and whispered, 'This could be the very first time that we take a patient out the house and he starts bloody beeping!'

I didn't let even a flicker of a smile touch my lips as I knew we were being watched very intently, and in a none-too-friendly way, by the anxious crowd standing over us.

I made sure our man's airway was clear, intubated him and started ventilation while Derek commenced CPR, attached a monitor and got a line in. The rhythm on the monitor was encouraging. It was a pulse-less electrical activity rhythm almost certainly caused by oxygen starvation. Our man had a chance but it was likely that his brain would have sustained some damage even if we got his heart going again.

We worked on as the crowd grew in size. The tubby tattooed guy came over and introduced himself again with another charming question, 'What the fuck are you doing? Take him to fucking hospital!'

I explained that we were doing everything here that a hospital could do, and that the patient had a better chance if we worked on him now before moving him. Our new tubby friend wasn't convinced and decided to offer some helpful encouragement.

'If he dies,' he said, jabbing his finger towards us, 'I'll fucking kill you both!'

I could see Derek was itching to get up and smack the guy, but instead he knelt to the floor and spoke into his radio, calling for the police and for the launch of the aircraft. Upon hearing the word 'police', Dr Tubby gave us his diagnosis: 'I ain't afraid of the police. I'll still fucking kill you if he dies 'cos you should have taken him to hospital!'

We ignored him and worked on in silence but I could tell that his opinion, wrong as it was, had developed some currency in the crowd. There was a low-level ominous mumbling that seemed to be on the verge of an ugly expansion. The whole scene was soundtracked by the constant loud sobbing of the man's girlfriend. Thankfully, within a few minutes we heard the familiar and reassuring whine of our Agusta approaching and landing close by.

A minute later, the familiar figure of Porky was shouldering his way through the crowded room. He glanced up at the wall – 'Nice telly' – and then down at our patient, 'And very trendy ankle bracelet.' He seemed oblivious to the atmosphere; I couldn't decide whether that made me feel better or worse.

Derek and I had completed another cycle of CPR and we stopped to check for a pulse. I put my fingers onto the side of our hanged man's neck and I felt a strong, bounding pulse at the carotid artery.

'Output restored,' I advised. Derek confirmed it by checking for a pulse over the femoral artery. 'Yep, all there,' he offered. I surveyed our patient. His pupils were dilated and did not react to light from the laryngoscope in my right hand. There were two possible explanations for this: either his brain had sustained damage or his pupils were dilated because of the high dose of adrenaline that we had given him during the resuscitation attempt. Given that he was not breathing yet, I suspected the explanation was brain damage. I reassured the crowd around us that their friend's heart had been restarted and he had a chance.

His girlfriend had by now all but finished chain-smoking the pack of cigs that she had popped out to buy. Her loud sobbing throughout the whole time we had been there only now started to subside a little. I felt sympathy for her, as she would no doubt feel some guilt about leaving the house, even though this wasn't her fault.

Two police officers arrived and joined the party. I gave them an update on the course of events and asked for their assistance in clearing the house and the street of onlookers. They obliged and were superb: forceful but sensitive. Clearly they knew this patch and how best to deal with the locals.

One of them returned and asked me how the patient was. I thought about it for a second and said, 'He's alive but his brain's likely fried.'

'Prognosis?' he asked.

'Well, best-case scenario: in a wheelchair and fed through a tube,' I answered.

Our conversation was cut short by Derek's familiar loud bark, '*BLEET*man! Give us a hand loading him, then.'

As we flew off, I looked down and saw the small pathetic figure of the girlfriend looking up, her sad features becoming indistinct as we lifted higher.

The next Sunday, we had a relief pilot on the aircraft. His name was Dan and he'd just completed his conversion training to the Agusta 109, having recently been in the RAF, where he flew Chinook helicopters. He told us that he had been a flight lieutenant. This was useful because everybody on the unit needed a nickname. His was obviously going to be 'Lieutenant Dan', said in an American accent that mimicked Forrest Gump's.

Barry was our paramedic for the day. We had just called online and sat down to watch *Top Gear* when the Bat Phone rang.

Shifts on summer Sundays were always interesting. They tended to be busy, with equestrians and motorcyclists occupying a disproportionate amount of our time, sometimes even together when a bike ran into a horse. Ketamine all round, then.

Even in good weather, many recreational pursuits ended in injury or disaster and a visit from the air ambulance. We attended paint-balling events, hill walking, mountain climbing, kite flying, scavenger hunting, orienteering, off-road cycling, angling competitions and traction engine rallies. We saw England at its quaintest and best, and most catastrophically fucked up.

By and large, we were made to feel very welcome at these events. People were generally pleased to see us and recognised that we were there to help. But on occasion, we were not treated well.

There had been a lot of public debate about foxhunting and eventually the Labour government outlawed it. I think everybody in the countryside recognised that foxhunting continued, albeit with some subtle modifications in a ludicrous attempt to disguise it. Most hunts seemed to carry on much as they did before but the participants and organisers were adamant that they were not hunting foxes, but instead exercising dogs. I think we can agree it's a pretty extravagant way to exercise a dog. And they were no longer huntsmen, they were horse riders supervising the exercising of a pack of retired hunting dogs. If, by chance, the pack of retired hunting dogs happened to encounter a fox and rip it into tiny bits, that could hardly be called hunting, rather an unfortunate sequence of events over which they had no control. The 'dog exercisers' on horseback continued to assemble on Sunday mornings, resplendent in their red coats, black riding hats, hip flasks and bugles. They charged across the country after a fox much as they had before the hunting ban.

From my perspective, nothing had changed. We attended a number of injured equestrians engaged in foxhunting both before and after the ban.

This day the Bat Phone call sent us to a fallen horse rider from a 'hunting dog exercise meeting' over the other side of the county. Lieutenant Dan was understandably nervous on his first HEMS mission. His flying style was very military. Recently discharged military pilots could take a while to understand that we needed to get into a landing zone quickly; often they would fly a couple of circuits around the selected landing site before committing to land. We were used to Porky and Chris getting us in very, very quickly to a scene.

On this occasion, it really didn't seem to matter. We had been advised that our casualty was conscious. There was a crowd of hunters with horses and a pack of exercising dogs towards one side of the field. Our casualty was lying on the ground and a lady in riding gear kneeling beside him. Lieutenant Dan flew the approach slowly so that the hunters would have a chance to move the horses and dogs away.

Lieutenant Dan gave us the thumbs-up sign indicating that we were cleared to leave the aircraft under the running rotors. Barry said something unintelligible as we walked across the field. 'Half past two, Barry.' I answered.

The first thing that struck me about this job was that there was an air of hostility – even more so than the housing estate job. The lady stood up from her kneeling position at the side of our casualty and, staring fiercely, said the last thing I would have expected to hear. 'Did you really have to make all that noise?'

Me and Barry looked at each other with mirrored she-cannot-be-serious expressions.

She galloped on, 'His lordship has been upset quite enough this morning!'

A scowl appeared on Barry's normally warm face. I knew him well enough to know that it would not take much to make him bite back if he was further provoked.

I tried to be polite and helpful. 'Good morning, my name is Tony and I am the doctor on the Air Ambulance. This is my colleague Barry, our paramedic. Try to explain to me what happened,' I offered.

She looked at me suspiciously. 'A *doctor*? What sort of doctor works on a helicopter? You certainly don't look like a doctor. Go and fetch a stretcher!'

Barry began to growl and I was beginning to already miss the good old days of tubby tattooed men telling me to fuck off. That was actually preferable to this insufferable crap. A groan from our injured lord interrupted my thoughts. I knelt down to tend to him.

The lord's lady saddled up her thoughts and cracked the whip with her tongue again: 'Don't worry, I'll find out where these men are taking you and I will phone Cyril.' She turned and pointedly informed me, '*Cyril* is surgeon to *Her Majesty the Queen!* Cyril doesn't fly around on helicopters, he has a clinic on Harley Street, where all proper doctors work.'

The lord asked where we were taking him. Good question, I thought. One of the key decisions that we take in the field is the choice of hospital. Patients with minor injuries will go to the nearest hospital with a landing site. Those with major injuries or complex medical needs we will fly as far as we need to get to the right hospital offering the specialist care that our patients require.

This man did not have major injuries but he was anxious and, given the mechanism of his fall and his advanced years, I thought that a more formal assessment in hospital and some X-rays of his spine would be prudent. And this was a good opportunity to involve Lieutenant Dan on his first HEMS mission. I asked him to plan our route, and it was decided to fly to a nearby hospital.

When I informed 'his lordship' of where we were taking him, his anxiety grew worse. He looked visibly shaken and upset.

'I can't possibly go there, that's my local hospital. Everybody knows me there. I'm on their board, for God's sake! If they see me in my red coat they will know I've been hunting. And it's illegal now that it's been banned by this left-wing, lesbian-loving, tree-hugging, Kumbaya-singing bunch of politically correct cocks that are in government! I can't possibly go there!'

Things got worse. Lady Muck called us 'Silly little men', and a crowd of their hunting chums gathered around us, some of them still high up on their horses, both figuratively and literally. They started heckling us in support of Lord and Lady Arse. I'd discovered a new collective noun: a clamour of toffs. It was like facing a firing squad, where the guns were loaded not with bullets but high-velocity irritating voices. They had plums in their mouths and they were all spitting them at us.

I don't consider myself to be particularly averse to any social group or class but the behaviour of this bunch was as bad as any. From country estates to council estates, the only real difference between upper-class twits and lower-class yobs is the accent they use to insult you.

Barry and I completed our examination of the patient and manoeuvred him onto a spinal board. We gave him a little morphine for his pain and an anti-emetic to reduce the risk of him vomiting mid-flight. Wouldn't want him messing up our nice clean Agusta. Or choking to death. In that order.

Morphine and other powerful painkillers can affect people in different ways. Morphine is very effective in dealing with the pain and anxiety that often consume people after injury. More so when we then made them lie down inside a noisy and vibrating aircraft. Morphine was also very useful in dealing with the anxiety and claustrophobia that our patients sometimes suffered in flight.

He reacted well to his morphine but became decidedly religious under its influence. For a brief moment I was concerned that these were early signs of brain injury but on closer inspection I reassured myself that this hallucinatory religious expression was due to the morphine that we had given him. He started to ramble and mumble; he seemed perfectly at peace but appeared to think he was talking to God or Jesus. On the flight he fell silent and snoozed. Me and Barry looked at each other, and giggled to let go of some of the tensions that this job had created.

CHAPTER 18

How to Kill Yourself Without Dying

It is actually quite difficult to kill yourself. I hope you'll take my word on that – there are some things it's better to take on trust.

Overdosing on tablets rarely works. Slitting your wrists hurts and it's surprising how ineffective it can be in producing enough blood loss to actually die. Carbon monoxide poisoning can work but the catalytic converters on cars have made this more difficult. And in the future when we all have electric cars, it's going to be even more difficult if you're sat in the garage for three days with the engine running and waiting to die – in fact, death will only come when you get the electric bill and drop dead of a heart attack.

People generally know that an overdose of paracetamol can kill you. But they think you swallow a handful of tablets, wash them down with a little alcohol before drifting off into Never-Never Land. Well, it doesn't happen that way. You need to swallow a fair amount of the stuff. If you don't sick it up, once in the system it will attack the liver, which if you've taken enough will pack in. Over the course of the next few weeks, your skin and eyes will turn yellow. You vomit and feel awful, eventually developing a tremor, clouded conscious level and a bloated, painful abdomen. Spontaneous bleeding will occur from every orifice as the liver is no longer producing clotting factors in the blood. Death follows in weeks while you suffer and hope that someone else will die and donate a liver to you, which rarely happens. That's an awfully long time for you to think to yourself about how silly you were swallowing a packet of paracetamol following an argument with your girlfriend or boyfriend, or because you wanted to scare your mum.

Fortunately, most people who present after a paracetamol overdose haven't taken enough to do any major damage. Those who do can be fixed if we get to them quickly enough with an effective antidote drug. In fact, it's quite difficult to kill yourself with any drug. I hope I've painted a rosy enough picture to put you off.

Of course, there are some people who are determined to do it, and we'd often be called out to clean up the mess. One morning we got the call-out to an incident on a nearby railway line. We found the scene and circled overhead as we waited for confirmation from Ambulance Control that the railway line had been closed and the power was off. From up above we spotted our woman lying on the railway tracks in two pools of blood. She was positioned just beneath a bridge that crossed the tracks at that point, which made it look as if she'd thrown herself off, but we'd already been told that wasn't the case. So it wasn't exactly what we'd been expecting. From up above we couldn't work out what had happened.

We didn't have long to puzzle over it before the all-clear came through regarding stopped trains. Crewe, our pilot for the shift, began his descent. This was a first – even back in my Israeli Air Force days of helicopter training, I'd never been in a craft that had landed on railway tracks. The tracks here were four lines wide and walled either side by high and steeply banking verges covered in trees and bushes.

Crewe skilfully hovered us down towards the tracks and into embankment shadow, 25 metres ahead of the bridge and between the walls of trees either side. It was, essentially, a long, treelined, man-made valley. We touched down on the gravel, the Agusta's wheels sinking in either side of the steel tracks. It was a weird feeling to look ahead and see the shiny steel rails disappear under the bridge and into the distance. The converging lines at the vanishing point looked far away but I knew it was much nearer than it appeared. Any speeding train that hadn't got the signal to stop would cut across that distance in a flash and completely destroy us and the helicopter. Fingers crossed all the train signs were at red, then.

I jumped out the doors under spinning rotors and ran towards the land ambulance crew, who were already near the bridge with our patient. As I approached I saw more clearly where the pools of blood were situated and immediately spotted what had happened. This woman had correctly worked out that the bridge, high as it was, might not be high enough to do her in with any certainty. She'd worked out what we already knew, that the only sure-fire way was a violent trauma inflicted on the body at a point of maximum escalation. One version of that would be a gunshot to the head; her version was laying down on railway tracks and waiting for a train to come along.

Her logic was sound. The train wheels passing over her body as she lay on the rails would pretty instantaneously bring her eternal peace and the pain would be too short-lived to be meaningfully felt. She must have known it would be messy, though. But it wasn't easy to get there; she'd had to climb over a fence and scale down the embankment towards the rails. This section of the rail network had four lines linked by some railway points.

She had obviously patiently waited for a train until eventually she'd heard it approach, whereupon she'd lain down across one of the lines – her arms resting on one rail, her body over the other, ankles on the adjacent line. Her logic in not jumping off the bridge may have been sound, but her implementation of the plan to kill herself by train wasn't so good. Which is why she was still alive. She had lain her body across the wrong rail and as it sped by the train just sliced off the end of her arms.

She was mightily pissed off and in a great deal of pain. I quickly loaded her with morphine and applied tourniquets to her bloodied stumps. Her face was grey and damp. As I tended to her, I studied her face and for a brief moment felt an overwhelming surge of compassion. I wondered what turmoil had brought her to this. And if she'd lain down there because she thought she'd fucked up her life, then God knows how she'd react to having to live with the fact that she'd fucked up her death, too.

About 50 yards down the track, we found her hands and forearms. We packaged them to take them to the hospital with their owner. I knew they couldn't be reattached but it was possible that some tissue might be used to close defects in the stumps.

As Crewe lifted the aircraft out of the shadow of the embankments, I looked down at our woman's blackened hands inside a plastic bag, like some off-cuts we were taking home from the butcher's for Derek's mad Alsatian dogs. And I glanced down at our patient. She was peaceful now with the morphine fully on board, her turmoil temporarily alleviated. But I knew she'd have to wake up soon to a whole new reality. And whatever had brought her to this would still be there, but now she'd made it even more difficult to try and kill herself again. Some might say that with the unreliability of the railway timetable she was bloody lucky that a train turned up at all. But in my experience if someone is determined to die, they will find a way.

Youngsters who take an overdose, or try to harm themselves in other ways, very rarely truly want to die. More often than not it's a cry for help. It's the old folk who really want to do themselves in. Sometimes this is very powerful stuff. Their lives are truly empty following the death of a spouse, their family have left, they have poor health and have really had enough. On occasion, I felt cruel saving them. They never call for help themselves, they are always found by someone. We get there and usually find a peaceful scene. The house is all arranged, documents laid out so that all their affairs can be easily dealt with after their death. There is sometimes a suicide note.

They are in bed or their favourite armchair. Sometimes a CD is playing on the stereo. And then we kick in the door, go charging in and save them. Some of them hate us for doing that. As soon as they get out of hospital, they just make sure that they won't get discovered the next time.

Sometimes we got what you might call an accidentally-on-purpose suicide; that is, someone who had tried to kill themselves for the wrong reason.

The call came in: 'Crew request – 69 year old woman – overdose of opioids – deeply unconscious'.

Mark, a relief pilot, the Bitch and I flew out to an address in the city. We landed on a smallish patch of grass near the house. After a short jog with the kit along the street, we turned second right into a cul de sac and easily identified the house from the ambulance parked outside. We entered the property and encountered a lady lying on the floor, breathing slowly and deeply unconscious.

Her worried husband showed us empty packets of Co-codamol, a painkiller that contains codeine. She had taken a lot. The paracetamol content of these tablets would also be a problem. A morphine derivative, Codeine shares many of the same characteristics: it reduces conscious level, slows breathing and makes the pupils constrict. We call them 'pinpoint pupils'.

I looked her over and found that she did indeed have pinpoint pupils. It seemed fairly straightforward. Her husband anxiously told us that she had felt awful for several weeks, feeling sleepy, restless and spending most of the day running to the toilet. Her eating habits had also changed and she frequently had to get up at night. She hadn't been herself in a while and had been very depressed, which he said was unusual for her. After seeing her doctor on several occasions she had given up on getting better. The consultations hadn't gone anywhere. There was talk of prescribing her some anti-depressants.

The husband said he'd woken that morning and come downstairs to find his wife snoring on a sofa in the lounge. He assumed she must be having a nap and went out to buy a paper. When he came back, she was still snoring on the sofa in the same position and he had been unable to rouse her. It was only then that he found the empty pill packets and had called for an ambulance crew, who had recognised that she was very ill – which is where we came in.

Given the potentially massive overdose of codeine in this lady, I decided that I should give her a large dose of naloxone into her muscle to reverse the effect of co-codamol, just as we had done for our 20-stone patient in the housing estate. I thought that the slow release of the drug from the muscle would help maintain her recovery. We drew up the contents of four ampoules of the drug and I injected it deeply into her thigh. We then started to squirt some into her vein. I was surprised that not much seemed to happen. Sure, her breathing picked up a bit but she remained deeply unconscious. Her pupils were no longer pinpoint but I was expecting her to do much more from the dose received. I repeated the dose into her vein. After a minute or two, she groaned a little but was by no means waking up as I had expected.

This wasn't right. Something was amiss. A body not reacting as expected or, indeed, as commanded by a drug they should not be able to resist, is a major warning sign. I quickly ran through the procedures again and could come to only one conclusion – are we missing something here?

'Check her BM, please,' I told one of the ambulance crew.

BM is a finger-prick test to measure blood sugar level. The ambulance man used the spring-loaded lancet to produce a drop of blood from our lady's right index finger. Then the little BM machine bleeped.

'Strange, it's reading 19.6,' he said. I agreed this was strange; it was a very high reading.

I learned years ago that the first thing to do when you get an unexpected test result is to repeat the test and make sure that you're doing it properly; test repetition is the only way to eradicate any unforeseen variables that might be throwing off the results.

'Do me a favour,' I said, 'clean her finger with an alcohol wipe, let it dry and repeat the test.' I did this because I knew the oddest things could fool you and the machines. For example, I'd been duped before with high sugar readings by sugar residue left on the patient's fingers after they'd been handling food, dunking a biscuit or eating a cake. I know there's Death by Chocolate but you'd be pretty pissed off if it did actually contribute to you dying. Always embarrassing to be offed by a gâteau.

Our ambulance man repeated the test. 'No, it's different!' he said. 'It's higher, 21.1.'

Must be the machine, I thought. But this was still confusing. I asked him to find another BM machine, which he did. The third reading was even more worrying – 22.9.

Even though this lady and me were now the centre of the attention of her understandably anxious husband, the ambulance crew and my own pilot and paramedic, who were all looking on expectantly, I was tuned out of that part of the scene as my mind raced through the signs, quickly looking for Sherlock Holmes-style eliminations and clues to this puzzle box.

The pieces of the puzzle began to fall into place. One, our lady had been feeling rough for weeks: sleepy, restless, going to the toilet all day and night, constantly eating. Two, she had sought help but it wasn't picked up. Three, she'd got into such a state that she tried to kill herself.

I suddenly realised that she was in fact killing herself because of a depression resulting directly from an undiagnosed condition; the same condition that explained *why* she hadn't responded much to the naloxone – she had undiagnosed diabetes and was in a diabetic coma!

All the pieces of the puzzle box silently clicked into place and the box automatically opened with the answer. There were at least three problems with this lady: the codeine overdose, potential massive liver damage from the paracetamol and now a coma induced by the diabetes.

I immediately changed tack on the case and started very aggressive treatment for the diabetic coma. After we'd stabilised her somewhat, we flew her into hospital and got a good reception and handover from the critical care team. I knew the elderly lady would do well.

I sat in the open door of our aircraft having a snatched and much needed fag and thought about how this was exactly the kind of critical-care-at-scene incident that our Helimed units were formed to provide. Flying the lady to hospital without any intervention would not have worked.

I've seen how tenaciously the human body can cling to life even when it's put in the most testing situations – mangled in a crumpled car wreck, for example   so to see suicidal people try their very best to overcome that innate survival instinct is something that gives you pause for thought about death: you can't stop it coming, and it isn't all waiting on us. So maybe we should and appreciate what we have.

CHAPTER 19

Death at Your Elbow

I see death almost every day. I find death fascinating. It comes in many forms. Death in the Emergency Department is quite different to death on other hospital wards. And death that we encountered on the Air Ambulance was different altogether.

Death in the Emergency Department often takes the form of an ambulance crew bringing in somebody who has collapsed in cardiac arrest. Most of the time, we knew that these people were dead before we even got started with them. We went through the motions of a few cycles of CPR and after an appropriate and decent period of pretending to hope that they might recover, we would start a well-rehearsed speech: 'Well, he's 86, his collapse was not witnessed, there was no bystander CPR and we've had a flat line on the monitor since we started so I don't think he has a good chance of recovery.'

We then have to wait for the grave nodding of heads from the resuscitation team members before continuing along the preordained path of graceful withdrawal from the indignity and futility of jumping up and down on the chest of a fresh corpse. Once you secure enough grave nodding heads you move onto the next stage: 'So unless anybody has any objections I think we should stop at the end of the next cycle.'

You wait for the second wave of gravely nodding heads and then you move on to the final part of the speech: 'So I think we should stop. The time of death is 10.53. Thank you very much for all of your efforts.'

Often you then have to speak to a relative brought to the hospital and contained within a quiet 'relatives' room' that we reserve for such events. Breaking bad news is probably the most difficult part of my job. Everybody has developed their own way of dealing with it. I found it easier to be compassionate but also firm and brief. You confirm that you're talking to who you think you are talking to and you deliver the bad news in one concise sentence: 'There is no easy way to tell you this but I'm afraid your husband has died.'

You then wait and allow the freshly bereaved relative to assimilate the information and go through the first stage or two of the bereavement process. This was beautifully described by the psychologist Elisabeth Kübler-Ross. The grieving relative will often be in denial, followed by anger then some bargaining and depression and finally, resolution. This process can occur very quickly or it may take months. The stages may appear in a slightly different order but they happen and you have to be prepared to deal with one or possibly more of these reactions. The more I did it, the easier it became to be utterly detached, so you were then left with the problem of having to feign caring. It's an awful admission but that's just how it was and that's just the distance you had to develop to survive emotionally.

Some deaths in the Emergency Department are far more tragic and dramatic so it's hard in some instances to remain detached. Once in a while we will deal with a child killed through non-accidental injury or tragic accident. Traumatic deaths from injury are actually quite rare. They perhaps happen once or twice a week at most in a busy Emergency Department. These are far more difficult to deal with in terms of breaking bad news because they are almost always unexpected and ugly, and usually involve youngsters. There is no easy way of telling parents that their son or daughter has been killed in an accident or assault.

On hospital wards, death is often expected. Hospital staff will have had a long time to prepare families for death. The process there can be managed differently.

Whenever we encountered death on the Air Ambulance, it was usually brutal and almost always unexpected. But there were exceptions. On two occasions we were called to nursing homes for patients in their late 90s, who were dying or who had just died. On these occasions, the temporary member of staff would freak out when checking on the elderly ladies and would dial 999 in a panic. On two such occasions, we landed in the beautifully maintained gardens of the nursing homes and trudged mud over the nice clean carpets to enter a resident's room. The kindest thing we could do was precisely nothing. We were there largely to reassure staff they had done everything that they should have done and we let the poor old lady pass away quietly and very naturally.

But a natural death isn't always an easy one. On New Year's Day we were called out to a farmhouse. The report was of a collapsed patient. Calls of this nature could be anything from very benign to ghastly in the extreme. Crewe piloted me and paramedic Jenny for the 10-minute flight to a rather splendid array of farm buildings in a remote part of the countryside. We landed and met a middle-aged man, who was waiting patiently for us. He explained that his father lived in a converted barn on the farm and that he had not seen him since Christmas Eve, having been away with his immediate family in the intervening period. He had returned to the farm and could see his father lying in bed from the window. His father hadn't moved and had not responded to repeated knocks at the door. The son did not have a key and could not get in. We sought his permission to break down the door and he agreed. He didn't seem particularly distressed and all parties there understood that we were likely to find a corpse.

As we approached the converted barn we heard buzzing. Stepping forward to look through the glass it was clear that there were many tens of thousands of flies in the little ground-floor room. The air was thick with them; some were flying into the window glass in their bid for freedom.

We were all reluctant to continue and could have called for the police to gain entry but they would ask us to confirm death anyway before our departure. The door gave way quite easily to a few kicks. We were all hit by that deeply penetrating and almost sticky smell of decomposing human flesh. More disturbingly, was the glimpse of two rats scuttling away as we gingerly stepped inside the bedroom. We could determine death from the 20-foot distance between us and the bloated, decomposing corpse lying on the single bed. The left arm was hanging towards the floor and some fluid was dripping off the extended middle finger. It was grotesque, as these things usually are. I felt for the son, seeing the grief and horror on his face. Not the best way to spend a New Year's Day.

I believe that death is a process that starts quite some time before the heart stops beating. One could argue that death begins when cancer is diagnosed or after the first heart attack, or indeed from the moment when you are born. It ends perhaps with decomposition in the grave or with the scattering of ashes. For practical purposes, watching an old person die in hospital or even a trauma victim bleed to death follows a process that has a beginning, a middle and an end.

Watching a cancer victim or a very elderly person slip away peacefully can be serene. Often it is a relief to the family and possibly also to the dead person, who might have been suffering or otherwise not had a meaningful existence for months or even years.

Traumatic deaths in younger people are brutal and often meaningless. The pain for the individual and those left behind is sudden and overwhelming. HEMS crews see it, deal with it and feel it on most shifts. On days like Christmas Day, when we could have been at home and warm with our families but we were instead trying to revive someone on a wet pavement by giving them CPR, you'd think it might make you think again about doing the job.

But you don't have to think about it too long for it to occur to you that these people – the victims of accident, crime, violence, idiocy, cruelty, bad luck, reverse serendipity, awful coincidence, or just their own failing health – were all going to fall prey to those events, whether or not we were there, so *much* better we were there. The gods of bad luck and broken hearts never took a day off so the HEMS had to be on just as constant a watch.

Motorcyclists seem to make up a good proportion of traumatic deaths. It's not for no reason that bikers are known among medics as 'organ donors'. Young bikers mostly died through their inexperience. The older 'born again' bikers mostly died through their experience, and the rest died mostly through no fault of their own. Or because of the inability of tarmac to grow under their departing wheels. There is one thing that's as fatal to a biker as running out of luck, and that's running out of road.

I began to coldly think of motorbikes as just these upright vertical engines that growled, barked and spouted tubes and pipes, and were perfectly designed to transport mostly young men towards their mostly early deaths. The motorbike was the impeccably disinterested but incredibly efficient agent of that journey of elemental obliteration.

Being a HEMS doctor certainly made one aware of the capriciousness of life and the devastations wrought by right-place/wrong-time syndrome.

Some of this was in my mind as Crewe lowered the Agusta gently into a field adjacent to the small country road. The call from Ambulance Control had been very clear – 'Motorcyclist with severe injuries'. It doesn't get more urgent than that. In the overhead, we could see that things were bad from the actions of the land ambulance crew. The tense, terse body language was all there, even from several hundred feet on the approach to land.

Sure enough, when we got there things were bad. The land crew had intubated and one paramedic was ventilating our motorcyclist. This in itself was a bad sign. Paramedics cannot give drugs to allow the insertion of an intubation tube into the throat. The fact that they had intubated without drugs implied that at best, the motorcyclist was profoundly unconscious as it's impossible to intubate a patient with any degree of meaningful brain activity. You needed powerful anaesthetic drugs to intubate patients that were even half dead. The other clues that all was not well were the floppy appearance of both multiple-fractured legs and the skin colour, which was very pale. The cardiac monitor showed the occasional flicker of activity.

As we approached with all of our kit, the second paramedic looked up from his position at the motorcyclist's side and said, 'I can't get a line in, can you help?'

We needed a cannula in a vein so we could give fluids to replace lost blood and to give drugs. This was an entirely reasonable request. Jenny went across to the patient's other arm and tried to find a vein to push a cannula into. With both of them working on the arms, I looked for other alternatives. Getting fluids into the motorcyclist now was an absolute priority; probably his only slim chance of survival.

I thought the likely reason that the paramedics couldn't get a cannula into our patient was that he had lost so much blood that his veins had collapsed. I pushed my index finger across the base of the neck, hoping to find an external jugular vein to cannulate. No joy. There was one option left. I had just introduced the EZIO, a new electric drill, into the service, which drilled into bone and allowed us to pump fluids and drugs directly into bone marrow. Fluids and drugs flow very quickly from the bone marrow into the circulation, replacing lost blood volume. There were several recommended sites for drilling. We could use the breastbone, the shin, the shoulder, the pelvis or even the elbow tip. As the bottom half of the motorcyclist was still clad in biking leathers, I chose to use the shoulder. Loading the sharp hollow drill bit onto the end of the little power drill, I blipped the trigger to test it spinning, and then pushed it into his skin in front of the shoulder until I felt bone. I then squeezed the trigger and the drill bit span and easily went through the head of the humerus. After unclipping the drill from the drill bit, I attached a bag of fluids, screwing the line in securely. Fluids went in, along with some adrenaline.

After a few minutes of fluids, drugs and chest compressions, it was clear that it was game over for this motorcyclist. We stopped and pronounced him dead.

It is only at this stage of proceedings, when you begin to withdraw your complete focus away from the patient, that you can start to see the details of the reality of the loss. Our motorcyclist was in his early forties. It looked as if he had come off at very high speed while negotiating a bend – luck and road ran out. At his age, he most likely had a job and a wife and children, and parents that were still alive. It was all over now. Soon the police would be knocking on a door and would have to tell a young woman and probably some young children that he was dead. A family would be devastated, a workplace would mourn for a colleague, several dozen people would mourn the loss of a friend.

The brain has its own instrument panel of dials with needles constantly sweeping to find the correct emotional register. There are directly proportional sliding scales of distress, horror and acceptance related intimately to the age of the patient; meaning of course that the older the person was, the easier it would be to accept their passing, the less distressing to see them go. But when we fell back down to the other end of the age scale and towards lives only just beginning, those ever-sweeping needles of distress and horror bounced right up into the red.

Child murders combined all the worst elements of human behaviour and strength of emotion. All needles dancing fully in the red. We attended a number of dead shaken babies. The culprit was usually at the scene, trying to absorb the scale of the disaster, giving us poorly formulated excuses. Other family members would inevitably show up and the dynamics could get very interesting. The dead child becomes evidence for the police and the natural grieving process is derailed by the forensic process. For this and other reasons, we always took the victims to hospital, even when we knew they were dead. The hospital was used to dealing with the death of an infant and the forensic process. It was all ghastly. I think the worst part for me was having the culprit present in the room. We knew that he knew that we knew that he'd done it. And we couldn't allow ourselves to be judgmental or accusatorial in any way. That's a job for the police and the justice system.

One summer afternoon we were despatched to a lido to reports of two drownings. On this particular day, I had James, a trainee military doctor, on the aircraft; one of the most talented doctors I have ever met. He was learning how helicopter medicine worked in the civilian sector before being sent to Afghanistan to fly on army Chinooks, retrieving wounded troops from the battlefield.

We landed on some wasteground nearby.

We got to the scene to find that one of the staff had allowed her husband and young son to go into the outdoor swimming pool after hours, despite the fact that the husband couldn't swim. He was playing with the child on the steps leading into the shallow end of the pool. The wife had left them there while she went about her duties. She had come to check on them after about half an hour to find the father floating lifeless in the pool and the child lying underwater in the deep end. Somehow she had retrieved them both to the poolside. The child, it seems, had slipped out of reach and got into difficulties. His father, presumably in desperation, went into the water and he too had got into difficulties in his attempts at rescuing the child.

The scene was one of the most disturbing I have ever witnessed. As we entered, the lifeless body of a small child lay closest to us. A paramedic land crew were there and had intubated the child and were performing CPR; the cardiac monitor demonstrated a flat line. Behind them, another crew were working on the father. I decided that I would take on the resuscitation of the child and asked James to work on the father. The distraught mother was being comforted by two police officers.

I knelt down and focused in on the child. The land crew knew me and it was easy to integrate into their efforts. One of them was an ambulance officer and he proudly told me that he had intubated the child. Fair enough, I thought. It is common practice to check the position of a tube in the windpipe just to make sure it really is in the windpipe and not in the gullet. This is recommended when taking over responsibility for an intubated patient. So I looked, listened and checked. The tube was nowhere near the windpipe; it was in the gullet and stomach.

'When did you intubate him?' I asked as I pulled the tube out of the little boy's mouth.

'We've been working on him for about 15 minutes,' he replied.

I knew then that he was dead. The crew had been blowing air into his stomach and not into his lungs, due to the tube being in the wrong place. When a child drowns, his heart will eventually stop as no oxygen is getting into the body. Within a small time frame, this can be reversed – if the lungs are inflated with oxygen and the heart restarted. Having effectively deprived him of oxygen for at least another 15 minutes by putting the tube in the wrong place, there was no realistic chance of him being saved. Had the child become very cold, the brain could possibly have survived in temporary stasis and this resuscitation perhaps had a slim chance of success. But this child was still warm. I intubated again and confirmed that I was in the windpipe this time. I gently squeezed the child's abdomen and with a long burping noise, the air that the crew had been putting into his stomach through the misplaced tube escaped, making it easier to ventilate him.

I said nothing but both crewmembers now realised that the first intubation had been into the gullet and they knew the implications of this: the child would not recover.

'Can you fly him to the children's hospital?' the ambulance officer appealed, more in faint hope than expectation. He added, 'I've alerted them… '

I knew he was dead and I was not going to let the drama continue into hospital to subject this little boy to further prolonged and futile resuscitation efforts. Tragically, he was dead and we all knew it.

'I think we should stay where we are and reassess before flying him. There's precious little that the children's hospital can offer above what we have here,' I offered.

I knew he was looking for a way out. He wanted the shame of his error to be flown away in our helicopter. I knew it, and so did he. He was hoping that in the mêlée and scrum that would follow in hospital, everyone would overlook the 'intubation'.

No, he wasn't going to hospital. But we continued to work on the child, rigorously going through our resuscitation protocols. There wasn't a glimmer or hint of heart activity on the monitor. It was time to stop. This was going to be difficult.

The ambulance officer tried one last time to get me to fly the boy to hospital. But as time went on a little longer, and our own adrenaline surge subsided, even he accepted that he was dead. I told the two paramedics that this child was dead. They were both silent. It was now a very tense and intense scene.

I looked up: James was still working on the father, a couple of yards away from us. The mother was sitting on a chair, quietly sobbing and looking at us intently, hoping for any sign of a miracle. I'd seen that look of desperate longing before in relatives approaching a reality they didn't want to meet. At that moment I knew they would give anything, even volunteer their own lives, to turn back time. The mother remained, flanked by two police officers. I took a deep breath and walked over to her. I gently tugged on the sleeve of one of the officers and she stepped away from the woman to allow me to speak confidentially to her.

'The child has, I'm afraid, died and I'm going to have to tell the mother. I needed you to know that first,' I said quietly. She nodded and stood closely behind me as I knelt down beside her.

'My name is Tony, I'm the doctor on the helicopter. I'm so very sorry but there is no easy way to say this: your son has died.' I felt a sudden but familiar surge of emotion within me that I had to immediately suppress. It always happened in situations like this but over the years, suppressing it had become easier.

I waited for her response. Her face contorted and reddened. She howled, cried and begged me to do something. This was classic acute bereavement and despair.

'I'm so sorry. I wish that I could offer you some hope but I can't,' I said. 'I'm desperately sorry for your loss.' That little surge of emotion came back again for a second or two. I held her hand. I knew that it was likely that James would be coming across in a minute or two to deliver the next piece of bad news that her husband was also dead. I disengaged to go and check on James.

He had run through the standard resuscitation protocols and there had been no reaction whatsoever from the father. Flat line. Dead. We didn't need to speak; a glance between us indicated that we knew. Time to call it. James had no difficulty in getting his crew to agree. As he stood up to walk over to the women to deliver the second bombshell, she had already worked it out, let out a gut-wrenching scream and slumped forwards, sobbing. That little surge of emotion inside me became more insistent. It subsided in a few seconds, as it always did, as James walked over and took the woman's hand, gazed into her begging eyes and told her what she already knew.

'I'm so sorry, your husband has died.'

James stepped back a little, predicting the next onslaught of pain and emotion from the loss of the woman's young family. It came, and it was raw. The police officer that I had spoken to earlier disengaged from this scene of utter grief and went into evidence preservation mode.

We went outside and sat on a wall to complete our paperwork in complete silence. Discussion would have to wait. It would come in time and would help us get through this. But it was premature, the scene too horrific. There was no way out of it. Especially for the poor woman. She was deeply in it in a way that we weren't.

I had other concerns. The failed intubation had damaged the ambulance officer's confidence and made him look incompetent in front of another paramedic. I would need to debrief him to try and help him get through this.

I found him standing silently by the dead child. Crime officers were now busying themselves around the swimming pool and were photographing the dead father and his son. I took the ambulance officer to one side and we talked it through. I tried to emphasise that intubating children was always a challenge and a missed tube could happen to anybody. The important thing, though, was to check. Apart from the emotional shrapnel, there was some other fallout from this job. The ambulance officer tried to avoid responsibility by suggesting that the tube had been fine and that I had somehow moved it when I took over. A sign of his guilt, it was seen for what it was. The powers that be in the Ambulance Service saw through it. It was never mentioned again.

Lying awake in bed that night, watching the occasional headlight beam sweep across the ceiling, it occurred to me how our position as HEMS doctors and medics gave us a unique perspective, literally, on these death scenes. Everyone else there – the police, the ambulance crew, the CSIs – drove laterally away from the scene. It receded behind them, quickly out of view, and that's if they even turned around to glance back.

We in the helicopter, however, rose vertically above it all. The different elements of the scene – ones that on the ground you are physically so close to, you deal with individually (the bodies, the pool, a chair, the officers, the mother) – from up in the air became locked together in a seemingly arranged pattern; an awful *mise en scène* of everyday horror receded below us in the noisy whirr of the rotor blades until those elements became abstract, and then small, and then vanished.

In addition to the horrors of a traumatic death, we dealt with people who had instantly become disabled. This was always particularly difficult when they were conscious and aware of what was happening.

We flew to the scene of yet another motorbike crash. A group of born-again bikers in their forties had gone out touring. I liked born-again bikers and always found them to be genuine and good blokes. In many ways I envied them their rediscovered sense of freedom. Usually, they were careful on the road but seemed to come to grief more often than the young guys racing around on high performance bikes.

Our motorcyclist had been knocked off his bike by a Range Rover reversing out of a petrol station on a country road. He had probably only been travelling at 30mph. He'd come off and landed on a gatepost, striking his back. He was lying on the road in a great deal of pain. Right away he knew that he had suffered a spinal injury: he had pain in his back but couldn't feel his legs. Morphine helped the pain and dulled the anxiety but his grieving process had already started. He began to talk about work, walking and sex: three things that he knew he would never do again.

Injuries like this happened fairly frequently. We saw a fair few born-agains with horrible injuries. One of them went on to become a significant figure in junior doctor education at our hospital. Raymond, who I first met by the side of the road strewn with the workings of his eviscerated bike, had come off his motorbike at speed when a van jumped a red light at a road junction. He was severely hurt. The job came in just after the aircraft had been towed into the hangar for the night so I responded with our paramedic, Sean, in one of the unit's rapid response vehicles. He drove us skilfully through the rush-hour traffic on blue lights and sirens.

Raymond was lying on his side, groaning and trying to push himself up onto his hands. We got him onto his back and carefully removed his helmet. He was agitated and combative; a tell tale sign of a significant head injury. This was bad. His chest was making abnormal movements, a worrying indication of multiple rib fractures, probably with associated injuries to the lungs. His skin was pale and clammy, a sign of blood loss somewhere. We got to work. I gave him a third of the dose of thiopentone that I planned to use to anaesthetise him. This controlled the agitation and allowed us to work. Sean was great under pressure. We worked almost in silence, knowing without speaking what the other was doing. I gave the anaesthetic drugs and Sean intubated without difficulty, performing his checks to make sure all was good.

Once on a ventilator and asleep, we moved on to deal with our patient's chest injury. I made small incisions in each side of the chest to drain the air and blood that had accumulated inside and was crushing his lungs. This too went very smoothly. Our motorcyclist was beginning to look a lot better. We moved on to manage his blood loss, carefully running in fluids until his blood pressure stabilised to a reasonable level. We splinted his broken limbs and gently got him onto a spinal board. Due to the proximity, we went to the hospital where I worked my day job and handed him over to my colleagues.

I kept an eye on Raymond's progress. It turned out that he had suffered a total spinal injury and would be in a wheelchair for the rest of his life. From time to time, I went to visit him on the ward. At first he had no idea who I was and no recollection of his accident.

Over time, we developed a good rapport and I explained what had happened, piece by piece, visit after visit. During my last visit to him in hospital, he told me that he had vivid flashbacks – remembering the pain and the sound of my voice talking to him before he was anaesthetised and went to sleep. But he remembered that his sleep was not deep, he had felt a tube in his throat and panicked but couldn't move, resist or tell us to stop. He had felt us cutting into his chest. I thought about this a lot. As doctors, we learn what to do and how to do it but sometimes give little thought to the poor sod on the receiving end. Clearly, my anaesthetic calculations had been conservative and Raymond hadn't been fully anaesthetised. I asked him if he would come back to the hospital to talk to doctors about his experience.

From time to time at the hospital, we arranged trauma meetings at which doctors from all specialities involved in trauma care would attend to review cases and the hospital's survival figures. There were surgeons, intensive care doctors, radiologists and emergency physicians in the audience: a crowd of about 80. I helped wheel Raymond onto the stage. The doctors and surgeons sat there in utter silence and with their total attention on the wheelchair-bound speaker about to address them. Raymond gave a steady narrative of his experience. The pain, the semi-awareness of the anaesthetic and the holes in his chest, the painful operations and learning to live his life in a wheelchair. He mourned the loss of his independence, his sex life and his job. He described having to empty his bladder with a catheter. It was a powerful performance that had a big impact on our doctors. This perhaps was the best thing that I have ever seen coming out of someone's pain and suffering. We invited him back several times to repeat his account at hospital meetings. I know that his experience educated and improved the trauma practice of 80 doctors in one fell swoop. I hoped that by relating it to others it had perhaps also helped him deal with his own misfortune.

One of the greatest weapons for dissipating the horror was the knowledge that from bad things good things sometimes came.

CHAPTER 20

The Cowboys Versus The Luftwaffe

The background noise of rivalry between our unit, Helimed 999, and the nearby and very established North Central Ambulance increased in intensity. We ran a doctor-led critical care medical model and we believed in it. We had succeeded in our aim of bringing the hospital to the patient and dealing with critically ill patients on the ground and in the air. North Central offered the more traditional paramedic-led service and a flight to take the patient to the hospital.

One bright spring day, and on one of my days off, our pilot du jour flew Helimed 999 to a busy and very serious crash job on the M1. A car had crashed between two articulated lorries, one lorry in front of it and one behind. A tarpaulin had been hung up to screen the mess from the public in their cars on the carriageway. Already there was one fatality and others critically injured.

They landed on the embankment to the side of the motorway. The traffic had been stopped on all carriageways and was backed up for miles. In front of an audience of thousands, the pilot decided not to remain on the embankment and instead lifted back up into the air, hovered directly over the motorway and lowered the Agusta down onto the tarmac. He landed, of course, in the fast lane. This move alone was probably enough to impress all the police, ambulance crew and members of the Fire Service who were watching, not to mention the public, who were by that time standing out of their cars. Unfortunately, that wasn't the end.

Next, the pilot taxied the Agusta *along* the M1 towards the accident scene to make it easier for the paramedic and doctor to load the patient once they were cut from the wreck. The big yellow Agusta slowly moved forward in the fast lane, the central barrier only a few feet to the right, and with the aircraft's rotor blades still spinning, it went under a motorway sign, past two police cars and then past the lorries and two ambulances and a fire engine to the left, the blades spinning above their roofs. Finally, he braked just beyond the crash scene.

It was an astonishing piece of aircraft control and an awesome sight to see the Agusta lowering down onto the country's premier motorway. Unfortunately, the shock and awe felt by everyone who witnessed the manoeuvre didn't remain at the scene. That kind of wonder that I mentioned earlier that people feel at the sight of a helicopter? Well, it inspired an occupant of a car in the stationary traffic on the other side of the motorway to use his mobile phone to video the M1 adventure. The video was then uploaded onto YouTube, where the whole world could see it.

The video is sound-tracked by two things: the noise of the Agusta and the voice of the young man filming it, whose comments give an insight to how it all looked at the time – '*Wow!* Damn cool, innit? Oh, it's clever. They're bloody clever the people who do that. Wow, you don't see that every day! *Look how close it is to the light!* – the *rotors!* Oh, he's gone under the thing (the sign).' And then there's an audible sharp intake of breath – '*Ooooh!*' – as the helicopter taxis alongside the stationary cars.

It went on to become the most viewed YouTube film under the search 'Air Ambulance' and racked up nearly 50,000 hits (and counting). And it proved that in our modern hi-tech world you couldn't even do a simple thing like land a bright yellow Air Ambulance helicopter in the middle of the day during rush-hour traffic on the M1 without someone bloody filming it! It also proved that the Agusta rotor blades did look to be spinning very, very close to an awful lot of things that wouldn't have at all appreciated being struck by helicopter rotor blades.

When the crew returned to base they were adamant that the foreshortened perspective from the video clip made it look much worse; in reality there had apparently been a lot more clearance than the clip showed. However, the bosses weren't there and the only evidence was the online film. Either way, the M1 episode combined with tales of Porky's helicopter aerobatics had enhanced our reputation as cowboys. The word was that our pilots were barnstormers and our doctors too gung-ho: the pilots flying at extremes and the doctors going around doing dangerous things to people who should only have those things done to them in hospital. The North Central Ambulance didn't like us, and we didn't like them. They were calling us 'Cowboys'. And we had started to call them 'the Luftwaffe'.

Although from time to time we met them at jobs that were big enough and serious enough that they needed both services to attend.

One late afternoon, our yellow Agusta 109 stood a few yards away from North Central's red Eurocopter 135 in a field close to the scene of a multiple car collision. It was a busy scene. North Central had attended first and then asked us to assist due to the number of seriously injured casualties. BASICS doctors had also attended. The combined clinical teams worked very well and there was a good rapport and the shared feeling that clinicians sometimes get when working in a team and everything goes smoothly and efficiently.

A local BASICS doctor and I established a field casualty clearing station close to the aircraft and I went over to the pilots to plan the order of evacuation and to spread the workload across three hospitals in the region. As I approached, I sensed some tension between the two pilots. Porky said slightly mockingly, 'Hadn't you better leave soon? It'll be dark and you boys don't fly at night, do you?'

I saw the crisp, ex-military North Central pilot grimace and reply, 'I hope you can get your wheels out of the mud. If you get stuck, I'll fly back and help you out.' He was referring to the fact that their helicopters had skids, not wheels – an age-old helicopter pilots' disagreement. The exchange was a little more competitive than just friendly banter.

After the job, as we few back to base from hospital, Porky told us triumphantly that he had 'pissed all over him' with the superiority of the Agusta 109 in terms of carrying capacity, avionics, flying skills and the powerful punch of carrying a medical team over a paramedic team. I feared our reputation as cowboys might have been enhanced by that encounter. It had, and things then got even worse.

There was a well-known Peak District trail at which many hill walkers fell and injured themselves. This area was definitely deep in the Third Reich district covered by the Luftwaffe.

One afternoon, we were dispatched to a fallen hill walker somewhere on the Peak District trail. Navigation was a bit difficult as we didn't carry a map for the area; we got there using the GPS and the grid reference, which was less than ideal. As Porky brought us into the high ground, we could see the trail. A mountain rescue team was at the base of the hill, waving to get our attention. One of them made clear hand signals for us to land on some flat ground at the base of the hill, where the team had assembled. He managed to convey through further hand signals that they would deliver the stretchered casualty from the trail to the proposed landing area. Porky brought us into a hover while he thought about it.

'They'll have to walk him down about half a mile if we land at the bottom of this hill. You see that small area of slightly less sloped ground about two-thirds of the way up the hill?' he asked. 'Well, I reckon I can get us on to it. Okay, doors open!'

I had some doubts. There was indeed less of a slope on the area Porky had pointed out but it was still quite steep. I wondered how much of this attempt to land there was driven by residual feelings in Porky of challenging the North Central pilot as this was the kind of work they would more likely handle.

The aircraft touched down in the centre of the slightly less sloped ground. I noticed that Porky kept his left arm tensed on the collective lever. The collective is the control that changes the pitch angle of all the rotor blades all at the same time, thus increasing the total lift from the rotors. The fact that Porky was grabbing onto it tightly suggested that he knew he might have to pull the power on quickly to lift us back into the air if we started to slide down the hill. And if we slid, we'd likely tilt, and if we tilted, the tips of the rotors would chew into the earth – and I didn't even want to think about what would happen to us then.

Porky lowered the collective lever very, very slowly, making sure that the aircraft was stable on the ground before he took off the power. He double-checked that the wheel brakes were on. I hopped out as soon as the rotors stopped (I wanted to be out of the aircraft just in case it started to roll backwards and topple down the hillside).

We were approached by the mountain rescue team and immediately got both barrels from their leader.

'You can't park there! I clearly directed you to our agreed helicopter landing area,' he advised us rather directly. 'We've used it for years. It's surveyed, and it's safe. North Central Ambulance always land there.'

'That's the advantage of wheels over skids,' Porky explained. 'The wheels act as a tripod, you see, and they anchor the helicopter into the ground. North Central's aircraft has skids which are a bit like skis; they will make the helicopter *want to* slide down hillsides.'

The mountain rescue man was unimpressed. I sensed that he would take this further.

Our casualty was treated, boarded and loaded. He wasn't particularly unwell. I got in first and guided his legs towards the rear of the cabin. I got him ready for flight and alerted the hospital.

While we loaded, Porky decided to remonstrate a little more with the mountain rescuer but as he got out of the front seat, I felt the aircraft 'give' just a little. There was a tiny movement rearward. I was terrified. Was this the first sign? Was it about to start a slide down the hill? What a way to go, sliding down a steep hillside inside the tin-can tomb of a helicopter! I knew any slippage would accelerate exponentially and before we knew it, we'd be done for. With Porky's weight in the front, our balance was just about keeping us attached to Mother Earth. Before I could object, in a split-second Porky was gone. And when he got out to verbally spar with the mountain rescue guy, the centre of gravity shifted perilously close to tip-over. I now knew I had an ethical dilemma. My every instinct was to jump out of the aircraft, but I could not leave our injured hill walker alone in the cabin facing the same risk. I moved slowly towards the side door and had a mental image of the closing scene in the film *The Italian Job*, with Michael Caine balanced inside a bus precariously overhanging a cliff-top drop.

I yelled loudly at Porky, 'We're ready! We *need to GO*!' Oblivious to the urgency and terror in my voice, he was still extolling the virtues of wheels over skids to the mountain rescue guy.

'We need to *GO*, NOW!' I pleaded. As I sat back down in the helicopter cabin to rejoin our casualty, I felt that little creak again as the wheels slipped a millimetre or two. I appealed to him again: 'And NOW would be good!'

Porky wandered back to the aircraft and got up into his seat. As his backside made contact with the pilot's seat in the front, the aircraft felt more secure. He started the engines and the knot of tension in my belly only started to come undone once I felt that familiar feeling of the aircraft wheels breaking with earth. We lifted into the air. I breathed, and looked back down the slippery hill. It was a long way, and from up here it looked even steeper than it had felt. I thought how great a way it would have been of confirming our cowboys' nickname if we'd tumbled and smashed all the way down the hill.

After delivering our patient to hospital, I knew that the story of our involvement in this job would soon reach the ears of the North Central crews and take our reputation with them to a whole new level. It took less than a week: our reputation was becoming tarnished.

We accidentally went one step further to establish ourselves as cowboys in the capital. Porky and I saw an advert in a flying magazine (which we often referred to as 'pilot porn') for the *Fly* aviation exhibition in Earls Court in London. We decided to go and have a look. I thought that if we were already in London, it would be a good opportunity to visit London HEMS to introduce ourselves and swap notes. I had called them the day before and they were very gracious. We arranged to be there early afternoon, giving Porky and I enough time to go to Earls Court and get some lunch before heading over to the Royal London Hospital, the home of London HEMS.

Porky asked me to pick him up on that Saturday morning as he'd been out drinking the night before and felt a bit rough. When I got there in my Ford Sierra Wicked, he did indeed look rough. Come to think of it, so did I. I had a three-day growth and was wearing a T-shirt and grubby, well-worn jeans. Which is exactly what I liked to do when I wasn't all trussed up in Helimed or hospital work clothes – slob out.

Throughout the entire journey down the M1, Porky had his eyes closed and his head was right back against the headrest. He didn't speak. We got off the M25 and as we slowed in traffic in leafy suburbia, suddenly he ordered me to stop the car. I braked smartly right next to a bus stop, where a queue of elderly folk were waiting patiently for their bus. They all looked at the car, wondering why it had pulled up at the stop as if it was about to pick them up. They soon realised why when Porky opened the car door, leaned out and vomited profusely and noisily onto the road. The vomit hit the road, the inside of the car door and the front of Porky's shirt. I looked out through the open door to see a dozen horrified elderly faces looking back. I smiled weakly.

'Right, that's better,' Porky said, obliviously, and closed the car door. I pulled back into the traffic hoping no one had taken the registration number. We continued into town. After a couple of coffees and a bacon roll, we both felt fine and Porky perked up a bit and seemed to enjoy the *Fly* exhibition. During lunch in Pellici's, I missed my mouth and got spaghetti bolognaise down my T-shirt.

We were in good spirits when we finally got to visit London HEMS at the Royal London Hospital. They were expecting us. As we got out of the lift, I could see our host's face drop. I extended my hand, 'Tony Bleetman, Air Ambulance doctor and consultant in Emergency Medicine.'

Porky extended his hand, 'Nigel Brown, chief pilot, Helimed 999.'

Our host was obviously not convinced that we were genuine. He looked at us with some disdain and could probably smell the vomit on Porky's shirt. I certainly could. He looked at my shabby attire that was accessorised with a fine array of bolognaise sauce decorations (model's own) on my T-shirt. Clearly he didn't buy our story and we got the schoolboy tour: 'This is a helicopter, and it takes the doctor and paramedic to help people,' he explained. He may perhaps have considered that we might have been genuine when we started asking him some pertinent questions and offered some professional comments and opinions. Either way, I don't think we made a very good impression.

But much worse was to come than whatever bad impression Porky and me might have made. Soon after, the unit was shaken to its core by Derek's suspension.

His sergeant-major approach to work was a double-edged sword. He was the ultimate inspirational leader and a superb clinician; the kind of man to trailblaze and build a working, operational Air Ambulance base on £800. But he was not what I would call a diplomat. He stood by us and got us out of the occasional scrape that we got ourselves into. He spoke his mind and was not always the best conflict resolver. Some of the land ambulance crews didn't take kindly to his direct approach when they did not deliver care to what he felt were the highest possible standards. We sometimes had to 'love bomb' ground crews with praise and encouragement to compensate for the ear-bashing that they could receive from Derek in full belligerent flow.

But then one disagreement in particular lit the blue touch-paper on a mound of fireworks beneath Derek that had been steadily building, all rockets donated by anyone he'd pissed off. At the first spark, everyone seemed to come out of the woodwork with their own box of matches. The flames took; we lost Derek.

In my opinion, it was a classic case of a right man for the job lost for the wrong reasons. Often the best people at their jobs are not the ones who are the best at office politics, and this was the case with Derek. It was self-defeating, and a great loss, for him to go. But we couldn't do anything about it.

The charity appointed Simon Paris, one of the established paramedics, as the new unit boss. A good paramedic and unit leader, he continued to do a superb job with Helimed 999. But with Derek gone, Chris gone, Porky and I somewhat under surveillance for unconventional behaviours, and things generally changing, I started to get the feeling that something was coming to an end.

A few of us attended the annual Air Ambulance conference in Droitwich. It was truly impressive. In front of the stage, there was an Agusta 109 and a Eurocopter 135. I sat next to Martin, our medical lead, who had just taken on the role of medical director for the regional Ambulance Service. On my other side sat Jeremy, the CEO of the helicopter company. He had heard of me and we chatted pleasantly.

The lights dimmed and there followed a very exciting short video of Air Ambulances in action accompanied by a wild rock music soundtrack. The video finished with indoor fireworks. The first bang made me flinch and the contents of my coffee cup were thrown over Julian, the man who ran the country's second largest helicopter provider. Obviously, he wasn't happy. This was not going well.

During a break in the proceedings, Martin took me to one side and said the regional Ambulance Service wanted a doctor to become clinical director for the three North Central aircraft in order to take them from the traditional paramedic-only crew to the medically-led service, as we had set up with Helimed 999.

I was elated. It was exactly what we all wanted to do – to roll out the same kind of service over a wider area of the district. And, hopefully, eventually over the whole country. I would be able to mould the service and lead three Air Ambulance units and bring them into the twenty-first century. There was only one problem...

If I took the job I would now be flying with the units that we called the Luftwaffe. In fact, I would actually be commanding them. I wasn't quite sure what to think about that, but the new opportunity certainly took some of the sting out of the break-up of our old Helimed 999 crew. Better still, it would give me the chance to try to continue the sterling and pioneering work of a team of pilots and medics that had set up an Air Ambulance headquarters with 800 quid and a talent for blagging. After all the work, not to say love, that had gone into establishing the unit, and then flying thousands of

missions and tending to desperately ill people – saving many –
I think we had a right to justifiably feel a little bit proud for a
few seconds.

Helimed 999 was now solidly established enough to carry
on without us. Maybe it really was the right time to move on
and spread the word.

EPILOGUE

Having left the Cowboys under a bit of a cloud hadn't held Derek back and he established his new HEMS unit in another area. We kept in touch and saw each other from time to time. I listened with a smile as he told me about his latest adventures with a new group of muppets and fuckwits that he had to whip into shape. He was doing well and asked me from time to time to join him there, which was also tempting.

One Saturday evening at the end of a long phone call with him, in which he told me more stories of battles won and battles lost, he said casually, 'Oh, me and the Bitch are getting married. It'll be in May. And you're the best man.'

I was speechless for a few seconds and Derek filled the pause (and echoed what he'd said when we first met) when he said, 'Which part of you're going to be best man don't you understand, fuckwit?'

On the day of the wedding, Derek phoned me in a panic: 'Bleetman, is Mrs B with you?' Well, get over to my hotel room, I'm struggling with my cufflinks!'

So Jacqui and I went to the rescue of a man who could intubate and anaesthetise a critically injured patient at the roadside but couldn't manage to fasten his own cufflinks.

We made sure we got him looking relatively human. Newly shorn of his moustache, he looked unusually smart. He needed to be at his best because Yvonne – Helimed's treasured Bitch – looked stunning.

After a very sweet and charming wedding ceremony, Derek got everybody outside in the grounds of the hotel not just for the usual photographs, but also for something rarely seen at a wedding – a bloody great Air Ambulance helicopter flying in to land! It was a magnificent entrance. The pilot came in low with the black and green helicopter and over-flew the wedding guests at high speed before taking the aircraft into a sweeping tight-left turn prior to landing in front of everyone. There was a lively atmosphere as the photographer posed Derek, Yvonne and the guests around the aircraft for some unconventional wedding photos with what looked like the weirdest-looking wedding car you've ever seen. I just didn't know how we were going to tie tin cans to the back of the chopper.

I stood up to make my best man speech. I'd thought about it a lot and decided that the best thing to do would be to deliver what is, essentially, the first chapter of this book: my first meeting with this strange, tall figure with the porn-star moustache and flying suit, barking into a mobile phone while pacing up and down in the chaos of establishing the new HEMS unit in a blagged fire station filled with blagged sofas and equipment. I also mentioned my first blue-light response drive. The words 'muppet', 'cock' and 'fuckwit' were all essential contributions to the speech. It went down well as most of the guests could relate to my experience of Derek.

I also mentioned the special guests we had in attendance: Chris, Porky, Irish Barry, Sean, Tom, Klaus, Crewe, Steven, Maurice, Simon and Jenny, the whole Helimed 999 gang was there. If any guest was going to choose today to choke on a chicken bone or have a heart attack, this was certainly the wedding to do it at.

At the end of the speech, I asked Jacqui to stand up and take a big round of applause in recognition of all her great support for me, and for feeding the crew better than they could have ever dreamed of every time I flew HEMS.

Later, away from the slow-dancing couples, laughing drunken guests and tables of empty wine bottles, I sat with Derek in the bar and we reminisced.

Derek, laughing hard, said, 'So I got a call from the police asking if I knew that a pilot was driving a clapped-out Ford Sierra on blue lights in fog! And then you fucking phone me up to brag about some life-saving heroics! Remember the bollocking I gave you?' I certainly did. 'And then the police phone me back to tell me that one of my response cars has T-boned a Transit van at a red light, driven by a doctor who should have been at work and whose insurance status was uncertain. And, best part, that was *all in just one night*. It was a bastard making that one go away.'

Then, a bit more soberly, he said, 'You didn't get to hear the fights I had to get into on our behalf when you lot went out and tore up the rule book. Mind you, I did a fair bit of that, too. More than my share, actually.'

'Yes, well we know what they say about making omelettes and breaking eggs. As we well know, after we royally fucked up all those chickens.'

I knew that Derek's battles with some of the authorities had taken their toll, probably more than the rest of us really could know, and I knew he missed the Cowboys. But we were laughing too much now to get maudlin.

I said, 'I'd never thought about it that way – about you hearing the other side of the stories when you weren't there... '

'Yeah, and only a few weeks later, I get a mad call on the radio from Barry in his Irish, which made it sound even madder because he's in a real panic – "Boss, Bleetman just jumped out of the aircraft in a hover, he landed deep in crops and we can't see him. I think he's feckin' dead!"'

'Did he really think I was dead? Silly fucker, he didn't tell me that at the time! Mind you, having said that, when I hit the ground like a sack of coal, *I* thought I was dead!'

'Well,' Derek continued, 'a few minutes later, Barry's back on the radio and he says, "Nope, Boss, I think he's alive. We can see the crops moving but we can't see his head, he's too feckin' short!"'

I told him how my son David had come good on his early promise as a potential medic and informed Derek that his reference had helped David recently get into St John's College, Oxford, to study medicine.

'That's brilliant, Tony! Now if we can just graft onto David some of your Laura's love of speed and flying, we might have another Helimed doctor on our hands.'

'That's true. And he's a foot taller than me so we wouldn't lose him in the grass.'

I finally told Derek that North Central had offered me a job as clinical director, responsible for their three aircraft.

'What, with the Luftwaffe? So you'd be in charge of them? Jesus, Bleetman, that would make you Herman Goering!' He thought about it for a second and then said, 'Tony, go for it! It's a chance for you to spread the word, take what we established at our unit and roll it out across more of the country. That's what we always wanted to do, isn't it? But don't forget your old Cowboy friends and don't forget us, 'cos we're your Helimed family.'

I knew Derek was right and it was the correct move to make, but that didn't stop him from egging me on one last time.

'What you waiting for, Bleetman? Do it, you *muppet*!'

ACKNOWLEDGEMENTS

I would like to thank my friends, Helimed colleagues and family – especially my father Gerald, my mother Rosalie, my brother Danny, my long-suffering ex-wife Jacqui and my children David, Laura, Rachel and Mim.

Lady Liane of Prestwich has taken me on and has changed my life so much for the better. She has my admiration and respect for her bravery and commitment.

My gratitude extends to the Israeli Air Force who taught me that flying helicopters is actually quite difficult! They also taught me that helicopters carrying medics save lives.

I have been inspired by a few great doctors who motivated me to become the best doctor I could. These include Professor Theodore Wijnitzer, Professor Sir Keith Porter, Professor Jonathan Benger, Chris Ellis, Martin Shalley, Howard Sheriff, Stuart Maitland-Knibb, Ruth Brown and, of course, Dr Hyman. A special mention for the late Dr Bert Binnie who 'did it right', from his time in the 8th Army through to General Practise in Glasgow and on to ophthalmology at Gartnavel Hospital. Had he not smoked and drunk whisky he might have lived longer than 94. A lesson to us all.

My Helimed chums are also 'family' and this book and my Helimed adventures could not have happened without them. You know who you are!

Thanks to Marcus Georgio for all of his expert help and guidance; my agent Andrew Lownie and, finally, Kelly Ellis and everyone at Ebury.

ABOUT THE AUTHOR

Dr Tony Bleetman (PhD FRCSEd FCEM DipIMC RCSEd) grew up in London and is a consultant in Emergency Medicine. A former Israeli Army medic, he has been a volunteer Helicopter Emergency Medical Services (HEMS) doctor for the last 10 years. He currently flies with the Air Ambulance unit in Bristol. In 2006, he won the Vodafone National Life Saver Bravery Award for saving the life of a woman who was trapped inside her car during a traffic accident.